The
Romance
of Publishing

The
Romance
of Publishing

An Agent Recalls Thirty-Three Years
with Authors and Editors

Alex Jackinson

Cornwall Books
New York • London • Toronto

Cornwall Books
440 Forsgate Drive
Cranbury, NJ 08512

Cornwall Books
25 Sicilian Avenue
London WC1A 2QH, England

Cornwall Books
2133 Royal Windsor Drive
Unit 1
Mississauga, Ontario
Canada L5J 1K5

The paper used in this publication meets the
requirements of the American National Standard for
Permanence of Paper for Printed Library Materials Z39.48-1984.

Library of Congress Cataloging-in-Publication Data

Jackinson, Alex.
    The romance of publishing.
    1. Jackinson, Alex.   2. Literary agents—United
States—Biography.   3. Authors and publishers—United
States.   I. Title.
PN149.9.J3A37   1986   070.5′2′0924 [B]   85-41059
ISBN 0-8453-4797-7 (alk. paper)

Printed in the United States of America

*For Matilda, who had loved our
"lusty family of clients," and
for the fellow and sister members
of my three valued organizations,
The Poetry Society of America,
The Mystery Writers of America,
The Authors Guild.*

Contents

Preface

A number of literary agents have written books about the craft. Richard Curtis's *How To Be Your Own Literary Agent* received publicity because it raised a titillating question: authors being cheated on royalties. Donald Campbell had called his book *Don't Step on It—It Might Be a Writer.* Even in satiric rib, such a title would never occur to me. Collectively, I hold that writers are a star-thatched breed. That some crawl, and some cheat, and some booze too much, and some need to be institutionalized—all that does not detract from the conviction that writers are the custodians of the greatest of all creative gifts. Words *communicate.* From the pioneering of Gutenberg to the Nobel prizes of the future, books form the gold carpet on which civilization treads—and often falls on its face (recall Hitler's book-burning).

In over thirty years of agenting I have placed books of the widest range one can imagine. In the process I met the most varied assortment of writers and editors. They will move through the pages of this book: the victors and the defeated, the conniving hoaxsters, and the splendid human beings who restore the heart.

Writers and editors learn to live on a jagged cliff, rejection. Yet the chimes constantly ring, even today, when publishing, like the theatre, or society at large, is faced with challenges that seem cataclysmic.

Each individual breakthrough echoes a universal empathy, for the heart vicariously feeds on visions of glory. In publishing's see-saw business of dizzying triumphs and bewildering declines, faith becomes the guidepost, the beacon.

As in a dream, the chartered-unchartered road seems very familiar until unexpected storms erupt. Trees turn into rocks, and mud sullies the lilac. But the poet's lamp does not go out. New paths emerge. New light and new horizons. The most magic of all cameras is the word. Meet some people who hold that Merlin instrument of communication.

Acknowledgments

The author is grateful to the following editors, columnists, and publishers for various permissions:

Publishers Weekly and Paul Nathan for generous permission to quote;

The *New York Times* for permission to reprint copyright material (16 February 1972, August 1977, and 8 September 1973);

Macmillan Publishing for permission to reprint four lines from "Nineteen Hundred and Nineteen." Reprinted with permission of Macmillan Publishing Company from *Collected Poems* by W. B. Yeats. Copyright 1928 by Macmillan Publishing Company, renewed 1956 by Georgie Keats;

Dow Jones & Co. for permission to quote excerpts from "Biography of Hughes" by John Keats which appeared in the *Wall Street Journal;*

Time, for permission to reprint "Kill! Kill! Kill!" Copyright 1979 Time Inc. All rights reserved. Reprinted by permission from *Time;*

Viking/Penguin for permission to quote from *Hoax* by Stephen Fay, Lewis Chester, Magnus Linklater. Copyright © 1972 by Time Newspapers Ltd. Reprinted by permission of Viking Penguin Inc.

The
Romance
of
Publishing

Part One
PUBLISHING:
A BIRD OF STRANGE PLUMAGE

1

A Long, Long Way to a Happy Ending: Placing the Book

No romance worth writing about is always a gentle walk down garden paths. Allowances must be made for rain, sleet, high winds, violent storms. So with publishing. There are those strolls through orange groves—and frenzied cries for survival. Let's take some looks at the sunny side, if only because publishing trade books is invariably—as editor Joyce Engelson has said—"a roll of the dice."

Doctors are trained not to become emotionally involved with their patients. This sounds reasonable, practical, but it leaves a vast uncharted area. Abraham J. Twerski, M.D., is a psychiatrist who I am sure would endorse the dictum that aloofness is not always applicable. Dr. Twerski is also a rabbi, a rabbi who, for the ten years that I have known him, has headed the Psychiatric Division of St. Francis General, a large Catholic hospital in Pittsburgh. By natural inclination Dr. Twerski takes a very *human* interest in people and their problems, and he writes books that reflect those sympathetic insights.

His first Prentice-Hall book appeared in 1976 under the title *Like Yourself (And Others Will, Too)*. It is a *successful* publication. Twice each year I receive statements. Always there is a check. But I did not place the book until its third trip to Englewood Cliffs. In all, fifty-seven submissions had been made in the course of over two years.

I was called about the third acceptance soon after the submission of *You May Not Be Neurotic* went to Prentice-Hall. By then he was "their" author, so fast action could be expected. But a very different story unfolded about that pivotal first acceptance. It was a book I absolutely *had* to place because, when Dr. Twerski had first contacted me (I had been submitting to Nelson-Hall for a long time, and Dr. Twerski had heard of me through a friend), he already had a contract. From Nelson-

Hall, a good, solid firm, described on its letterhead as "Publishers Of Educational Books and Courses, Established 1909." In June 1973 they wrote:

Dear Dr. Twerski:
    Your manuscript on the general subject of the negative self-image syndrome has been read with care and approval. Therefore, I am enclosing two copies of our contract. After you have signed both copies please return them to us for execution and then one copy will be immediately returned to you.
    There is one thing we decided I should write in this letter, that the book is too short, too concise for our particular program. Any book we publish must be approximately 70,000 words in length, yours is approximately 42,500. This means a hardbound volume of about 250 pages long. This we know from experience does not postulate any padding; any book which should be read, can be read, by the intelligent layman, needs all kinds of case histories as operational definitions and other written devices to make more understandable what the author has to say.

William C. Staubing
Acquisitions Editor

    I wrote to Mr. Staubing:

    Dr. Twerski "just" became a client, and hence he placed in my custody the matter of securing a publisher.
    That Nelson-Hall offers only a token Two Hundred dollar advance does not bother me; my chief concern is with the publication of a book which is apt to do the most for Dr. Twerski in terms of his work, and the prestige which should grow out of a successful publication. Toward that end, I would like to see the widest possible distribution, and so let's exchange some views.
    Once the book will be "built out," what audience do you plan to reach? And how do you reach it? Mail order? Book stores? Library sales? If the book is to be classed as a *trade* book, will Nelson-Hall allocate an advertising budget?

In his reply Mr. Staubing was courteous, but it was clear that my questions were not entirely welcome. He stressed that, because of the time-lapse, the book would have to be reevaluated as a new submission. This left Dr. Twerski and me somewhat dubious because the door was neither closed nor fully opened. I suggested that we look elsewhere. I assured Dr. Twerski that he had a good book, and that I would find the right publisher.

Some typically mixed reactions followed. From William Targ, then with G. P. Putnam:

Dear Alex:
    Sorry to return a negtive answer on COPING WITH THE NEGA-TIVE SELF-IMAGE. It's a respectable and interesting book, but al-

most hopeless in the commercial market. Sorry, and thanks for the chance. Please try me again.

Bill.

From Nahum Waxman, then with Harper & Row:

Dear Alex:
   The book is an interesting one that could find a substantial readership. Oddly, quite apart from my knowledge that Dr. Twerski is a rabbi, it struck me that this was a book that might be suitable as a new style religious title. I would like to send it over to Clayton Carlson in our Religious Books Department if I may. He may have some further comments of interest. One of us will write you again shortly. Best wishes.

Nach.

The Religious Department did not see it as "quite right for us."
A host of other scrambled reviews followed, which was very familiar to me but clearly bewildering to Dr. Twerski. This forced me to once again write to William Staubing:

   Since I am returning with Dr. Twerski's rewritten and retitled manuscript, this would seem to be a difficult covering letter to write; actually, such is not the case. And it isn't because I am going to be perfectly candid, and where one is candid, what is there to fear? Or hide?
   I sent Dr. Twerski's book to Macmillan, Scribner's, Houghton Mifflin, and half a dozen more. I could have had a contract, and still could have it, if Dr. Twerski were to bend a little; that is, hoke-up the self-improvement angle. This Dr. Twerski will not do. His reply was: "Please send the book back to Nelson-Hall." So here it is.
   If it will facilitate matters, I will step out as the agent, and you could deal directly with Dr. Twerski, as per the original agreement.
   Thanks for the new hearing.

Net result, rejection.

I thought about other possibilities. Prentice-Hall is a conglomerate sheltering many divisions, including Parker Publishing, whose speciality is self-help. I had placed many books with them, but I could not show them Dr. Twerski's work because he frowned on what is called self-help. His case histories are intended to steer those troubled to seek professional counsel. Spectrum Books was another possibility.
I thought about individual editors as well. The large firms employ many editors; I invariably submit to one or two within each house. That way a bond develops. Not that a book is ever accepted due to what outsiders call "the personal contact"—a book has to fill an editorial need. But getting to know an editor has its benefits. You become aware of

individual quirks, tastes, and prejudices. At Prentice-Hall I had exceedingly close ties with Bram Cavin. We had negotiated a number of contracts. I was "sure" Bram would like Dr. Twerski's book; he didn't. He wrote:

Dear Alex:
    I am returning Dr. Twerski's COPING WITH THE NEGATIVE SELF-IMAGE. I'm afraid this is one of those cases where we disagree sharply; I cannot see this as a trade book at all. I hope you turn out to be right, and I wish you the best with it.

After Bram left Prentice-Hall, "my" editor became Tam Mossman. I worked well with Tam, and we worked out some contracts. I resubmitted the book. Tam also declined. I still had a number of publishers to contact.

Where, one might properly wonder, lay the basic problem? Was it the theme? The writing? The handling? The theme had universal appeal—people on all economic and intellectual levels suffered from a negative self-image. The writing was fine. The handling was a matter of viewpoint. And here are some additional insights, into both publishing and the diversity of the editorial psyche.

Thomas H. Lipscomb, then a partner in Mason & Lipscomb:

    Thank you for submitting COPING WITH THE NEGATIVE SELF-IMAGE. We have published one or two books in the self-help area, but it isn't a field we particularly enjoy working in. Dr. Twerski's language skills are pretty much limited to the type of social-psychological phraseology that drives me up the wall. I think he has some excellent points to make and I can see this being an extremely successful mail order possibility under a headline such as STOP HATING YOURSELF!, but I really don't want to get involved with this project.

From Joyce Engelson, then with The Dial Press:

    I read through the Twerski manuscript and I agree with you that there is sound material here, possibly even commercial material. But this is not a book for Dial. I don't think that we'd know how to market this kind of special religious/inspirational/psychiatric material that this should be placed as. In fact, I can think of no better place for it than Harper's. I encourage you to send it there. But thanks for letting me see it.

From Joyce Hartman, then New York's Houghton Mifflin editor:

    We've given very close attention to COPING WITH THE NEGATIVE SELF-IMAGE, but regretfully there wasn't sufficient enthusiasm for the project here to warrant our making an offer for it. The author seems to have considerable knowledge of his subject and the case histories are interesting and well-chosen. However, there appears to us to be no new departure or technique presented, and I'm afraid we feel the book is too over-simplified for an educated audience.

Finally, Prentice-Hall, again, but this time I went to Lynne A. Lumsden of Spectrum Books. Ms. Lumsden sent the manuscript for evaluation to a firm called Growth Associates, headed by Dr. Dov Perets Elkins. Dr. Elkins is also an ordained rabbi, as well as the author of several books. He reported:

> Let me share with you my reactions to Dr. Twerski's manuscript. I enjoyed it very much, and would highly recommend it for publication. Here are some general as well as specific reactions:
> 1. The approach, focusing on self-image, is innovative and exciting, a genuine contribution to the field of psychology. Yet, it is easy to read and not academic or overly complex.
> 2. The author uses many cases to illustrate his points, and keeps the reader's interest thereby.
> 3. Profound psychological and psychoanalytic concepts are woven gently into the work, made palliatable to an untutored reader.
> 4. The author refers to later developments in the book as he goes along, arousing interest in later chapters.
> 5. There are abundant excellent analogies to help readers understand his points (ex: wearing green glasses re difficulty in perception; alcoholism as a car with sand in the crankcase, etc.). The chapters are short, wide-ranging, and touching many fields of endeavor.

Lynne Lumsden had sent me a copy of the report along with the contracts. I read what Dr. Elkins had to say, and smiled. How could one *not* feel a glow? And subsequent sales proved that he had been right.

The book received publicity. Peter Leo, a *Post-Gazette* (Pittsburgh) staff writer, wrote:

> He has the sparse, ascetic look of a Talmudic scholar. The long, grey beard, the sidelocks, the ancient Hasidic garb proclaim devotion to an older, immutable world. He is an orthodox rabbi, immersed in the "timeless truths" of the Torah.
> He is also a psychiatrist, immersed in grubby and searing problems of the 20th century, and the author of "Like Yourself and Others Will, Too."
> Some might find a contradiction in all this. Dr. Abraham J. Twerski and his family—10 generations of rabbis stretching back to 18th-century Poland—is the story of a family that has approached the American melting pot in its own unique way.
> It has at once avoided "assimilation" while firmly planting itself in the mainstream of secular society, fiercely upholding age-old religious

practice in a country that has a way of making and unmaking tradition overnight.

It is a story played out daily in Pittsburgh, where Abe Twerski applies the Hasidic principle of concern for the common man as clinical director of psychiatry at St. Francis General Hospital.

And on a wooded hillside near Aliquippa here stands in mute testimony to his social activism that Gateway Rehabilitation Center for alcoholics, which he founded six years ago.

For Twerski, the different worlds that he functions in have an underlying unity.

"Almost everything I have picked up psychologically, I've subsequently been able to find in the Torah, Talmud and Scripture," he says.

"In effect, I became a psychiatrist to do what I'd hoped to do as a rabbi. . . ."

Dr. Twerski's second Prentice-Hall book, *Kindness Can Be Dangerous,* grew out of his work with alcoholics. In it he shows that when members of the family join an alcoholic in denying that a problem exists, the assumed "kindness" can be dangerous both to the alcoholic and to those close to the drinker.

The third book dealt with the "impaired physician"—alcoholism among doctors. *Doctors Do It, Too,* was published by The Hazelden Foundation, specialists in books on alcoholism. The topic was too close to the Prentice-Hall book. The fourth manuscript was hand-delivered by Dr. Twerski when he was in New York, where we met for the first time. I had seen pictures of him, and was not surprised to see a tall, lean, rabbinical-looking figure. He had a benign smile, a smile that recognized, had learned to live with, the double spires of existence symbolized in the rose and the dagger. It was a smile one could expect of a man who might have been chums with Spinoza.

On the title page of the manuscript he dropped on my desk I saw: *Committed, but not insane.* That is the theme, patients diagnosed as insane when actually they suffered from a somatic illness. Later there was a note from the author:

This is just to advise you that the title of the book is being changed, because it refers to other patients than just committed cases. The new title is "You May NOT Be Neurotic."

2

Shattering a Publishing Myth: Assistant Editor or the Editor on Top?

Many submissions to publishers return with a rejection letter signed by the assistant editor. I hesitate to pass on such notes to authors because I know how authors reason. *Assistant editor,* the reaction invariably runs. *Ah, if only the editor on top had seen it!* This is one of many publishing myths.

When Nancy Coffey was fiction editor at *Cosmo,* she wrote to me (2 July 1982), "I absolutely *loved* 'Tender Sex' by Donald Jordan, but, alas, Helen didn't, so back to you." It was Nancy Coffey who had italicised "loved." The identical thing happened with "The Teacher," a story by Clark Howard. Ms. Coffey was for acceptance; the editor on top, Helen Gurley Brown, decreed, No.

Years ago, I sent a story to *McCall's.* Beverly Jane Loo was then fiction editor; Helen Johnson (later DelMonte) was her assistant. It was to Helen Johnson that the submission was made. Helen had previously taken me to lunch to get acquainted and to get first look at better stories. Helen had phoned and said, "I loved DECISION PENDING by Sara Grimes. So did Jane. The story is now with Mr. Mayes."

Herbert R. Mayes, the boss, killed the sale. And that taught me a valuable lesson. Everything else being equal, I prefer to submit to an editor at the lower rung of the editorial spiral. Senior editors are more likely to dismiss new work and less likely to pursue other possibilities.

What does an assistant editor hope for? The answer should be self-evident—to climb up the ladder. So he or she *works harder.* Nothing pleases assistants more than to discover writers who would prove to be an asset to the firm.

Senior editors at large firms have assistants, who come in as many varieties as spring flowers. Obviously the aides will differ in temperament, ability, ambition. Some never go beyond the role of secretary.

Some read manuscripts—not slushpile arrivals but submissions from agents, which go directly to an editor and thus warrant courteous treatment. Agents are supposed to do prior screening; still, there is ample room for disagreement. Tastes vary. So some assistant might be wrong; but, by and large, the aides are both competent and cooperative.

Even at the slushpile, fledgling editors begin to read submissions very carefully, and they delight in passing on manuscripts worthy of further consideration. They might not have to go beyond page three to establish that the style is hopelessly wooden, and the story-telling too amateurish to merit consideration. Where this happens, the fault is squarely with the author.

A manuscript might be utterly hopeless, but to the novice it represents a great deal of work. Hope. Without exception the dud goes off to Random House, Simon & Schuster, and other top houses. This hurts other authors, because more and more publishers refuse to accept unsolicited submissions. But where an author shows promise, assistant editors are happy to assist. Many go out of their way to help.

A submission to some senior editor may arrive when the traffic is slow. Then he or she might do the reading, but responding about the book is left to the assistant. Or a manuscript might come in when countless other boxes are piled up. (Agents submit manuscripts flat, in a box, because that is the way editors prefer it. They do not like a bulky manuscript to be bound. Binding is fine for a play or a movie script; anything over two hundred pages becomes burdensome to handle.) Often as not, submissions are turned over to an outside source, or a first reader. The rejection letter, promising or negative, is based on the report. First readers are not on the firm's payroll; they are employed on a free-lance basis to analyze specific projects. And most do it competently.

Not all editors serve the same function. Some read and some edit; acquisition editors have special tasks, one of which is to woo away profitable authors from other houses. And many highly placed editors began as subordinates, so the assistant of today is the senior editor of tomorrow.

Raboo Rodgers writes on two levels, juvenile and adult. I am handling adult novels for him, and each submission has to be offered as a *first novel,* an extra slippery hill to climb.

The letter quoted below from Houghton Mifflin was in response to a short story by Rodgers that appeared in *Boys' Life* magazine.

March 16, 1982

Dear Mr. Rodgers:

I recently had the pleasure of reading your story THE MOST PRECIOUS GIFT that appeared in the December, 1981 issue of *Boy's Life* and wanted to let you know how impressed I was with the skillful way you handled the suspense in the situation. While I realize you're probably involved with your own projects, I'm wondering if you have ever considered writing a full-length novel for children or young adults. If you do have anything in the works I'd love to have a chance to consider it for our list, either now or in the future. In any case, though, congratulations on that gripping short story and all the best wishes for continued success with your writing.

Sincerely,
Andrea E. Cascardi
Assistant Editor
Children's Trade Books

Could such a letter have gone out from an editor at the top? The Houghton Mifflin acceptance—thanks to a very special alertness—is going to make placing the novels a lot easier. Raboo made his break-through.

Each book I handle becomes a challenge, especially if it is a first novel. I was expecially anxious to place *The Zoo* because it had come to me for co-agenting from The Reece Halsey Agency of Hollywood.

I often have three copies of a novel circulating simultaneously, to a hardcover house, a paperback house, and the movie people. Each submission is designed to help the other. *The Zoo* went to Ken McCormick, dean of senior editors at Doubleday. Mr. McCormick wrote:

Dear Alex:
We are getting interesting reports on THE ZOO by Terry Brykczynski but the general feeling is that it isn't quite right. The quite right part comes with the love relationship between Steven and Amanda. Could this be expanded and developed a bit more romantically?
There is a sort of strain on one of the scenes towards the end of the book. There is definitely good story-telling talent and if he can turn his attention toward some corrections I hope we can give serious consideration to this book.

Mr. McCormick was sufficiently impressed to invite the author and me to his office. He offered some suggestions. The changes were agreed upon, and made. I resubmitted the story, and awaited the verdict.

But at the large houses no single editor accepts. Where promise of a successful publication shines through, the editor first prepares a report. Then the offering is discussed at editorial meetings. Often the decisive vote is cast by the salespeople.

While waiting for word from Doubleday, we received a response from the paperback end:

Dear Alex:
Thank you for sending me THE ZOO. I'm afraid it's not for us. I've read several zoo novels, and something in them generally doesn't

work. The best I've read—and also edited—DOCTOR RAT by William Kotzwinkle demonstrates the difficulty of the genre. It's hard to get the story going from the proper point of view.

Perhaps it takes the hand of a master writer to pull it off. I sincerely don't believe Mr. Brykczynski to be that kind of writer. I appreciate your thinking of us for ambitious fiction.

> Yours sincerely,
> Robert B. Wyatt
> Avon Books

The Doubleday verdict came; it too was a rejection. *The Zoo* was finally published by Crown, with the title changed to *Caged*. The editor who piloted the book through new revisions, and then to contracts, was Jacob Fondie. Mr. Fondie had to convince Nat Wartels and others at the top echelon that this *first novel* would make its mark. And it did. There was a quick movie option. Fondie succeeded where editors at the top did not.

Back in 1957–58, John Rearick of Paramount Pictures used to sign his letters, "Assistant Story Editor." Then I noticed: "Play and Story Editor." I phoned him. Was Paramount interested in *plays?* Yes, they were—as backers, and then as producers should a film version result. I stressed that I was handling the play version of Stephen Longstreet's famous novel, *The Pedlocks*. Mr. Rearick was anxious to see it. I wrote in my covering letter:

> In the original Simon & Schuster edition, THE PEDLOCKS sold 100,000 copies and over a million in the Pocketbook reprint. So it is quite a property, one from which Hollywood shied away because of the story's "Jewish angle." So all of us concerned turned our eyes toward Broadway, where the handicap could turn into an asset. Should the play succeed, the real or fancied fears could well melt away.

John Rearick was strongly for acceptance, as was everyone else in the Paramount Story Department. The veto came from the ultimate decision maker.

Stephen Longstreet had given my client, Maurice Stoller, the right to dramatize the Pedlocks saga. Nothing happened in the time-span Longstreet had stipulated. But it's a classic demonstration of how an assistant went to bat for something he believed in.

Another letter from Andrea Cascardi.

> August 12, 1983
>
> Dear Alex:
>   Here are Raboo Rodgers's contracts for THE RAINBOW FACTOR. It's a thrill to be be getting the ball rolling on a new novel of his!

3
Angry Writers

The subject was poetry, a favorite topic with me. I said to my friend Lillian Geldman, "Placing even an excellent collection of poems is on a par with buying a lottery ticket. I'm thinking of the brand-name houses." "Would it help if poets picketed publishers?" she asked. "Lil," I replied quickly and emphatically, "the fault does not lie with *publishers*. Publishers would be happy to publish poetry, providing the books could be sold." The plight of the average *published* writer—in any genre—has never been worse than at present, but publishers are not the heavies.

Writers as a group have earned the right to be angry, but at whom should the arrows be aimed?

—At the literary quarterlies where some of the finest writing in America appears? These journals cannot pay unless they are heavily subsidized. Most are sponsored by universities, but college endowments are down. Some are independently managed, and barely survive from issue to issue.

—At poets who write poetry, but fail to buy books of poetry? Or subscribe to poetry magazines?

—At publishers who must first of all study the ledger?

—At the educational system which teaches literature so badly, most Americans lose total interest in a book once schooling is over with?

—At the Reagan Administration for cutting endowment funds, with libraries a heavy casualty?

—At individual editors who must first think in terms of what would be profitable for the firm?

—At critics who will give precious space to the newsworthy book rather than the *deserving* book?

If screenwriters could be organized and organized very effectively, why not the writer at large? A *New York Times* headline (May 27, 1982): ANGRY WRITERS TALK OF FORMING A UNION.

The *Times* story had run the pictures of four authors—Robert

Ludlum, Helen Yglesias, Toni Morrison, and Gay Talese. Helen Yglesias would join essentially because rare is the author who has not piled up a list of grievances, and it is generally against a large publisher. Ludlum, who is "for" a union, needs union representation like a healthy baby needs an attack of colic. Ditto for Gay Talese and Toni Morrison. Best-sellers have transformed them into NAMES. NAMES have become the hub around which the publishing wheel spins.

In Hollywood for every one hundred pictures made 80 percent lose money. The same ratio applies to trade book publishing. The aim is for the blockbuster. Blockbusters make many birds sing, and the tra-la-la transcends religious-political or liberal-conservative lines. The trouble is, neither the manufacture of books, nor filmmaking, can live on block-busters alone. Publishing is a jungle of many trees. Many animals, with some welcome and unwelcome lizards crawling around.

Geraldine Ferraro announced on a TV show that she would write a book based on the 1984 Presidential campaign. Publishers, being a competitive lot, wanted the plum. They acted instantly. Two days after the announcement, an eleven-hour telephone auction followed. The $800,000 floor bid soon escalated to over a million, with Bantam Books snaring the gold ring. Anything *wrong* in that? Viewed one way, it could be hailed as a classic success story. Over a million-dollar advance! Viewed another way, the speed with which it was all done could cast an obscene shadow over the pantheon called publishing. What stands out is the making of a best-seller before parts were ready to be examined.

Did anyone bother to ask whether Geraldine Ferraro could write? A book needs to have some sort of a style, other than that supplied by the ghost. Did any publisher think that even this NAME should first submit a chapter or two? For the sort of Proctor & Gamble merchandising which would follow, it simply was not necessary to observe established house rules.

Let's linger a bit on the matter of NAME.

No exact statistic exists, but I'd guess that 90 percent of published trade books revolve around the big NAME author, or the book by an unknown which, through one way or another, leaps to national focus. These are the books at the center of the ballyhoo syndrome. These are the authors sought for the major talk shows, and for whom Waldenbooks (used symbolically) spread the red carpet. Item: wholesale book buyers inject a major voice in editorial selection. Editors may disclaim it publicly, but on manuscripts which raise a question in Sales, copies are shown to jobbers-book buyers. A negative response at that end will prevail over Editorial.

Bookstores have become cousins of big business. The *old* book store has gone the way of the Mom and Pop grocery. Modern stores have modern realities to contend with; rising rents and taxes. Higher wages. So they concentrate on the books which they could quickly dispose of, and since ours is a totally business-minded society, who could fault bookstore owners?

The growth of the chain store outlet would seem to be good for distribution; unfortunately, it is good essentially for the touted title. The stores do not stock unknown authors, and there is almost a taboo on *first novels*, unless, miraculously, that novel, or other type book, somehow managed to attract attention.

"Midlist authors," an inner-industry term, are competent writers who produce neither flops nor best-sellers. They are needed on a list, if only because the supply of Sidney Sheldons is limited. These midlist authors are less important to the industry than they used to be, but they still have to be reckoned with. The Pathmark equivalent will order a few midlist titles, but the major focus will fall on the "promotable" book.

Not all TV viewers dote on soaps: a segment will turn to Channel 13. Michael Jackson has one audience, Zubin Mehta another. Similarly, some book buyers are readers of poetry and are aware of literary worth. But like television, publishing is governed by ratings. Book buyers (pitifully few in proportion to the population) respond to the author who has achieved fame. Then there are the numerous non-authors who get by the publishing gate as Authors. They are celebrities—Hollywood folk, newscasters, politicians, rock stars, evangelicals, M.D.'s who merit media coverage, especially with some faddish diet book. Crime figures must be included, from Joe Bonanno to the many Sons of Sam who pop up with shocking regularity. One feature predominates, a recognizable NAME. Readers have been so conditioned, and publishers carry only a minimal complicity.

Jacqueline Onassis is not a writer, but she is an intelligent woman, capable of an autobiography. How many millions would her story be worth? Three? Five? Ms. Onassis is an editor at Doubleday, and she *edits*. At the start, it is a safe guess that the former First Lady's services were not required to pull disjoined sequences together, or to correct authors' errors. Famous people know other famous people, an excellent base for an Acquisitions Editor. Refinement and adjustment to the job come later. She had started with Viking.

Editors, it could be said, are *made*, not born. After I had been agenting for some years, I decided to take a course in editing. It was at NYU's Professional Writing Center. The teacher was Beatrice Cole. Before turning to teaching, Ms. Cole had been editing *True Confessions*, then under Fawcett sponsorship. She remembered having bought a lot of "Sally Breen" stories from me, but the point I am making centers on the class, the student. They formed a very wide range. The men and women came from all walks of life, and were of varying ages. I'd guess that no new Maxwell Perkins emerged, but most of the students probably went on to get jobs in some phase of publishing. All had a desire to edit. The technique part is an easy craft to learn.

Supposing that Elizabeth Taylor decided to tell her story? As with Ms. Ferraro, who would care if it was a "good" book or "bad"? The drums would start beating. Publishers would stumble over each other to be first on line. The same would apply to a book by Johnny Carson, or his ex-wife, Joanne, who has become a celebrity in her own right, especially since Truman Capote died at her home.

Iacocca's book surpassed expectations. Joan Rivers's novel, *The Life and Hard Times of Heidi Abromowitz*, made many birds happy. So would a book by any NAME living on today's Mount Olympus. I crossed off Richard Burton, but his memoirs (should they turn up) would command rapt attention.

Burt Reynolds claims that he wishes to write his own autobiography, but he has been so busy making flicks, after being a year overdue on delivery, his lawyer returned to Arbor House the first part of a substantial advance—less, it should be noted, the agent's 10 percent. The agent, the famed Swifty Lazar, defended his position. "I've done my job, I brought Burt and the publisher together. Should the agent who did his job and got him a million dollar advance not get paid?" The $250,000 already paid to Mr. Reynolds represented the first installment on his advance.

It is not difficult to trace such a gross distortion of *values;* a lot of angry writers would become a lot angrier. But whose head should properly be on the block? Books inevitably mirror our society, and Burt Reynolds is simply another *product.*

The clock is not going to be turned back to days when a publisher was primarily concerned with *writers.* There had always been the successful novelty nonbook. Simon & Schuster had sunk a foundation on the crossword puzzle. I remember Chic Sales's *Outhouses* and *21 Delightful Ways to Commit Suicide.* But there was balance. In those days publishers took risks on a promising writer. A good-sized book could be published for three or four dollars, and publishing was in the hands of people who loved books. The bottom line was a term reserved for merchants. Publishers were always *merchants,* in that the books had to be sold, and there had been problems. Publishers folded, merged, and went under, just as they do today. But independent publishing, as traditionally understood, can be called a thing of antiquity. Such firms as are left must compete in the marketplace, and they find the going extremely difficult. To survive they concentrate on the specialty book. Fiction is very much on a back burner. A few firms stand out as survival curios. In the broader social context, NAME-worship was not created by publishers.

The ills of publishing are many and varied, and the dislocations can be traced back as far as one wishes to go. While I have been agenting for thirty-three years, I have been close to writers and publishing for over fifty. Who today remembers V. F. Calverton or that fine magazine he had edited, *The Modern Monthly?* Who remembers the Macauley Company? Or Robert McBride? Or magazines like *Pagany? Contempo?* And at the totally opposite end, *Manhunt* and *Nugget?* All were important to me when I had started out. Oddly, what stands out is that *the author* had always been crushed at the bottom of the income pyramid.

The Little Magazines simply could not pay, then as today. Niggardly circulation. As a first reader for Macauley and McBride, I gained some insights into payments for authors. Edna Ferber and Fannie Hurst were two of many big earners, but the average published author—again, I stress *published*—earned less than the average actor, musician, artist, or composer. This applies today as it did forty years ago. And where authors bleed, publishers also need mouth-to-mouth resuscitation.

ASCAP is so structured that the highly successful songwriters willingly pile up a kitty to help the less fortunate. There can be little doubt but that the "dividend authors" would be glad to help those struggling at the bottom by the creation of some fund. Americans are notoriously *giving*, and writers are even more so because writers tend to be more socially aware.

Lawyers can bemoan dislocations in the legal system, but there is little an individual lawyer could do to change things. So with authors. Much was made of the fact that *Princess Daisy* had fetched $3.2 million in paperback rights. Competition among authors and publishers being what it is, and egos being what they are, no individuals could be singled out. Collectively authors lament that publishing is a lopsided see-saw, with rewards unevenly distributed. The producers of bellringers feel—not a sense of guilt; for what should they apologize? But there is a manifest desire to help. So they would not balk at making some gesture of support. If it should take the form of an endowment, it could be the underwriting of a few hard-to-sell novels. Or some collections of poems. Or short stories. It would boost some. Perhaps the winners of a competition?

This would have little to do with *unionism,* which is a topic apart. Some clear distinctions should be drawn. There are unions and there are protective guilds, and it is essential to remember that one is often in sharp conflict with the other.

The agent who represented Ludlum could ask for the moon and get it gift-wrapped, delivered by some speedy overnight service. That is "now," after Ludlum proved that he could turn out hit after hit. But the agent who represented a new Robert Ludlum, offering a *first novel,* as Ludlum had once done, would be apt to get the door slammed in his or her face.

Breaking in was infinitely harder in 1984 than it had been when Ludlum had been on the outside, looking in hopefully.

Furriers, plumbers, screenwriters, or anyone else, are not equally skilled, so income varies. When I cut broadtail coats for a living, I was good at it, and earned more than most other cutters. A union was indispensible. Not to protect a Harold Robbins but the weak worker. It helps in industry, but the author without box office clout is not going to be helped much by a union. Then, too, unions are split into locals. Here the locals would not be geographic; they would be based on earning power. On track records.

Unions have business agents. Does the successful author need a *business* agent, a literary agent, or a tax-contract lawyer? And lawyers *do* represent most of the successful authors. Successful authors form only one finger of the publishing glove. The basic discontent lies with the huge cadre of non-NAME authors who would be on breadlines if they did not hold down some job, or have a sympathetic mate who was employed.

George A. Plimpton, who is neither poor nor a "poor author," said of Project Pushcart: "I'm all for anything a poor author can do to push his books." So he joined other famous authors who banded together to sell their books off a pushcart. The demonstration was held in the pre-Christmas shopping rush of 1972. The purpose was to dramatize what the disgruntled authors called: "Publishers' ineptitude in distributing books." The demonstration brought ample publicity, but did it bring *results?* Some twelve years later the "same" situation not only persists, it has become worse.

There is one branch of the book industry on which authors and publishers agree—that distribution is faulty for all trade books save the big seller or the specialty book. But there will be violent disagreement about where lies the blame.

A union is a desperate reaching out for some degree of equity. It is not a new idea. In England there is the British Society of Authors. Here the talk cohered into action. In 1983, a year from the first announcement, a union *was* formed, The National Writers Union. It has a membership of 2,500 and 11 local chapters. The overall aim could not be more noble, to give writers "the compensation and respect they deserve."

As could be assumed, the union boasts some very prominent NAMES: Norman Mailer, E. L. Doctorow, John Kenneth Galbraith, Marilyn French, Philip Caputo, and many others. There is much that a union could do to correct inequities, but it depends on *for whom.* The New York local had some strictures on work for hire: writers for hire and packagers (which do most of the hiring) form a separate branch, or level. Publishing is made up of so many tiers and layers it becomes bewildering, especially since the levels must of necessity overlap, merge, separate. It's like sperm and ova floating in a vacuum. With fertilization, dwarfs and cretins as well as beautiful children emerge.

Are authors cheated on royalties? This is the sort of a slippery eye-catcher which attracts attention, but which needs considerable qualification to be fully pinned down. To get as close as possible to some valid answers, "publishers" will have to be split up like cuts of beef into Grade A, Grade B, Grade C.

Two individuals band together and publish a new software book, for which there is still an expanding market, plus a book on how to improve your golf, for which there is a very steady market. So a new publisher is listed. The firm may or may not survive; the mortality rate among new publishers is lamentably high. And this must be considered.

Agents regard many publishers as sheer salvage markets. Submissions that have failed at the top are scaled down to the last choice, since "bad" publication is better than *no* publication, or publication by the vanity houses. Only the professional writer depends on writing for a living. At least the harried author did not have to dig into savings. But expectations must be lowered, and allowances made for some dishonest returns. When it comes to the Grade A publishers, publishers who have been around for some time, and are apt to stay in business (though perhaps merged), authors will be angered by sums withheld for possible later returns; they will rail at books having been killed by what they call inefficient promotion and distribution. The complaints are not without merit, but when it comes to the semi-annual accountings, I have always found them to be accurate and in full compliance with the signed agreement. Does this mean that here and there a mouse will not creep through some hole? Yes, some mice are exceedingly devious.

This broad topic of authors' complaints will be covered in more detail as we advance from chapter to chapter. I will cover all the diverse outposts: sales and returns, editorial selection, writers for hire, the frenzied hunt for a Hollywood bid, book auctions, take-overs and take-overs after the take-over; the threat to books from the computer and other HighTech offshots. And I will return to the theme of writers and a union, whom a union could help, and whom not.

4

Hollywood, Hollywood: Fantasy at the Tip of a Knife

Dorothy Dandridge

Hollywood lives by razzle-dazzle and gets a bloody nose for a variety of reasons. Hollywood is lice and legend, Barnum and Cinderella. It is where roses turn to ash—and, on the balancing side, ash to roses. Once a picture is released, a lot of puffed-up Hollywood hype is expected. It's the law of exploitation, if not the jungle. But let's take a few looks at some film-flam where no picture has been made.

To the author of a published book a movie option is the first step toward Mecca. Statistically, only some 10 percent of optioned properties get to audiences. Why the sun does not shine more often splinters into many shards, or reasons.

At the time that a producer's option check goes out, hopes hang high; or, it follows, the investment would not have been made. The producer hopefully envisions a particular star. A NAME director. A veteran screenwriter comes to mind. A "package" needs to be assembled: script, star, director. This has been the mode ever since the old Hollywood went the way of the ostrich feather, the Toonerville trolley, the dinosaur, or any other behemoth faced with new conditions to which it had difficulty adapting.

Production became a collective affair, mostly in the hands of bearded young men with new ideas, and fresh out of college where they had taken courses in new film techniques. Some brash young women had also broken the old mold. Collectively they all became the New Breed. Once these Indies had something to work on, the scarred and scattered studios could be approached for distribution. Or the tax shelter people could be called in. It all takes time. Options frequently have to be renewed, but more often than not they are allowed to lapse. While the

sun is out, ads are placed in the trades; producers lean heavily on *hope* as
well as hoopla. Study the full-page ad *(Hollywood Reporter)* for *The Dorothy
Dandridge Story,* placed by Cannon in 1981:

> The Cannon Group Inc. Presents JAYNE KENNEDY in a Leon
> Isaac Kennedy Production of a Michael Schultz Film. Produced by
> James T. Aubrey, Leon Isaac Kennedy. Executive Producers Menahem
> Golan and Yoram Globus. Directed by John Barry. Lyrics by Carol
> Connors. A Cannon Films Release. WORLD PREMIERE: CHRIST-
> MAS 1981.

Wouldn't one surmise that a production was now *assured?* Guess again!
When plans were torpedoed, I was ready to head for the wailing wall. It
was another setback in a long series of disappointments.

The current owner of the book, *Everything and Nothing: The Dorothy
Dandridge Story (1970),* is Harper & Row. But the publisher originally was
to have been Bernard Geis, whose byline would have read: "By Dorothy
Dandridge, written with Leo Guild." Guild, an authentic Hollywood
character, is a publicist, publisher, author, and ghost. He has ghosted
many celebrity books, the best-known of which was Hedy Lamarr's
Ecstasy and Me. However, Geis had some second thoughts. He began to
prefer a *better* writer; he wanted Earl Conrad to be the collaborator.
Conrad had done many impressive black-white books, including *Scotts-
boro Boy.* Guild stepped aside—for a consideration. A cash sum plus 10
percent of royalties. A similar sum was to be paid Earl Mills, who had
been Dorothy's manager, and who also served as a literary agent.

Like Conrad, I had always sympathized with the oppressed—even
before it became chic—and Dorothy Dandridge had come smack up
against the spears. Dorothy had an absorbing story to tell: a badly
retarded child, two ruptured marriages, several abortive affairs with
prominent white men, some cripplingly bad investments, a career that
rose and ebbed.

A highlight of Dorothy Dandridge's career was being on the cover of
Life (November 1954), billed as "Hollywood's Fiery Carmen Jones." That
elevated her to stardom, but problems ensued. Her colleagues, Pearl
Bailey, Sidney Poitier, Harry Belafonte, and Sammy Davis, Jr., could play
all sorts of roles, but a leading lady is a thing apart. Dorothy was not
Caucasian. In the mid-fifties the breakthrough had not been made—if,
indeed, it has been made.

Conrad worked long and hard on the book. Subsequently, the depressed actress-singer was found dead on the floor of her bathroom.
Without the star to help promote the book, Geis, addicted to the big
promotion, lost interest. The manuscript floated in a limbo familiar to
writers, editors, and publishers. With a dead manuscript on his hands,
Earl Mills recalled that we had previously been in touch, and he invited

me to come in as co-agent. This I was happy to do. I had seen *Porgy and Bess* and *Carmen Jones;* I was moved by Dorothy's gifts and beauty and the flagrant prejudice of society and her peers. I quote from Earl Conrad's Foreword:

>   There is a story, but not for complete telling now, how friends of the late Dorothy Dandridge unintentionally hastened her death by warning her that if she told her story she would hold back the march of black womanhood for a long time. All that she wanted to do was to tell her life story and in the course of it to speak of a few friendships and romances across the color line. But these friends, learning of her decision to do an autobiography, landed upon her in full force, telling her that her life was a disgrace to black womanhood, and she should keep quiet.
>   She was rendered so sick by this opinion and advice that she went to bed crushed and for three days she lay near death. She recouped— partially—from that illness and decided that she either had to tell her story now, or lay down and die then and there. She was actually about eight or nine months dying from the shock and frustration—largely that—of that experience. In those months, torn by what she discovered her friends believed about her and hurt by this, and fearful of the effect her book might have, she intensified her decline with drugs, champagne and pills. She entered deeply into the valley of the dolls and she died on September 8th, 1965.

There were Dorothy's own words as well: "Not knowing which way to turn or how to recoup, desiring death more than anything else, I took pills. Pills to pep myself up, pills to slow myself down. The concept of self-destruction became a permanent part of my psyche."

The book so touched me, I was determined to find a new publisher. And I did—after the usual see-saw of rejection: Abelard-Schuman, a small but active quality house owned by a husband-wife team, Lew and Frances Schwartz. Lew was busy running some profitable trade magazines, mostly for the alcohol industry; Frances concerned herself with juvenile books. (Their trade books editor was Joyce Engelson, and that was where I first established contact with her.)

How did Harper & Row become the owners of the book? First, Intext (International Textbook) Company, successful publishers of textbooks, wanted to branch out into general trade books. On the hunt for profits, Intext absorbed John Day, Ballantine, Abelard-Schuman, Criterion Books, and Steck-Vaughn of Texas. The Intext purchases proved to be a disappointment because they brought prestige but no profits. Following a familiar pattern, Intext itself was put up for sale. Then the firm was gobbled up by T. Y. Crowell. Crowell, despite its ancient history, fine backlist, and some notable titles, found itself deeply in red ink. Subsequently, the firm merged with J. B. Lippincott's trade book department.

The New York branch became Lippincott-Crowell, and in time the combine—and all the firms I have just mentioned—found itself in the welcoming jaws of Harper & Row, which in turn is owned by a foundation.

(Many writers are left hurt, stranded, and bedevilled by so many mergers, but editors and publishers are left bleeding by the swing of the same ax. Staffs are cut, offices consolidated. More important, the marginal book is almost all but totally bypassed.)

With the intensely dramatic material of Dorothy's life story, it was inevitable that there would be movie interest. The first concern was shown by the late Al Zimbalist. The producer and I met in my Manhattan office, where a contract was negotiated and mutually agreed-on press release drawn up. I mailed a copy to Paul Nathan.

The book was not yet published; I sent out page proofs and some strong promotional material. There was a quote from Ruby Dee: "*Everything and Nothing* held my attention from beginning to end. It is fascinating because Dorothy Dandridge was a contemporary, a black actress and singer caught simultaneously in two crazy, damaging, stupid and frustrating battles—the woman battle and the race battle." Zimbalist had a top-rate production in mind. He was deeply fascinated by the woman whose life was a constant teetering between jewels from Tiffany and trinkets from the bargain basement.

Zimbalist and I agreed that here was a true *black* American tragedy, which means a true *American* tragedy. More correctly, it could be called a *global* tragedy, for racism is one loud carryover from pre-Biblical days. I recall Zimbalist saying, "In today's racial climate [1969] I doubt whether Gershwin could have written *Porgy and Bess*. Catfish Row is authentic history, but thinking blacks are now increasingly sensitive to black stars playing prostitute roles and having the focus fall on poverty and degradation. It's why Harry Belafonte turned down the role of Porgy."

"But Sidney Poitier did it with success," I cut in.

"Well, sure, there isn't any *one* opinion. It's what makes the story so controversial."

I again interrupted. "Publishers are even more timid. I encountered it in placing the Dandridge story, and even more so in my Howard Hughes book."

Zimbalist had his thoughts formulated, and went on. "I just want to be sure of my facts. I have no fear of opposition from Otto Preminger or Peter Lawford. They won't deny that D. D. was magnificent for an affair, but they were afraid of something Dorothy wanted, the stability of marriage. However, I *am* afraid of Pearl Bailey, Belafonte and other blacks."

"I think they'll welcome an *honest* dramatization."

"As soon as I return to Hollywood, I'll contact Phil Moore, her arranger, and I will try to get a black dramatist for the screenplay. It's what I'm banking on, a strong, *honest* story."

Paul Nathan ran the release in his influential *Publishers Weekly* column. But the movie deal was never consummated. This was explained in a subsequent letter:

Dear Mr. Jackinson:

With reference to the Dorothy Dandridge story which you submitted to me; and for which I committed myself to a bonafide offer; please be advised that I hereby revoke such offer in behalf of myself and my company.

This is being done principally because during a meeting with Mr. Mills I learned that there could be no transaction until and unless he was included in the package as CONSULTANT.

Thank you for your courtesies and perhaps sometime in the future we can conclude arrangements on some other property without encumbrances.

Kindest regards.

Alfred N. Zimbalist

Two days later there was another letter, this one a lot friendlier in tone, but more searing in content.

Dear Alex:

As you no doubt noticed, a copy of my formal letter went to my attorney, Gregson Bautzer. Incidentally, Greg knows you very well, and asked to be remembered.

My enthusiasm for D.D. did not diminish; it increased. But Earl Mills is a key figure in her story. I had to meet with him. Call it the wrong chemistry. Fact is, Mills rubbed me the wrong way. You are not aware of it; or, I am sure, you would have told me; Holloway House is coming out with a Dorothy Dandridge paperback, PORTRAIT IN BLACK. The author? Earl Mills!

I got an advance copy. It's sleazy and sex-sational. The proper title would have been, PORTRAIT FROM THE GUTTER. I was ready to look toward the stars, Mills has his sights set on the toilet bowl. I also learned that *Tattler* had run some "excerpts from a book by Dorothy Dandridge" which would have made the singer sue, were she alive. Need I say more?

Mills' views on D.D. and mine are so opposite, I decided it was best to call it off. The last thing I need are shackles. It's a tough project to start with, but its very toughness is what attracted me in the first place. Good luck with the book, and I hope that Mills beating you to market with a paperback will not kill a proper reprint sale.

Regards,

The next interest was shown by Freda Payne. Ms. Payne announced on Mike Douglas's show that she was going to star in the Dorothy Dandridge story. I did not know of the broadcast until made aware by Vivian Dandridge, Dorothy's sister, with whom she had been in a vaudeville act, The Dandridge Sisters. Their mother was Ruby Dandridge, once a well-known character actress.

The Freda Payne interest was protracted, with many letters passing between myself and Stanley Handman, her business manager. The interest was still simmering, though on a back burner, when I received a call from the William Morris Agency. Were the rights available? They were. Lola Falana was the interested party. The book went out. Nothing happened. Stars welcome the free publicity entailed in an intent to purchase.

Next, I was contacted by Rudy Tellez on behalf of Jayne Kennedy who, like Freda Payne and Lola Falana, showed a desire to recreate the fascinatingly tragic life. A new deal was set.

In the span of an option, generally a year, a lot could happen. The producer's enthusiasm could wane; the theme could become dated. Or the financial backers could develop box office fears. Or the desired star and director could be unavailable. Here the star *wanted* to see the picture made. Here the "package" seemed to be extremely glittering, but unforeseen obstacles developed. The differences were sharp enough to sink the ship.

The Cannon option expired on 1 August 1981. Two days later Rudy Tellez phoned me to say that Jayne Kennedy wanted to take a new option, in her name, and that a check would be along in a few days. On September first, I found myself in conference with producer Stephen Graham, the son of Katherine Graham, and his astute associate, Fran Pillersdorf.

Ms. Pillersdorf came up with what I thought was a really brilliant idea, to stage Dorothy Dandridge as a first-rate theatrical entertainment. She mentioned the success of Edith Piaf and Lena Horne. She was thinking of "A Night with Dorothy Dandridge." Whoever would play the lead would sing the old Dorothy Dandridge classics. The men who played major roles in her life would be portrayed in the dramatic interludes. Should the production succeed, a film was bound to follow.

Since Stephen Graham and Ms. Pillersdorf were primarily interested in the stage, I hoped to work out a co-production movie arrangement. This was not possible, because they did not regard Jayne Kennedy as a *singer*. They tagged her as an attractive show personality who could sing, but the producers had in mind not particularly a star, but a gifted singer-actress who had the capacity to rise to stardom. This made sense to me.

When the Jayne Kennedy check arrived, I had to return it, and I wrote to Rudy Tellez, her manager;

As you know, I have been with EVERYTHING AND NOTHING so long, it has become a passion to see an actual production. In my measured judgment, I feel that this will best be achieved by going the "new" way. I'm sorry, because I regard Leon Kennedy as a producer with a vast potential, and his wife, Jayne, as capable of going far beyond her cast role of sportscaster.

I had written to Menahem Golen that I was planning to write on the subject, and he replied;

> Announcements regarding forthcoming projects are customary in the industry. Even major companies drop projects one after another, after they have been announced. We do not believe that even 10% of motion pictures announced by producers in America ever get to the screen. Cannon's average with regard to this is much higher. Actually it is very seldom that projects announced by us are not produced.
>   We still have interest in THE DOROTHY DANDRIDGE STORY and hope one day to get back to it when the right package can be put together. We of course will then negotiate the acquisition of the book rights.

In that period I was contacted by two women, both black, both eager to portray Dorothy Dandridge. They were Arteena Rubenstein and Gwen Mitchell. Neither could effectively translate the *wish* to a concrete purchase.

For all the early enthusiasm for a Lena Horne–type stage production, in the end it all added up to zero. But while the zeal waxed high, I was invited in 1983 to the home of Stephen Graham, who threw open his lavish Sutton Place apartment to a huge ensemble—those who might have roles in the play. The men and women entertained; it was a gala evening. I saw many hopeful faces—being chosen could make the difference between recognition and anonymity. I met Leata Galloway, whom Fran Pillersdorf had favored for the role. Once I heard her sing, I agreed that she was a fine choice. But everyone connected with the theatre, or publishing, is geared to expect the rumblings that seethe under the surface.

Through the years, both Arteena Rubenstein (who calls herself Arteena Jones) and Gwen Mitchell continued to show interest. The trouble was, neither had the right backing. Arteena had twice been to my office. She is a beautiful ex-model who had studied acting under Lee Strasberg. And her husband, once in the record business, had switched to moviemaking. Financing would come from West German filmmakers. Finally, she had the means.

During March 1983, when the Graham option expired, Jayne Kennedy had made two announcements on ABC that she was going to produce and star in *The Dorothy Dandridge Story*. She had not contacted me. She did not have to; she had optioned that Earl Mills paperback. The Conrad book option went to Arteena Rubenstein.

Arteena wrote to me: "Try to see and hear Lonette McKee. If I do not play the role, I am considering her for Dorothy Dandridge."

In May, actress Esther Ryvlin was in my office.

"There are so few roles for black actresses," she complained. "Dorothy Dandridge offers a great role."

Ms. Ryvlin was so right. I recommended her to Arteena. In June, I caught Lonette McKee on "Live at Five." This co-star of "Show Boat" and *The Cotton Club* would be another ideal choice. Also that month I saw Leata Galloway on the Merv Griffin show. I had taken it for granted that this actress-singer would inch her way to stardom. She had been in the West Coast *Sophisticated Ladies*.

Who will win out? Will there finally be an actual production? Certainly the talent is available. The hope flag is out.

Six Against the Rock and *The Arm*

Let us focus for the moment on "the true account of the most ingenious, spectacular escape attempt in the history of American prisons, the forty-one hour ordeal on Alcatraz Island, May 2, 1946."

On 25 April 1979, a full-page ad appeared in *Variety:* "JOHN PEARSON, ARNIE FRANK AND FRED MINTZ CONGRATULATE QUINN MARTIN ON HIS MAJOR MOTION PICTURE BASED ON THE INTERNATIONAL BEST-SELLER." Below the large type was a picture of the book: *Six Against the Rock* by Clark Howard. At the bottom: "Exclusive world representation: John Pearson International/Cinephile."

On 2 May 1979, *Variety* ran another full-page ad: "QUINN MARTIN FILMS PRESENTS—Starring Glenn Ford, Ernest Borgnine, Joe Don Baker, Jack Warden, Stacy Keach. . . . Principal Photography Commences on Alcatraz, Fall 1979. For release in 1980. . . ."

The variables of filmmaking can be likened to crossing a dangerous, uncharted shoal. Paramount Pictures beat the market with an Alcatraz film. It was *Escape from Alcatraz,* starring Clint Eastwood. Then one was announced from Pierre Cossette. But these were not the main reasons the *Rock* project never got out of the womb. Co-producer Fred Mintz (head of Cinephile) and producer Quinn Martin began to exchange acrimonies. Friendship and loyalty being such frail flowers, wreaths can easily displace valentines.

A distinction must be drawn between Quinn Martin as an individual and *Quinn Martin Films.* Martin had sold his interest in *Q M Productions*, the firm he founded, headed, and ran very effectively. *Rock* had always fascinated him, and he said that he was determined to make the picture. A new option was negotiated after the old one lapsed, but the new one also withered on the vine.

Clark Howard's first published book, *The Arm* (1964) was subjected to similar treatment. The novel was published in hardcover by Sherbourne Press of Los Angeles, a firm that has long been floating in the Dead Sea of extinct publishers.

Cully, the central character, was a dedicated crapshooter (an "arm" is a professional dice-thrower). *Publishers Weekly* said in its review: "*The Arm* is a shocking novel grim with the truth about today's underworld and filled with stark portrayals of the viperous people who inhabit it. . . . Reminiscent of 'The Hustler' and 'The Cincinatti Kid' . . . the reader is held firmly by the pace of the novel."

Film rights were originally to have been bought by Gordon Kay. Peter Thomas, then connected with the Evarts Ziegler Agency, the Hollywood agent who had represented Sherbourne Press, phoned me about the Kay interest. It was to have been an outright purchase for $40,000, then an impressive sum. Thomas called again, to say that the producer was having those familiar second thoughts, but that he, Thomas, wanted to break in as a producer, and he would take over on the same terms. Thomas worked out a deal with CBS Films, which assumed control. The purchase check came from the network.

Clint Eastwood made news by announcing that he wanted a million to star in *The Arm*. In 1967 the sum carried clout; escalation was yet to come. The million was agreed upon, and Dennis Murphy (of *The Sergeant* fame) was tapped for the screenplay. This was during the period that the networks decided to do their own producing. After a few costly box office failures, plans were abandoned. Outside packagers would do the producing. So rights to *The Arm* passed on to Four-Star International. Four Star, heavily geared to television, failed to mount a production, and the property was resold, this time to ABC. ABC encountered similar difficulties. The story was too violent for the tube. After holding the rights for several years, a new assign evolved, Gerard Lebovici, of Artmedia, who operated out of Paris. In a letter of 7 June 1979, Lebovici wrote: "We bought the film rights for one of our clients. The director and writer are working since several months to establish the screenplay. . . .I read the novel a few years ago and I liked it very much. I was always sure that it would be a wonderful vehicle for a picture."

In the fall of 1979, a news item appeared in *Variety:*

"Mike Wise as producer has acquired film rights to The Arm, original screenplay by Dennis Murphy, in association with Martin Poll. Pic will be produced under joint banner of The Production Company and Martin Poll."

I thought: *At last!* Mike Wise and Martin Poll were not primarily television people, locked into limited concepts. Since the Dennis Murphy screenplay could not be used without acquisition of rights to the book, I wrote at once to Martin Poll. Then to Mike Wise. I learned soon enough that neither producer had *The Arm* on his schedule. They never acquired the rights. The notice does not constitute an *ad,* but it does fit the pattern.

Producer Gene Kraft showed an interest in *The Arm.* I wrote to Gerard Lebovici in Paris. He replied by cable.

FURTHER YOUR AUGUST 26 LETTER ABOUT THE ARM WE SHOULD BE READY TO SELL WORLDWIDE RIGHTS FOR U.S. DOLLARS ONE HUNDRED THOUSAND BEST REGARDS
   GERARD LEBOVICI

Hollywood has been called everything under the sun, from Dream Factory to Nightmare Lane, depending on who does the calling. It has earned applause and censure in equal proportion. In the broader society, no one cares much if truth in advertising is bypassed like some dead cat in an alley. When it comes to options, it can be questioned whether any "sure" ads should be run before producers are really *sure.* It can be likened to that term one constantly hears—"highly affordable."

Like the Dorothy Dandridge project, *The Arm* has the hope flag out. It is now under option to Gene Kraft and Harold Schneider. Schneider, who had scored at the box office with *The Entity,* and thus acquired the right to be listened to. The moral involved is clear and stinging—in choppy waters, faith must be tied to the compass.

5

The San Francisco "Zebra" Killings

A book I had wanted very much to publish was Clark Howard's *Zebra*. The review by Edwin Warner in *Time* (15 October 1979) graphically describes the story.

Urban killing is as old as cities; today the accounts of street crime have grown so familiar that death has lost its sting. In a book that should prove this year's Helter Skelter, Crime Writer Clark Howard restores to this now routine event a primal horror. His pounding narrative meticulously describes the so-called Zebra killings of 1973–74, when 23 white San Franciscans were murdered or maimed by a group of Black Muslim extremists. In the retelling, the cold jargon of police files leaps starkly to life.

It is not only the murders that makes this narrative so gripping, but Howard's exploration of the group mind behind them. There are risks involved in attempting to re-create actual conversations and inner musings in the now fashionable style of the non-fiction novel. But the author's dialogue has the shrill, soul-chilling sound of truth. The killers are followed step by bloody step from the time of their initiation into the cult, which preached a fanatical hatred of whites based less on actual injustice than on a mystic prediction of black world dominance. All the young men are impressionable, violence-prone, and this particular Muslimism appeals to their worst instincts. Three are trained in the precincts of San Quentin, where they listen to cassettes urging the destruction of whites and learn how to kill with a single blow to the larynx, chest or neck. Since all these activities come under the heading of "religion," prison authorities are prevented from interfering.

Upon their release, the trio are invited to a meeting in a warehouse loft. There an itinerant upper-echelon Muslim urges them to start executing whites in order to achieve the elevated status of Death Angel, a role that confers a kind of perverse respectability. Each of the neophytes must kill nine men, five women or four children. Murdering the young earns more points because the act requires more "heart." On the eve of the killing spree the loft becomes a staging arena for a combination of horseplay and unfocused hatred: " 'Kill! Kill! Kill!' The chant was low, murmured, sloshing across the room

44

like dirty water in a flooded basement. It came from mechanized mouths below mesmerized eyes, robotlike, hypnotic, uncontrollable."

The new recruits, whose desolate backgrounds may have deprived them of a childhood, begin playing their lethal game. Victims are selected at random: women, children and frail men who cannot fight back. The murderers shoot or stab from behind, often leaving their victims in agony. They chortle over each attack, showing remorse only when they fail to kill. Then their eyes fill with tears. The more blood they shed, the more they seem to crave. One youth is picked up on the street, taken back to the loft and butchered piece by piece. The remains are trussed up like a frozen turkey and thrown into the sea. Their new-found religion forbids the recruits to rob or rape their victims, but that scarcely deters them. One of them removes a blood-specked ring from a woman he has hacked to death and gives it to a friend for his new bride.

The city is soon immobilized with fear; the police are frustrated. They cannot conduct a legal surveillance of the mosque because it is constitutionally out of bounds. While they find it impossible to infiltrate the sect, the Muslims have no difficulty placing members in the police department. In exasperation, an enterprising homicide detective, Gus Coreris, violates departmental rules by producing sketches of the killers from his own imagination. One of them resembles a real killer, who is thrown into such a panic that he considers informing on the others. Then the police launch Operation Zebra: stopping and searching black youths who bear any likeness to the sketches. Overreacting to a desperate effort to deal with a genuine menace, the American Civil Liberties Union and various black groups indignantly denounce the police action as racist. In response to a lawsuit, Operation Zebra is declared unconstitutional, but under increasing pressure, the worried informer turns himself in.

On the basis of his testimony, as well as that of surviving victims, four killers—Jesse Cooks, Larry Green, Manuel Moore, J. C. Simon—are sentenced to life imprisonment, though Howard states that other Death Angels have murdered an estimated 270 white men, women and children in California and few have been apprehended. The four prisoners have subsequently shown no sign of repentance and in prison they have been troublemakers. Yet they are up for parole in 1981.

Howard is clearly unhappy with that possibility. For the true villain of his book is a criminal-justice system that fails to protect society from its marauders. There is, however, another villain in Zebra—one that Howard somewhat slights. In concentrating on the crimes, hideous as they are, he does not really grapple with the social ecology that may drive ill-educated, rootless men to acts of such brutality. Still, Howard's pronouncement echoes like a scream on a dark street: "California (has) a bad habit of letting its convicted killers out to kill again."

The publisher was Richard Marek, then a bright star in The Putnam Group constellation. Dick Marek, one of the most knowledgeable of present-day publishers, said of *Zebra:* "This book will be big. Or very big." The sentiment was echoed by key people in editorial, sales, publicity, and promotion. This was months before actual publication.

Publishers have ways of gauging a book's potential long before it is presented to readers. When galleys are ready, they are sent to magazines, reviewers, reprint houses, motion picture people. The various responses become a pretty accurate indicator. Enthusiasm, or lack of it, determines the advertising budget. Early responses to *Zebra* had been more than good; they had been super, and so the book was launched with extensive promotion. *Penthouse* featured a segment in its November 1979 issue. Metromedia had gotten wind of the book and lost no time making inquiries. They were told that softcover rights would be auctioned off.

Before an auction, copies go simultaneously to the leading firms. A date is set. Then, whoever does the auctioning stays glued to the telephone. If $100,000 is offered (as for *Zebra*), that becomes the floor price. When a higher bid comes in, it is passed on to the concerned parties. The exchange spirals until the final sale.

No one at that time knew even approximately how many copies of *Zebra* were apt to be sold, but all signs pointed to a blockbuster. The first printing was to be 75,000 copies. How the book was placed illustrates what all of us in the book world learn to live with: sharply divided opinions.

It all began with a nineteen-page book outline.

The Marek firm had shepherded Clark's previous book, *The Wardens*, then in the process of being published. So I owed them first refusal under the next book clause. Normally it is ethical as well as sound business to give that publisher an exclusive. But in the tangled-spangled world of publishing, rivalries are so keen it is often necessary to take a few detours simply to cross an alley. Clark had written to me: "The writing of this book will involve sifting through thousands of pages of information, conducting numerous lengthy interviews, spending considerable amount of time in San Francisco visiting crime scenes, etc. It will probably take a year to put together. For these reasons, I am going to have to be somewhat inflexible about financial arrangements. I will do this book for a minimum of $25,000 payable $15,000 on signing, $10,000 on completion." I did not think that I could get the Marek firm to go that high.

Recall Burt Reynolds and Geraldine Ferraro: the large advances go exclusively to proven money-makers. Clark grew in status and earning power from book to book; still, he had not produced a best-seller, or a book that came close. That *Rock* was called an "international best-seller" was simply a bit of industry chest-thumping. The book did well, but not nearly *that* well, and income is the barometer publishers measure by. So I was faced with some formidable problems. To have as strong a bargaining hand as possible, I took a detour. Other copies went out, but I made it known that Joyce Engelson had first refusal.

Let me roll back a few years. From Abelard-Schuman, Joyce had moved to Dial Press, and I kept submitting to her. It was at Dial that she had gotten to like Clark as a storyteller. At the time that I was seeking a publisher for *Zebra,* I told Joyce that I was making other submissions. She objected. I pointed out that all she had to do was make a better bid.

Frederick Hills (then of McGraw-Hill) had been captivated by *Six Against the Rock,* published two years before. I thought that Hills would have welcomed *Zebra.* A copy also went to Jo—Josephine—Leondopoulos, the (then) movie and TV tie-ins editor at Ballantine Books. Ms. Leondopoulos had become impressed with the author's story-telling ability when she was Eastern story editor for Universal Pictures. Dial Press, too, received a copy.

Richard Marek had long been the publisher at Dial. He had held key posts at Macmillan and at World Publishing before he received what he called "an offer I could not refuse," which was to head his own firm. (It became a growing trend for key editors to have their own imprints.) Financing would come from MCA/Universal. Marek books would be distributed by Putnam, also under the vast umbrella of the movie people. Robert Ludlum went with Marek, his long-time editor, and Joyce Engelson, the editor-in-chief, wanted to continue working with Clark.

Did Dial regret losing Clark? Did they bemoan losing Ludlum? It's what makes publishing a bird of such rare plumage! To fulfill a contractual obligation, I had gone to Dial with Clark's next book proposal. It was a turndown. (So I did not want to show them *Zebra.* I was *forced* to.) A copy also went to Columbia Pictures. Columbia had bought a Howard story outline aired on CBS as "The Last of the Good Guys." This was the project Dial had rejected. Bob Gilbert had been my Columbia contact. He was responsible for the initial interest, and but for him the project would not have gotten to Renee Valente, then the Columbia TV head. Anticipating a high bid from The Linden Press, I sent a copy to Joni Evans, who headed that major Simon & Schuster imprint, and whom I had gotten to know when she was a fledgling editor for the *Ladies' Home Journal.*

Dial Press responded first. Juris Jurjevics, the editor-in-chief, wrote:

Dear Alex:
    I thank you for letting me see *Zebra.* Unfortunately, I don't think it is a strong enough subject at this point in time. There is something dated about it. Having watched Sonny Gross's Harlem Mosque book sink some months ago does not inspire confidence either. Sadly, oddly, I don't think the public cares that much about racial murder and seems to have less and less interest in police-work and dramas concerning it.

So, as chilling as the subject may seem, I truly think the public will turn
from it and that the book will not have a wide audience. It is oddly too
soon for it and too late, if you know what I mean.

Jo Leondopoulos also reported negatively:

Dear Alex:
    I am returning herewith the book proposal for *Zebra* by Clark
Howard. Unfortunately, I have to pass on this one. We just do not feel
it is right for the Ballantine list at this time. Thank you for giving us
the opportunity to consider it. Kind regards.

The rejection is polite, evasive, and utterly meaningless, as most rejection letters are. But the report on which the letter was based tells a totally
different story:

This is a book with which I would hate to be connected in any way. It
purports to be the true story, never before revealed, of a gruesome
series of murders that took place in San Francisco several years ago. It
describes the murders—random, gory, brutal—in great detail and
then the investigation and capture of the murderers. These turn out
to be Black Muslims dedicated to a reign of terror to wipe out the
"blue-eyed devils." The explosive nature of the material is supposed to
be the subject of Black Muslims and their threat to our society. I can
see it as an article in the Times Sunday Magazine, no more. What's the
point of polluting the atmosphere with more graphic gratuitous violence?

At first glance this would seem to be benevolently "liberal." The events
described are horrendously evil, and why not turn away from it? The
question could just as easily be turned around. Why not explore, probe,
try to learn from the events?
    From the first days that man started to crawl out of the caves, to the
Johnstown suicide-murders, the most heinous slaughters were race-re-
ligion motivated. No one race or religion is at fault; weapons are hurled
over *interpretation*. The Muslims who avenged ancient wrongs by ran-
domly picking white targets were taught the most incredible distortion of
Allah's doctrines. Who benefits by suppression?
    A magazine article? Howard's book ran to over five hundred typed
pages, and that was barely enough to tell the full story of the reign of
terror which had all but paralyzed San Francisco.
    Columbia Pictures also rejected. Bob Gilbert wrote: "*Zebra* is much too
risky a project for us. Murders with racial overtones is a very touchy
subject."
    My many years of agenting have inured me to conflicting opinions. I
had known from the start that some publishers, and some producers,

would be scared off the reservation; I also knew that other editors, and other producers, would see *Zebra* as a book which *had* to be published. It was a book that could not have been written before the three key police officers agreed that the time had come for the public to know the full, uncensored story. At that point hitherto classified material was going to be made available.

When Clark had the opportunity to digest the stacks of material, he viewed it through the eyes of a writer-journalist. He did not want to do the book in the sense that certain themes make a special appeal. This was an exceedingly nasty story, with many victims, many deaths, many maimings. But on the whole, *Zebra* formed a challenge Clark felt that he could not run from. He did what any professional would have done: summarized the vast data into an outline, and left it for me to probe the publication waters. I was so impressed with the promise, I told Clark that I expected to have a deal set within a month, but if he wanted an *immediate* contract, Impact Press would do the job. Why were my associates and I anxious to publish the book? Because it promised to be profitable? That is only a partial answer. Basically, where a topic is worthy of discussion, I am against censorship and suppression. Also, *Zebra* was a story that had already been told—told in blood, in voluminous court records, and newspaper clippings. Clark did not *create* the story; he simply had an opportunity to assemble in full how the attacks were planned and carried out. When the death knell ended, there were thirteen dead and seven wounded. Once the trial started, it became the longest in California history. The jury took 210 courtroom days to reach a verdict.

When the Marek firm was ready to contract, I regretted that I could not say that I had higher bids from McGraw-Hill or Simon & Schuster; both had reservations. McGraw-Hill wanted to see some sample text before reaching a verdict, and Joni Evans found the material "too harsh, with not enough sympathetic characters." I had to accept the Marek advance, which was less than I had asked for; but, to my great delight, Clark went along.

Months tumble over each other, and soon *Zebra* was a third written. Then half. Clark's progress reports were optimistic. The more deeply he delved into his material, the more interviews he held with survivors, witnesses, police officers, families of the dead, and convicted prisoners, the stronger grew the conviction that he would turn in a dynamic work. Some prisoners were surprisingly candid. And there was much manifestly good police work. Later the law enforcement people received an unexpected break which made the subsequent convictions possible.

One of the "Death Angels," Anthony Harris, began to have doubts about the wisdom of random killings of whites, or whether it was really

Allah who gave the attack directives, as the accused had imagined. Harris had first heard of the "Death Angels" while in San Quentin. The band, he was told by an inmate, was a select group of Black Muslims, many of them members of the "Fruit of Islam," a paramilitary organization that protects Nation of Islam mosques in cities across the United States. They were dedicated to the murder of "grafted snakes" (whites) to avenge what the white man had done to the blacks. Once Harris turned sides, he became a Muslim target and had to be hidden by police.

Hollywood and paperback scouts cover each major publisher, eager to get a scoop on the competition. Because *The Wardens* was prominently featured in the Marek catalogue, I began to receive requests for galleys. Ten sets went out to producers; one request was from Nona Brown, then director of development for Metromedia Producers Corp. When the package went off, I mentioned in my covering note that Clark's next book would be *Zebra*. I briefly described the contents. A few days later Ms. Brown phoned me, to say that *Zebra* interested her. Could they get the author to Hollywood to talk about the book? I stressed that Clark had decided not to show parts until the book would be completed. But, I added, I could show her the original outline. It went off. A short time later there was another call—that they wanted to contract for *both* books. Consequently, I would be hearing from Business Affairs. The double deal was consummated, and it ran into impressive figures.

Zebra carried this dedication:

> For Joe Buffer, fellow writer, fellow Marine,
> friend, the catalyst who made this book possible.

Buffer had become a client almost as soon as I became an agent. A war-hardened ex-Marine who had seen plenty of action in World War II, he wrote tough, gutsy stories which I sold to the best men's magazines. His first published novel was *Skull*, a hard-hitting suspense-thriller contracted for by Pinnacle Books. Buffer is also a prominent collector of antique guns who holds exhibits throughout the country. It was through mutual liking for weaponry that Joe had gotten to know writer-director John Milius, and this same fondness brought Joe close to several high-placed members of the San Francisco Police Department. One friend suggested that Joe do the book. Joe, in turn, thought that Clark could handle the story more *objectively*. I had brought the two together when Joe was holding a show in Las Vegas, Clark's home base. Clark also had an interest in guns.

Like Buffer, Clark had lived through war activity, but his baptism had been in Korea as a bazooka gunner at eighteen. His interest in guns remained. The war over, Clark availed himself of the GI Bill and took a college course in creative writing. His career began with short stories, most of which appeared in *Alfred Hitchcock Mystery Magazine*. When Clark decided to turn to books, he asked the (then) editor, Victoria Benham, to recommend an agent. Vickie replied that it was not ethical for an editor to pick one agent out of many, but she sent Clark a copy of my first book about my "adventures" as an agent. I think Clark was impressed with the fact that, in my free-lance days, I also wrote crime-detective stories. Our long association began then.

Once *Zebra* was completed, and I received my copy, I could not put the book down. The drama was riveting. The story-telling sharp. I knew for sure that we had a winner. The promise suggested in the outline came through with dazzling brilliance. The manuscript went post-haste to the Marek office where my enthusiasm was shared, and a copy went to Metromedia as well.

When I called some days later, Nona Brown had just returned from a vacation. "I have not yet read *Zebra*," she said, "but others in the organization have, and I have been getting some good feedbacks." There followed a letter in which she stated that the networks had some dire fears—since all the villians were black, the story might be considered as being anti-black. I replied:

> If *Zebra* was anti-black, I would not have wanted to be the agent, and Clark Howard would not have written the book. Similarly, Richard Marek (and staff) would not have wanted to be the publisher. All of us are reasonably "enlightened" individuals. We are not anti-black, any more than we are anti-Catholic, anti-Moslem, or what-have-you. We are against psychotics using the gun to settle social sores, current or ancient.

When it comes to television, an agent can deal with any number of producers, but each producer is at the mercy of the Three Kings—ABC, CBS, NBC. If these nabobs say No, it's the end of the line. Channel 13 is an outlet apart, and Channel 5 is only the kernel of a future Fourth Network. Cable TV was not then the threat it became a few years later. But producers have an alternative—to produce pictures for theatre release. *Zebra* has too much *story* to be confined to a single TV feature. The answer was either a mini, or bypassing television altogether. Many producers calculatedly choose filmmaking, where they have much more freedom.

Do the letters from Dial Press and Ballantine "say" anything to not only writers but to the broader audience of those interested in books? Especially teachers of Creative Writing. The letters say a great deal.

Some common sense needs to be used. Jo Leondopoulos's letter, for example, is utterly innocuous, and so I can safely name her. I do not name the other Ballantine editor because she could very well squirm a bit. She had obviously misread the signs. The outline in no way suggested that the involved Muslims "posed a threat to our society," but they certainly aimed some poisoned spears at the citizens of San Francisco. To miss that distinction is to throw the whole ball game. Still another factor figures in—*the right to know.* The right to know what went on. Also the right to know that editors guess wrong about as often as they guess right.

Berkley/Jove won the *Zebra* paperback rights. They simply outbid other firms. At the time it seemed that the paperback end would do exceedingly well. It didn't, despite an extensive and an expensive promotion campaign.

Three years later, what was the final tally?

On total, *Zebra* did well. The first royalty check was in the amount of $53,000. But given the dramatic theme, the large ads in the *New York Times* and other papers, and that excellent review in *Time, Zebra* did not do nearly as well as it should have. The book simply did not catch on. The number of returned books was massive, which was a heavy blow to the publishers. The paperback end showed a net loss. Metromedia Producers dropped their option. That Dial summation was as much on target as not.

6
Impact Press / Pushcart Press

Project Pushcart had caught the fancy of editor Bill Henderson, for he adopted it as the name of his then newly formed firm, The Pushcart Book Press. His first title attracted considerable attention: *The Publish-It-Yourself Handbook: Literary Tradition and How-To . . . Without Commercial and Vanity Publishers* (1973). The large anthology lists the many authors who have published their own books, and it covers a very wide range. Henderson describes my own firm, which has some very special goals, in a chapter called "Impact Press—The Literary Agent as Self-Publisher."

I became a publisher (on a moonlight basis) for the same reason that I became a literary agent—the challenge was inviting. I survived more than three decades of agenting.

The origin goes back to 1964, when Hazel Lin, M.D., was in my office. I had placed for her, *The House of Orchids;* her two previous novels, *The Physicians* and *The Moon Vow,* were already published. I happened to remark somewhat casually that, if I had the means, I would publish some books, books which the large publishers turned down as "good but not salable." This happens to be my most frequent single lament. And there was a much broader objective. I had long felt that segments of our society were becoming soft, gutless, easily intimidated—and publishing had been infected. There was too much fear of controversy. Some controversies were innocuous and spelled press coverage. Such were welcomed. Where views might offend racial or religious groups, however, there was a manifest lack of courage—much too little gumption to take a stand.

Dr. Lin, a rather shy, nonaggressive individual, had no stomach for becoming embroiled in causes, but she understood perfectly rejection based on "not sufficient commercial appeal." Her own novels had gone the route. She offered to become a partner.

Dr. Lin's investment was nominal, $6,000, against which I put my office and know-how. A limited overhead gave me an advantage; still, to survive I would have to balance the books that I wanted to publish, mostly poetry and offbeat novels, against the books I thought might sell. I planned to publish one of each, starting with nonfiction.

I had then a skimpy manuscript, *Is Divorce an Evil?* by Jack Greenhill, a retired Los Angeles lawyer-poet. Ours was a poetry friendship; we appeared in the same poetry magazines. I considered the manuscript completely unsubmittable. It was not full enough to be offered to the trade, and also too dated, having been written in 1932. Editing could work wonders, but it occurred to me to add a second part, to consist of essays by individual contributors on divorce-marriage. Mr. Greenhill agreed.

Letters began to go out, invariably to people I had previously been in touch with. The response was generous.

Assembling my anthology, I learned that Fannie Hurst had contributed an essay on divorce for a book on the subject published in 1931 by John Day. She and I had met in Pittsburgh at a miners' relief benefit given by the magician, Thurston, in 1928. She was covering the mine situation in the anthracite coal regions for the Hearst newspapers; I was doing the same for the *Daily Worker.*

A few years later I reviewed Miss Hurst's *Anitra's Dance,* and sent her a copy of the review. She thanked me. In that far-off period, I had the answer to social dislocations—change the system! Society's ills troubled me. One of many social sores was the heritage of slavery. In one of Fannie Hurst's novels I encountered an image which I thought was glaringly racial. I cannot recall the exact words, but this is very close . . . "Like lipstick on a colored girl; not wrong, but questionable." As a Marxist I was understandably more concerned with race. Miss Hurst took the criticism gracefully. When I started Impact Press, I let her know. She not only wished me well, she even recommended Gertrude Schleier, an author who had had a novel published by Simon & Schuster. Planning the anthology *Is Divorce an Evil?,* I asked if she would like to write something new. Yes, she replied, and hers was the first to arrive. Within a short time I had the following:

Frank S. Caprio, M.D., "Divorce or Martyrdom"
Leo Wollman, M.D., "Hypnosis in Marriage and Divorce"
Hebert A. Glieberman, attorney, "Marriage—Divorce—Disaster"
Erwin Di Cyan, Ph.D., "Divorce—Depression—Drugs"
Thomas Bledsoe, "Love is a Four Letter Word"
Harold Cross, Ph.D., "Divorce in England"
Alfred Dorn, M.D., "90% Unused"
Judge Roger Alton Pfaff, "A Personal Message to Parents"
Fannie Hurst, "Divorce Has Many Faces"

I now had a book!

Richard Taplinger, whom I had gotten to know quite well, was to be the distributor. Tom Bledsoe, then a senior editor at Macmillan, had introduced me to Dick. Tom would do the copy editing. Stanley Leeds, a highly experienced book promoter, would handle publicity. I secured a good artist for the cover and a top advertising agency for cooperative ads with the Doubleday and Brentanto bookstores. Impact Press was set.

Soon the jacket and a mailing piece for the book, now titled *Some Syndromes of Love,* went to the contributors. To my complete astonishment, two days later a letter arrived from Fannie Hurst's lawyers:

> Our client, Miss Fannie Hurst, has forwarded for our attention your memo to her of September 23, 1965, together with book jacket of the proposed Work of Impact Press entitled *Some Syndromes of Love* which you advise will be published on Friday, November 26th.
>
> Neither Miss Hurst nor this office is aware of any authority by which you may include the article by Miss Hurst on the subject of divorce in this proposed Work.
>
> Please be advised that in the event you or Impact Press proceed with plans for publication as stated by you, we shall on behalf of Miss Hurst, take all steps necessary and appropriate to stop the publication and recover such damages as may be incurred by her.
>
> We await word from you that you are not going forward with this project. . . .

As a consequence, I had to engage a lawyer, who replied:

> My client, Mr. Alex Jackinson, has asked me to reply to your letter to him dated September 28, 1965, in which you question his right to include in a forthcoming publication an article written by Miss Fannie Hurst.
>
> Mr. Jackinson has also forwarded to me his file containing correspondence with Miss Hurst, and after examining it I have concluded that there is no question but that Miss Hurst has given her consent to this publication.
>
> Our offices are only a few blocks apart, and I shall be glad to show the file to you if you will let me know when it will be convenient for us to meet. I think that this is preferable to an extended exchange of letters and preferable, also, to telephone conversations in which we could not both be looking at the same papers.
>
> I shall look forward to hearing from you. . . .

Fannie Hurst had no case, save that the book she agreed to appear in was called *Is Divorce an Evil?* What accounted for that lawyer's letter? It was no news to her that publishers habitually changed titles. My feeling was that she had suffered a mental lapse or seen the jacket and called her lawyer before taking the time to *think.* But lawyers always find an issue, and hers came up with the dodge that no contracts were signed. There

had been a formal agreement only with Jack Greenhill; to the contributors I outlined terms of payment, that 50 percent of royalties would be
set aside for distribution to the many authors. Those I approached either
sent in an essay or declined. Some, like Lucy Freeman and Dr. Edward
R. Pinckney, declined. Fannie Hurst had not only accepted but also had
edited her own pages. She clearly had acted before seeing that the book
offered essays by qualified people who had something trenchant to say.

It all would have blown over, save that a copy of the first letter went to
Taplinger; with a direct threat of litigation, Dick refused to distribute the
book, and I could not blame him. I could arrange for no other distribution; Taplinger was printed on each copy. Stymied, I nevertheless went
ahead. Review copies went out, and the book was reviewed. Not in the
key places, but it was reviewed. The book was put on recommended
reading list by *MD,* the most prestigious of the medical-oriented magazines. A prominent author-psychologist who taught at Franklin Pierce
College wrote to me: "I have not only read *Some Syndromes of Love,* but
have made eleven 8″ × 11″ pages of notes for use in my classes. There is
much good and little nonsense in it." A reviewer wrote: "The book is a
must for college students and educators who deal in human relations,
and it is a must for the average layman's library."

Having no case, Fannie Hurst's lawyers ultimately settled. She had
"won" absolutely nothing, but Impact Press lost very heavily. By the time
this detour was removed, and I wrote Taplinger that we now had the
green light, the assembly-line method of book distribution caught up
with me. This was the reply:

Dear Alex:
I don't know what we can do with *Some Syndromes of Love* at this
point. We started to sell it and had some advance orders, but found
that we could not distribute it with any degree of legal safety, and now
since the book has been published it will be impossible to get decent
publicity coverage for it, and it is also impossible to re-introduce it to
the bookstores. In view of the rather confused situation, I suggest you
continue as you have been doing.

Sincerely yours,
Richard Taplinger

Lacking distribution set off a chain reaction. The book promoter, Stan
Leeds, who had been a friend since the thirties and who took a very
active interest, questioned the use of publicizing a book that was not in
the bookstores. And he disagreed with Dr. Lin's firm resolve not to sue
Fannie Hurst for damages. We had what I considered a perfect case, but
I could not budge my partner. To do *something,* Stan ran a joint Impact
Press–Doubleday Book Store ad in the *New York Times. Syndromes* did not
sell; the book was not known and thus was not asked for in sufficient

quantity. There hadn't been that coordinated punch of an ad plus publicity, so that the book might get talked about. A few copies were sold by mail-order, but a short time later the book was remaindered at thirty-five cents a copy. It had cost us $1.35 to produce each book.

Impact Press was left comatose but still breathing. There were no funds to put other books into production; I did not want to operate on credit. After four years of inactivity, Dr. Lin withdrew as a partner. But that was not the end of it.

Alfred Dorn, an active psychiatrist, got his publication start with his essay in *Syndromes*. He was grateful, and he took over Dr. Lin's original role. Dr. Dorn wanted to see Impact Press revived, and he was ready to make funds available.

Impact Press was unique in many ways. Neither my new partner nor I wanted to "make money" out of the firm. That is, not for personal gain. Each of us had another source of income. The original concept remained—to publish worthwhile books that the commercial publishers bypassed. Dr. Dorn especially shared my views that too many publishers bowed too easily to intimidation. We wouldn't. So we became a firm in search of that *special* book. My inclination remained to publish poetry, to which there was no objection, provided a proper balance was kept. If we published a novel, it would have to be a book we would take pride in sponsoring. Also, we would want to see movie possibilities and a paperback sale. If nonfiction, the book would have to boast considerable punch. We believed in solid distribution, which meant putting considerable money into advertising-promotion. This could cost much more than simply publishing a book. To start, we needed a trailblazer. It was my own book, *The Barnum-Cinderella World of Publishing* (1971).

Impact Press has published no books since, and that was twelve years ago, but there are some compelling reasons. Dr. Dorn and I often wonder what might have been the end-result had Impact Press done *Zebra* by Clark Howard. We are certain only of one thing, that it is a book we would have loved to have sponsored.

For fear of attracting unsolicited manuscripts, I did not want Impact Press listed in the market guides. Nevertheless, I receive many submissions. Some authors have read *Barnum-Cinderella*. Or the Pushcart Press book. Others look into the phone book and submit "blindly," not knowing, and seemingly not caring to find out, what we would consider, and what we would not consider.

A writer proposed a sleazy sex book. I replied that, as an agent, I did not act as judge or censor. My job is to place books, whether I personally approve of the subject or not. As a publisher I exercise personal taste. Sex, yes, most assuredly, but not anything from the basement.

If a book on the order of *Future Shock* came along, it would receive top professional handling. For distribution I would seek a link with an established house. But simply to publish any book holds no appeal.

For different reasons, contracts went out to Ken Edgar and to Marjorie Holtzclaw. They had encountered a lot of rejection, and needed the assurance of publication. I suggested Impact Press, if I could not get them a main-line firm. Impact was also ready to publish Dr. Dorn's *Stress and DIStress,* written with another psychiatrist, Alfred E. Eyres, M.D. In the end, A. S. Barnes published the psychiatry book; Prentice-Hall did Edgar's *End and Beginning* and Berkley Books published Marjorie's *Go Naked To Eden.*

Give Impact Press a *reason* for coming out of limbo, and it will.

7

Linking Three "Unlikely" Writers: Ezra Pound, e. e. cummings, and C. David Heymann

In February 1972, I received a letter from Carroll F. Terrell, of the University of Maine, written on the *Paideuma: A Journal Devoted To Ezra Pound Scholarship* letterhead.

Dear Mr. Jackinson:

The enclosed invitation speaks for itself. Since all efforts to give Mr. Pound some honor in this country have come to naught, we believe *Paideuma* can help make up for the terrible way America has treated one of its greatest poets and men of letters.

Because the amount and kind of material *Paideuma* can print will depend on circulation, we hope to obtain support outside traditional academic circles. Harry Meacham tells me you might like to join our efforts in some of the following ways:

1. Subscribe to *Paideuma* and persuade a few other people to do likewise. A postcard will bring you more copies of the invitation.

2. Contribute to a special fund to be used for one thing only; pay Ezra Pound as much as possible for any of his work we either print or reprint. Checks should be made and sent to the National Poetry Foundation, Inc., and are tax deductible. . . . When one remembers that Mr. Pound has done so much to help others while he himself has lived on the edge of poverty most of his life, one despairs that the world will ever change in the way it treats its greatest artists and poets.

3. Participate in the efforts being made here and in Europe to get Mr. Pound a Nobel Prize before it is too late.

I drafted a reply:

Dear Mr. Terrell,

You write eloquently of Ezra Pound the poet. If it were *only* a matter of Ezra Pound the poet, a check would accompany this letter. Alas, I must also remember the Rome broadcasts. If his side had won, I would have "assuredly" rotted or died in a concentration camp, or gritted my teeth and somehow endured.

In America? Yes, in America. Perhaps *especially* in America if one has researched the Palmer Raids of 1919.

Man is a divine creation. This two-legged complex of genes is Man, the artist. Man also holds a very bloody knout. This facile creator-destroyer awaits his turn in America as he had waited for his chance in Moscow, Munich, Paris, Rome, and other sectors where free exchange was eclipsed. It takes only a given set of circumstances for holders of the Streicher guns to seize control. Here many minorities would suffer, including the eternal scapegoat. I was never schooled to stay silent.

If you have handy Charles Norman's *The Magic-Maker*, you will see me in the book, and you will note that I am very cautious about bandying about accusations of anti-Semitism. I quote parts of an article I had written back in 1951. It had appeared in *Congress Weekly*.

"Cummings composes poems which scorch dollar-sign patriots (who so expertly wave the flag with one hand while mulcting the government on war contracts with the other): he blasts bureaucracy in its hydra-headed forms. But throughout his work, Cummings' sympathies are also discernable. One feels instinctively that he is passionately against youth being blackjacked by poverty, against slums marring the April lilac smell. Cummings is wholeheartedly for more freedom, joy and laughter. Of course, that would not stop him from also being anti-Semitic, since even rabid Jew-haters love music, nature, and feed crumbs to birds.

"If Cummings lampooned only Jews, the brief against him would be truly glaring, but his satiric barbs spare no one, from Uncle Sam to Buffalo Bill. A question then poses itself; if Cummings is to be pardoned, nay, extravagantly praised, for turning a bright searchlight on the billboardish foibles of our day, on what grounds should he be expected to pull his punches on the Fritz Finklesteins who, for good or evil, form a colorful segment of the mural, *Americana?*

"It could be pointed out that Jews wind up in slaughtering pens, and hence a restraint not applicable in satirizing other people, is in order. But compassion is a matter of inner conviction, and cannot be imposed upon from without. Then, too, to put the Ikey Goldbergs on the satirist's exempt list is to endorse the open or covert separation of the easy-dollar Jew from other, matching, native fauna—a move which would be resisted by the principals involved on grounds that they are Americans first, Jews only by the technicality of heritage. Hence they are entitled to be treated like Christian, but otherwise similar-striped, fish.

"Cummings, it must always be stressed, makes poetry out of the nomenclature of the street; the gutter, if one wishes. In each of his many books one can find enough slang and colloquialisms to make the squeamish blush. He has poems in the Italian dialect, poems that satirize the English (Lord John Unalive), and other nationalities. To him nothing is sacred. This may still not excuse his poking fun at Jews, but when viewed (as it should be) as a part of Cummings' larger mural of peans and prejudices, it is his collective good taste more than his alleged anti-Semitism which becomes suspect. . . ."

Realistically speaking, Mr. Terrell, anti-Semitism is not going to be eliminated until and unless other prejudices sheathe the knives. This means that we will have to wait until one black tribe will stop jabbing spears into another. Or white or oriental tribes. Moslem against Hindu. Arab versus Arab. And what is the slaughter in Ireland but prejudice clinging to ancient blood-lore? In the moons of our time, blacks will be called "niggers" by my Hasidic brethren, and Gentiles will be *goyim*.

I do not want to try to predict what future dawn might usher in a society in which prejudice would don more tolerant vestments; I am concerned with "now," the segment of history to which I am a witness. There is an anti-Semitism with which I could live, and one that I *couldn't* live with. There is that Fagin-type "literary" heritage which runs through the pages of many British writers of note. And American. I can cope with the polite drawing room anti-Semitism of an Eliot.

There is also the gas-chamber venom of a Joseph Goebbels. Having in my youth embraced Communism, I know the totalitarian mentality in ways that a free-wheeling liberal could never know it. Pound's anti-Semitism carried the swastika imprimatur, replete with Auschwitz trimmings. If it is argued that America had treated Pound in a "terrible way," how did this literary Benedict Arnold treat America? Pound's war broadcasts from Rome have been made available and were why he was indicted for treason. All who are interested can check for themselves.

Pound's supporters feel that he "had served his time" by being confined to St. Elizabeth Hospital in Washington, and that bygones should be yesterday's wind. Pound was judged too *mad* to stand trial, and that in a sense was true. But if the *Cantos* side of this schizophrenic is to be accepted, I cannot ignore the other side of the coin. Pound often said that his poetry and his politics were one. The two blend in his fulminations against Jews and what he called the "Jew-war"— World War II. Pound has many apologists, people who want to forget his political role. To them the traitor part was (is) unimportant. To me it *is* important.

I did not need Watergate—the great 1972 headline—to make me aware of some deep moral decay, a process long in the making. It affects publishing, of which a vital artery is a free press. It was the freedom reporters enjoy which uncovered the coverup. With a controlled media it would be time to head for the hills. And for the more militant ones, to start digging trenches.

Leading Watergate witnesses gave clear evidence that a totalitarianist embryo was ready to burst its shell the moment the "communist threat" threatened to become actual. It never was more than a surface sore because the American radical movement was too fragmented, too programless. The Party proper had no mass following. The Trotskyite splinter group made up in militancy what it lacked in followers. Mostly, "Reds" were led by individual self-seekers, not a cadre trained to discipline and self-regulation. Lenin had a phrase worth recalling: "infantile leftism." This explains the SDS and Weatherman bombings and black shootouts with cops—acts of desperation which ultimately prove to be self-defeating. Vietnam had fanned most of the fires. But though the "threat" to Washington was only rhetorical, recall how easily the panic button was on hand to be pressed. It wasn't only *subversives* who were spied upon; it was also the other political party, conceived by some rightists to be "Left."

At one time I thought that communism offered mankind a more equitable social system; once that fantasy exploded, I feared *any* dictatorship, be it of the Left or Right. Each requires conformity. In America, the threat had to come from the liddy-hunt echelons. Banded together, those with a storm trooper mentality could form a vast army. At the Left, it is one thing to be *vocal*. This means having University professors join anti-Establishment demonstrations; it is something else to have a *power base*. This our radicals never had, for Labor is, and had been since Gompers, notoriously anti-revolution.

The cascade of muddy Watergate ink made me recall that old *Congress Weekly* article. From my subconscious there were echoes of how deftly Cummings had satirized our multiple hypocrisies, foibles and danger signs. I had to smile as I reread:

> a hyperhypocritical D
> mocra
> C (sing . . .

Of Pound, Cummings wrote me in 1950:

> My affection for Pound began in the Paris of 1915, and will not change because some Wolfes are preying. Pound will eventually die as an individual—and emerge as a cult, war animosities not withstanding.
> You are a yid with a (seemingly) bright lid on your shoulders, but could you persuade a wholly roller that he isn't rolling right?

My letter to Mr. Terrell was drafted, but not completed. I had in mind some changes. Not that I wanted to soften my political stand, but that *Paideuma* letter had mentioned Harry Meacham, and on the letterhead I saw names I greatly respected, especially Hugh Kenner. Did I owe *them* any special courtesy?

When my 1951 article was published, I was a free-lance writer; two years later I had become a literary agent. By the early seventies I had been an author's representative for over twenty years. I had written two autobiographical books: *Cocktail Party for the Author* (1964), and *The Barnum-Cinderella World of Publishing* (1971).

As an *agent,* I did not usually "handle poetry," but I was heavily involved with poetry. I wrote poems, and, of course, I tried to place collections for clients who wrote both prose and poetry such as George Abbe, Carolyn Forbes, Stanton A. Coblentz, and Harry Roskolenko. I continued to be profoundly interested in Ezra Pound and e. e. cummings. A third name had to be added: C. David Heymann.

Over the years I had read Hugh Kenner's *The Pound Era.* Then I received from Carolyn Forbes a copy of *Ezra Pound: The Last Rower,* published by Viking. Carolyn is an old "poetry friend." Our association started when we had both published work in a poetry magazine edited by the late Alan Swallow. Carolyn wrote me (4 December 1976): "The copy of [C. David Heymann's] new book on Pound looks a bit frayed; that's because it is a review copy I had picked up in a furniture store which also sells old books."

Noting "By C. David Heymann" reawakened memories. I went to my files. To Carolyn I wrote:

> Because you are so concerned with 'writers, writing and selling,' note from the attached that I had once been Mr. Heymann's agent. So I turned with great interest to his book. Here let me break off into a tangent more private. As you know, I have in the making my third book, tentatively called: A PERSONAL INVOLVEMENT: Twenty-five Years With Authors and Editors. The book will contain a chapter I'll call: AUTHORS I HATED TO LOSE—CLIENTS I WAS DELIGHTED TO BE RID OF.

In *Barnum-Cinderella,* I had gone into the legal status on letters. Here it is in capsule form: If you receive a letter from John Doe, the letter is *yours.* You can sell it if you wish, and can find a purchaser, but publication rights remain with the author. Thus, you need permission to quote, but obviously a bit of common sense needs to be applied. I can safely quote Mr. Terrell's letter, as I had quoted other letters, but I could with safety quote only *some* letters from Mr. Heymann.

He had come to me in his beginner days. I had tried very hard to place his early work, especially his first novel, *Inside Out* (1969). He had written me many letters, some couched in salty terms. If I quoted verbatim, I'd be apt to hear from his lawyer. What it essentially boils down to is an individual assessment of what is proper and improper. "Ethics" is an appropriate word, and it was the measurement used in my previous books. My audience is always writers and others who are interested in learning what happens in the bizarre world of publishing. Having a book published by Viking is a great credit. Heymann *arrived,* but I am showing you a letter written when he was as green as a ripe cucumber:

Dear Alex Jackinson,
    Small triumphs are better than none at all. I'm enclosing a copy of METROPOLITAN REVIEW. I won a short story award in it and

there's also a poem by me. Also, I've had a rather lengthy essay accepted by THE COLORADO REVIEW. As I said, small triumphs, but better than nothing.

Lately, I've been turning what time I have to short stories. On the basis of the story I wrote in METROPOLITAN REVIEW, I wonder if it would be worthwhile to send any of them to the larger magazines, such as *Esquire*. What do you think? And would it help my chances if you sent them?

I've been doing research for a book which I intend to start this summer. It's a rather serious subject, a historical novel on a rather controversial figure. I'll give you the details in person sometime. I'm still toying with some of the minor ideas I mentioned to you over the phone, but it's difficult for me to write about something if I'm not really enthused about it. Unfortunately, I can't write just to sell. THE CONFESSIONS OF A MALE CHAUVANIST PIG simply didn't work out after a few chapters. I'm still giving some thought to the book about the Catskills.

That's essentially it. Anything new on INSIDE OUT? And what do you think about the short stories, think it's worth sending one or two to Esquire?

Best wishes,

I replied to that letter:

Thanks for the copy of METROPOLITAN REVIEW. Having a short story there is, as you note, a small triumph, but better than nothing.

Yes, let me see those stories you think might be for Esquire. I know well the Esquire fiction people. As to INSIDE OUT, I had a talk with a top editor at Avon. Many paperbacks are eager to capture the sophisticated campus trade, and so Avon will get to see your book. The top copy is with Mary Walsh of John Day. She is a bit more receptive to the emerging "quality" writer than most editors at the commercial houses. So we have a chance. A slim chance, but a chance.

I handle dual submissions with extreme tact; hardcover, soft cover, with each submission designed to help the other. I told Mary Walsh that you would be a 'continuing' author, which is what publishers seek. I stressed that I would soon have a second novel to show.

I never received that second book. I lost contact with Heymann. When I learned that Viking was going to publish his Pound book, I assumed that the author had done what other writers do; drop the agent who had been associated with a series of early rejects. Some stick to an agent; to others loyalty is an entombed word. So he became a client I regretted losing. But after reading *The Last Rower*, I was glad that I was not involved as the agent. Parts of the book simply did not ring true to me.

1983 update.

In December of that year C. David Heymann was flung into a lot of media glare over his ill-fated Barbara Hutton book. Mr. Heymann will be picked up in a later sequence, but for now let me return to Mr. Terrell. I had shelved my reply as a task started but not completed. Then Pound died. There seemed no point in replying.

If *Paideuma* came up today, over fifteen years later, how would I react? On Pound the *politician,* emphatically the same way. On Pound the poet, there would be much of the old ambivalence, for he *was* a pioneer, a trailblazer, a madman tainted with genius.

Man's creative talent can claim some magnificent advances, in numerous fields: space, missiles, medicine, computer technology. Nobel Prizes still go out for literature. But the *destructive side* is more heinous than ever. Count the mass massacres, in Lebanon, India, with spillovers that stain (and shame) many sectors of the globe. Note the amount of "small" wars, the indiscriminate bombings; the proliferation of religious more than political hates. Though the sociological lines are blurred, the threats to freedom come from many arrows.

No new Ezra Pound emerged, but his viper brand of anti-Semitism is very much with us, a good deal of it stemming from the Soviet Union. And no new pathfinder like Cummings emerged either, but a chapter on poetry will come later; this is more a tocsin for anti-totalitarians to stay alert, especially in the domain of books. Books, more than any phase of the arts, communicate more directly.

I am covering several themes. First, there are the three authors, who are about as different as a boa constrictor from a mouse, and a mouse from a monkey. Cummings and Pound were poets of totally disparate gifts; the link is that their work poured over into politics. One dealt with social satire, the other loaded dynamite into his pen. Racial TNT can translate into disaster. To repeat, had the fascist side won, there would have been an iron lasso around that part of the sun which still rotates freely. And the danger remains ever-present.

Mad or sane, Ezra Pound is now kin with Homer and Euripides. Let them judge. And perhaps Cummings will be sitting in. Smiling. C. David Heymann will have to be judged by a totally different set of measuring rods, as we shall see in chapter 13.

Part Two
HOWARD HUGHES

8

That Clifford Irving Book

As a day to remember, 8 December 1971 will not make the history books, but that morning my subway ride from home in the upper Bronx to my Manhattan office was punctuated with visions: I was about to become a wealthy man! McGraw-Hill had released their first notice on what had quickly gotten to be widely known as THAT BOOK—the Clifford Irving biography of Howard Hughes. The *New York Times* report sounded convincing even to me, a confirmed Hughes watcher and an agent who was greatly hoax-conscious, having escaped by the narrowest of margins being a party to a swindle revolving around Dr. Jonas E. Salk which would have eclipsed the notoriety achieved by *God's Broker,* the Barbara Hutton withdrawal, or any other recent book debacle.

Howard Hughes is now beyond approbation or censure, but our theme is less the man or the legends he left behind than the fascinating and repellent dragon, publishing. The lid on Hughes's coffin had not yet been sealed when a new round of exploitation began. Clifford Irving's hoax was instantly bought for the movies. Books that Howard Hughes had stopped from being published surfaced like electronically charged corks.

From direct involvement, I knew that during his lifetime, the Odysseus-like mythmaker had strongly opposed the publication of books about him. His aides were in a position to block some biographies, such as the one which I had agented; some they couldn't. The books that appeared up to December 1971 had to be constructed from published bits and scraps, interviews with old friends and ex-associates. So the books had varying degrees of worth. Hughes's *own book* (though as told to) had tremendous news and money value, as events so dramatically established. If Irving's book was authentic, I stood to collect 10 percent. And a million dollars had already changed hands. Thus my euphoria on that subway.

Think what you will of the man whose gross eccentricities evoked

highly conflicting reactions, but trying to dismiss him offhand, dead or
alive, is like calling the Grand Canyon simply a hole in the ground.
Hughes could be viewed through assorted binoculars, and what added
greatly to the fascination was that he could be viewed but not seen. He
was *there,* and yet remote even to his closest aides. Before the final
breakdown, little of importance happened in the world of which Hughes
was not aware, and very keenly aware. Sick as he constantly was, he kept
a large staff busy keeping him informed. And in his own quarters, the
television was on more often than off. Even from a wheelchair he
worked long hours, and his weak but super-charged electronic fingers
touched currents on the highest national levels.

I was a victim of his autocratic whims, and also a beneficiary of his
largesse.

Some sixteen years before, I had agented a Hughes biography which
was garroted before publication. As a consolation prize, I had reached an
agreement with Gregson Bautzer, an attorney for Hughes, to the effect
that, if ever Hughes agreed to have a book written about himself, I
would be the agent. It did not now seem likely that McGraw-Hill (along
with *Life* and Dell) could have been duped. Each had an alert legal
department, and the editors knew that no individual's word should be
taken at face value. That subway ride in December 1971 made my pulse
quicken—10 percent of at least a million was a considerable spinoff. But
an even more important consideration was involved.

My written agreement with Bautzer is dated 21 October 1957; the
origin goes a bit farther back. How the compact came about forms a
story that stands out even by the bizarre standards of marketing books.

"Howard Hughes does not want a book about him written."

The words were uttered by Jack Goodman, in 1954, an editor close to
the peak of the Simon & Schuster pyramid, in response to a proposed
biography of Hughes to be written by Robert N. Farr. Goodman had
more to say: "Hughes is a public figure, and so anyone can write a book
about him. No permission is needed. There's a catch, though. As soon as
his people will hear of a book—I know of several such instances—there'd
be an invasion of privacy suit." Goodman paused, gathered some additional thoughts. "Hughes couldn't possibly win, but he could make
litigation so costly, it just wouldn't pay us to tangle with him." Looking
doleful, he returned the folder which contained the outline of Farr's
proposed book.

I next went to McGraw-Hill. Although this was in my salad days, I
knew firsthand how editorial opinions differed. Mr. John P. R. Budlong,
then a top McGraw-Hill executive, phoned me to say, "You brought over
a very interesting proposal! We don't want any costly litigation, but if you
could get Mr. Hughes's consent, come back here and write your own
ticket."

I was turned down at E. P. Dutton for essentially the same reasons. Then I probed for interest at Citadel Press. To acquire so promising a book, they were willing to take calculated risks. Morris Sorkin had put it: "If Hughes sues, it does not mean that he will win."

Philip Foner, then the other Citadel partner, phrased it a bit differently. "We pay our lawyer on a yearly retainer—and we're not afraid to challenge Hughes in court."

A book on Howard Hughes!

My agency was catching on. Clients with strong professional credits were coming in; publishers were becoming aware of me. I was placing a variety of books for a variety of clients, but, at that time, my shiniest hope was Robert N. Farr. Farr was then also doing a book which would feature Dr. Salk's name—or so we were led to believe.

Who is Robert N. Farr?

On 9 June 1977, a *New York Post* story was called to my attention:

JAIL TERM FOR AUTHOR ON CRIME

Robert Farr is a self-proclaimed expert on white-collar crime, having given lectures and written a book on the subject.

Farr is on his way to a federal prison today under a four-year sentence. It seems he tried out some of his own theories. They worked—but only for a while.

The 56-year-old resident of Old Greenwich, Conn. who pleaded guilty to submitting false information on loan applications to two banks here, was sentenced yesterday by U.S. District Judge Robert J. Ward.

Farr admitted providing false tax returns and financial statements to the Bank of New York and Chase Manhattan to get loans approved there.

The Bank of New York granted him an $8,800 loan and Chase approved a $5,000 loan, but Farr was apprehended before he received the money from Chase.

TIP OF ICEBERG

Asst. U.S. Attorney John S. Siffert said these loans represented only a small part of Farr's scheme.

The prosecutor said in a pre-sentence memorandum that the original indictment involved attempts to defraud six banks. The government believes Farr was responsible for defrauding a total of 19 U.S. and foreign banks of about $250,000 by using the same methods.

Siffert said Farr sought to impress bank officials by showing them a portfolio of articles written by him and news clippings describing his expertise in white-collar crime.

Farr claims he wrote a book, "The Electronic Criminals" on the subject.

DISMISSED COUNTS

The other counts in the indictment—which were dismissed when he pleaded guilty to the two charges—involved loans from Morgan Guaranty for $49,500; Citibank, $10,000; Barclay's Bank, $3,500; and a loan application to Chemical Bank which was not granted. He received other loans from banks in Europe by also submitting false documentation, according to the prosecutor.

Farr said before he was sentenced that he was most disturbed that his reputation was ruined.

His lawyer, James Schreiber, said his client was "a borrower, not a thief," but Judge Ward ignored that argument.

The dedication page in Farr's "The Electronic Criminals," published by McGraw-Hill, carries this tender passage: "To Betty, my love and my wife, for her patience and understanding, and to her parents, Bert and Jane, with thanks for letting me take her from them."

Farr had originally written to me on stationery of St. John Vianny Minor Seminary in Ohio. He explained that he was a recent convert to Catholicism and a teacher at the school. He had a novel in progress about a priest, but he stressed that his major interest was nonfiction, and especially writing on science. He wrote in 1953:

My father, Clifford Farr, was Professor of Botany at Washington University, St. Louis, Missouri, until the time of his death. My mother, Wanda K. Farr, is one of the leading women scientific investigators of our day. In 1936, as head of the Cellulose Laboratory at the Boyce Thompson Institute, Yonkers, New York, she discovered how plants manufacture cellulose. In 1954 she was the recipient of the Marie Curie Award, given to the outstanding U.S. woman scientist of the year.

Aside from writing and teaching, Farr wrote that he was also a scientist. A *successful* one, he impressed upon me. In a letter to me dated 27 July 1954 he wrote, "After a rather busy week, I am back on the book [his novel]. I had to go to Washington in connection with my application for a U.S. patent on a process of keeping cigarette tobacco fresh—on which one company has just taken a $100,000 option. So, in addition to being a busy week, it was also an exciting one." And I was quite certain that Farr would be a highly exciting client!

To achieve better laboratory facilities, Farr shortly moved to Pittsburgh and began to use the equipment at the University of Pittsburgh, where Dr. Salk was working on his much-anticipated polio vaccine. Then, in 1955, it seemed that the ferocious polio beast was about to be defanged.

Farr shelved work on his novel for something that promised more immediate results; it was to be a modern "Microbe Hunters," written in collaboration with Dr. Ralph Buchsbaum, who taught biology at the university, and who could double as a publisher. His still-active firm, Boxwood Press, publishes mostly sociological works meant for the serious reader. *Men Against Disease* was to be the book he was reputedly doing with Farr.

I quickly went to Macmillan. W. Holt Seale, who then headed the medical books department, showed keen interest. Farr reported that a personality clash had developed between the co-authors, and they had stopped collaborating on *Men Against Disease*. Disappointment is a common commodity, but it shows up more glaringly in publishing, where loudly heralded books flop and unsung geese lay golden eggs. For another industry where chance plays such a major role, you would have to consider Wall Street, song writing, or go to the truncated Broadway Theatre.

In our time the conquest of polio is taken for granted, but it was a horrible scourge in the period I am covering. Books on polio generally wound up as publishers' remainders because the *solution* remained enshrouded in crepe. But Dr. Salk seemed to be on the verge of victory, and a large number of readers were apt to respond to a book featuring his name. Farr wrote that Dr. Salk agreed to supply three chapters to a symposium on polio. It would be as told to Robert Farr. The other contributors would have also been major names in the field: Drs. Albert Sabin, John F. Enders, Thomas Francis, and others.

Anthologies rarely excite publishers, but *this one* promised to rate among the exceptions. This was a book that was bound to get talked about, and reviewed in the key places. Libraries would need to have it. Thus at least some modestly good sales seemed assured. Mr. Seale was most interested; at the same time he insisted that he could not commit Macmillan to a contract before he could see some text. Farr stressed just as strongly that he needed a contract—and an advance—before he "bothered" such extremely busy people as the involved doctors. It seemed plausible.

I had then just become familiar with Citadel Press, and I was impressed with the aggressive know-how of this small but active house. To offer such a potential winner, they were ready to take the same risks as with the Hughes book. Farr thought that Citadel would be fine. A contract was negotiated, the customary advance paid. The "Dr. Salk chapters" arrived. They read so well, a successful publication was indeed indicated.

Both the book and the "polio story" ran into some unforeseen difficulties. Polio was not conquered as easily as wishful thinking would have had it. Children still fell victim; some died. The bitter controversy that had raged underground between exponents of the "live" v. "dead" vaccine came into the open. Dr. Salk's popularity ebbed; Dr. Sabin's rose. As interest in the promised *cure* waned, Citadel decided that it would be best to postpone publication. And in just that period of fog, a long letter arrived from Farr stating that he had bought from an ex-secretary of Hughes a complete file on that singular autocrat. If I could stir up an advance, he was ready to bat out a book.

A book on Hughes clearly suggested a "name" house. I tried three. I could have continued the hunt for a publisher who did not fear expensive and extensive litigation, or I could again try Citadel. Farr was against losing more time.

Once I knew that I would have a Hughes book on the stalls, I wanted to learn all I could about the ghostly mystic. That meant spending nights at the library, opposite my Forty-second Street office.

When the anticipated biography was delivered, there was some keen disappointment. Despite the intrinsically exciting material, the book lacked zest, cohesion. Lillian Freidman, (then) a shining light at Brentano's, was called in as a consultant. Sorkin and Foner invited me to the luncheon where Lillian was to render a diagnosis. She offered sound revision suggestions. Farr agreed that a rewrite was needed.

Before the new version was ready, my star client wrote that Citadel Press was not acceptable to Howard Hughes as a publisher. Farr did not explain why, and I did not ask. I assumed that it was based on political grounds. Most authors would be totally indifferent to a publisher's political views, as long as those views did not infringe on marketing. How Howard Hughes felt about "communist subversion" is well known. His political views were and remained strictly rightist. He would not even permit RKO theatres to show Charlie Chaplin's *Limelight*. In the mid-1950s, while he might not have heard of Citadel Press, his aides no doubt had.

I was glad that the Citadel partners proved to be willing to cooperate. Farr soon wrote again:

Dear Alex,
    I have your letter of Friday, November 5 [1955] following your chat with Dr. Foner in Grand Central. If the agreement which Citadel will agree to under the terms I suggested—$750 now and $750 in 30 days—will preclude us from submitting the book to another publisher, do not pay them the $750 at this time.
    I might say that the money to buy off Citadel has not been put up by me. I have been requested not to reveal who has put it up. Perhaps you can guess, but I can't tell you if you are right or wrong. It has been handled in such a way that there is no possibility of the money being traced back to this party. Nor does this obligate me in any way, morally or otherwise, to materially change anything connected with the text or content of the book. I have complete freedom to put anything into the book that I feel ought to be there.
    If Citadel's demands had been $3,000, for example, the instructions I received regarding payment would have followed the same pattern—$1,500 now and $1,500 in 30 days.

So I again found myself in negotiation with Foner and Sorkin.

"The revise might make the book a best-seller, but we don't want any reluctant authors on our hands," said Morris Sorkin. "You want to repurchase the contract; we agree in principle, but surely we're entitled to some compensation?"

"I agree fully," I concurred. "I mentioned five hundred to Phil. The first advance was a thousand; we'll give you fifteen hundred."

"It's a deal."

"I already have my instructions," I detailed. "And a check for seven hundred and fifty, with the second payment to be made in 30 days. Meanwhile I want to be free to submit the book elsewhere."

"Agreed," Sorkin said, "if you give us your note for the balance."

Reluctant to lose time, I signed a note. The investment seemed assured.

The book rewritten, retitled, and the contract repurchased, I was set to resume the hunt. Before I could move, however, in late January 1956, Robert Farr wrote again. This time the "Dear Alex" gave way to something more formal.

> Dear Mr. Jackinson:
> I am in receipt of your letter addressed to me here [St. Clairesville, Ohio], I plan to be in New York over the weekend on my way to Richmond on a brief business trip and will try to get in touch.
> Within the past few days, I have learned much to my loss and sorrow that there is no possibility of ever publishing my biography of Howard Hughes. Very strong influences and considerable pressures have been exerted upon me to abandon this book entirely, with threats of dire consequences if I ever publish it. This has nothing to do with the accuracy of the text. If anything, I think that it may be caused by the fact that I may have been a little too truthful in certain parts of the book. I have discussed and argued and blasted representatives of Howard Hughes since early in this month, but this man is just too powerful for me to risk open warfare with. I must drop this book, and have dropped it. Hughes has paid me no money at all for doing this. There has been no pay-off and I do not expect any.
> As for the note you signed at Citadel, my letters to them and to you at the time of the $750 payment do not mention that I authorized you to sign such a note in my behalf. This was your own idea, and I do not mind telling you that I was surprised at the time, but I could say very little because I thought that you knew what you were doing, and that it was just a token arrangement.
> Since the Hughes book will never be published, I do not feel that I ought to be indebted to Citadel for any bonus. I think that my indebtedness should be limited to what they paid to me and to you in commissions. I will take care of this and my indebtedness to you just as soon as I can obtain the necessary funds.
> I can say no more, except to repeat that it is certainly in everybody's interest—yours included—that the Hughes book be dropped. It ought

not to be mentioned again. I can probably clarify the picture for you a little better when I see you or talk to you on the phone, and I will try to do so. This has been a terribly nerve-wracking experience for me. I could not have believed it possible in this day and age if it had not happened to me. You may expect to hear from me further in regard to these matters within the next ten days. . . .

This was like an adder unexpectedly creeping out of a picnic basket. Or a machine gun going off during a May-pole rally.

Losing a contract, withdrawing a book, is a "normal" trade hazard. But here some strange shadows loomed. Who had threatened Farr? *Why?* Just a while before there was every reason to think that the book would win Mr. Hughes's approval. So I fired some pertinent questions, and drew no reply, satisfactory or otherwise. Puzzled, I went directly to Mr. Charles McVarish of Carl Byoir Associates, the public relations firm that served Howard Hughes until the very end.

Once introductory formalities were dispensed with, McVarish showed me a copy of a long, legal Agreement drawn up between Robert Farr and Richard Dorso, a television producer. For the sum of $6,000, Farr relinquished for all time all rights to both versions of his books. The producer, I knew, needed the "research" material like I needed a second nose. I glanced again at the date, 2 January 1956, and said, "On January 2d I was very much Farr's agent. He sent his so-called dismissal letter three weeks later. So I'm entitled to six hundred commission. I also have letters authorizing me to buy back the Citadel agreement, which meant seven hundred and fifty out of my pocket."

Mr. McVarish was completely sympathetic.

"You certainly have a case against Farr. I suggest you see one of those lawyer fellows."

"Consider this," I stressed. "If I sue Farr, I will also have to sue Hughes."

"Then sue Hughes. Mr. Hughes will never pay a penny to settle Farr's debts."

I decided then and there to engage a lawyer as soon as I left Mr. McVarish's office. Passages from Farr's letter kept spinning in my mind: "considerable pressures," "threats of dire consequences," "this man is too powerful for me to risk open warfare with," and they led the lawyer to believe that he could build a case on grounds that through his representatives Howard Hughes interfered with my legitimate efforts to place a book on the market. Was I ready to sue? Yes, I said, basing matters on principle.

"What are my chances of winning?"

"Against Farr, your case is legally unassailable; against Hughes there is a question, but I think that I can build a strong case."

"Build it. I'll send you a retainer when I get back to the office. I'm determined to get at the root of the mysterious pressures of which Farr complained."

"Don't expect any quick action," I was warned. "These suits tend to drag a long time, and you will have to post a large bond."

"I'll do whatever will have to be done," I assured the attorney.

9

I Agent a New Book on Hughes

My paper has been the *New York Times* ever since the old *World* folded. I generally read it subway-bound to the office. My lawsuit still in progress, one morning in 1957 I found myself glancing at the *Daily News,* held by a girl sitting next to me. The attraction was a feature on Howard Hughes, replete with photos. Alighting at Grand Central, I bought the paper. The article, part of a series, sparked an idea. Why not a book for Paul M. Fitzsimmons?

The Ladies' Home Journal had given Paul his first impressive sale: at that time Paul was a professional writer, in that he had no income save from his writing. And his stories saw print in a variety of magazines. He steadily produced quality stories, which meant that only a fraction of his output was acceptable to the commercial magazines. Beacon Press was going to issue an anthology of his short stories.

The *Journal* policy then was to pay a thousand for a first story, twelve-fifty for the second, fifteen hundred for the third. After that it became a matter of negotiation between the editors and author or author's agent. For stories that really *pleased,* there was no ceiling. And what the slicks sought in those halcyon fiction days was the steady producer, the steady producer of the pleasant story. Stories had to be well-written and well-constructed, but the editors especially wanted stories which would give their readers a *lift.* That explained the upward scale. Paul rarely tried to slant. If a story clicked, fine; if it didn't, he went on to something else.

A second *Journal* story was accepted. That was a big check; most checks were small. I managed to find many diverse markets for rejected stories; *Family Circle, Argosy,* other men's magazines. Between sales Paul "starved," which is the lot of most free-lance magazine writers. The stars form only a small percentage.

Fitz was a relative newcomer to writing. After each good sale came another series of setbacks. More editorial trips, and more sales—but the

No's predominated. There was no third *Journal* check, though I tried repeatedly. Fitz's gas and electric had been shut off more than once. So after seeing the *News* article I thought: why not ease the recurring strain via a promising book? Paul was ready to tackle a book. After the thought germinated sufficiently, a letter went off to Thomas A. Bledsoe, then editorial director of Beacon Press.

> Dear Tom,
> For the Fall list, '58, would Beacon be interested in a title I con-cocted:
>
> ### GOLD-PLATED SNEAKERS
> #### A Biography of Howard Hughes
> I have not spoken to Paul about this, but I will show him a copy of this letter. The main thing now is to get your reaction. Knowing the material, I can be reasonably certain about delivering a zippy yet thought-provoking book—about the playboy tyro who learned how to produce exciting pictures; Hughes the star-maker, the capricious wrecker of RKO, the foreward-looking aviation expert, and the ultra-reactionary business tycoon.
> I already agented "such" a book, and I will brief you on details if we get this project going. Essentially, the book had to be withdrawn because Hughes does not want a book about him to appear. So he will not authorize a biography. Without official sanction, publishers fear an invasion of privacy suit, which will almost certainly follow. But suppos-ing a publisher refused to be intimidated? Here Beacon's Legal De-partment should take over!
> Is the subject worth the trouble? I think that a book on this bizarre character is long overdue. Despite the color and the hupla, a bad book will lay an egg; a *good* one should sell like mad. If that is to happen, I want to benefit by it. I would like Paul to benefit, Beacon Press. I'll put at Paul's disposal much data, independently accumulated. Paul would do his own supplementary research so that, when distilled, it will be *his* work of art, in every way different from the book I previously had on the market.
>
> Regards,

Tom Bledsoe was so intrigued he phoned me immediately. Great! And Beacon Press was ready to pit their lawyers against the Hughes's set. It was Fitzsimmons who could whip up no enthusiasm.

"I'm a *creative writer*," he stressed, "not some library historian. Besides, to me Hughes is a half-ass hero."

"But the job will call for creative writing," I insisted. "Hughes is not likely to make available his private files. That means working with news-paper clips, magazine articles, transcripts of the Congressional Hear-ings. To give this re-hashed material freshness will require *extra* fine writing."

"I know a book on Hughes will sell. I spoke to a lot of people. There's strong interest in the guy. God knows I need the money, but I still think I'm being miscast."

I wanted to bang Fitz on the head, but also admired his strength of character. So broke, and so pledged to principles.

"Tom thinks you're exactly right for the job; I think you'll be terrific, Paul. I've a lot of privately accumulated data, and copies of Farr's books. There isn't a thing he could now do with them!"

"What's with your suit?"

"The case is very much on. Frankly, if you do the book, I'd prefer to get my investment back that way."

"Jeez, I'd like to accommodate you. And Tom. Myself. But I've those doubts. Why don't you approach some of your other writers?"

"Because I don't think that they're right for the job. I consider you perfect because, fundamentally, you and Hughes are motivated by the same driving force. You're out to prove something if it kills you, that you could make the conformist slicks take you at your nonconformist terms; his egotist's peak is wrapped up in women, movie-making, aviation, missiles, electronics."

Egotist's Peak.

That could be the title!

For some time an idea had been bubbling in my mind. Why don't *I* write something on Hughes? I now thought the time had come to act.

"I still regard Hughes as a nobody," Paul insisted. "He *inherited* wealth; he didn't earn it. What has he ever done with his loot that's worthwhile?"

"You read," I reminded him, "that he started that Hughes Medical Center in Houston. Unless he will have children, with his death, everything will go for medical betterment."

Paul grimaced. "I'll bet that medical center is more a tax dodge. Sure, he helps a few bright students, but that's just showboating, like his daredevil aviation."

We got off the subject.

The term, *Egotist's Peak: A Candid Look Into Howard Hughes,* stayed on my mind long after Paul left. I gave it additonal thought as I went about my other tasks. That weekend, the article "wrote itself," as the cliché goes. I had lived with the material for so long, it became a mild compulsion to get something written. Ready, I first tried *Esquire.* They had something scheduled on Hughes. I then brought the manuscript to George Wiswell of *Nugget,* a Playboy-type magazine to which I was steadily selling.

Not long after, Paul was again at the office.

"Changed my mind," he said. "I kept saying to myself, what right have I got to be a prima donna about writing?A pro should be able to handle *any* theme. Tell Tom to draw up a contract."

I pulled open a drawer of the file adjoining my desk, took out a heavy folder marked O.W., the abbreviation for "Own Writing."

"Here's a copy of a piece I did on Hughes, but it will in no way interfere with your book."

Rather than a contract, an option would do in the initial stage, and we negotiated one. It called for a substantial advance, with a first payment of $500. The balance would be paid as copy was delivered.

Subsequently there was a phone call from George Wiswell.

"I'd like to buy that piece on Hughes."

I grinned broadly. "Fine. I'll be glad to sell it to you."

"What can you tell me about the author?"

Because I dislike any impression of "pressuring" editors with whom I trade, my own work goes in under a pseudonym. This time I chose "Stanley Phillips." To Wiswell I said, "You happen to be speaking to the author."

The editor laughed. "Hello Stanley Phillips."

"I'm not happy I chose that particular name, but let it stay."

And it did. The article, rushed into the next issue, bore the date, October 1957.

I gave Fitzsimmons a bit of time to get started. Then a letter went off to Charles McVarish. I explained that I had instituted a new biography, and I gave him all the pertinent facts. The Carl Byoir associate lost no time calling me. He wanted to discuss this new book, but he added; "I'd like a man from the Hughes organization to be present. This will be in two weeks."

"Swell," I said. We made an appointment for the afternoon of 3 October. I wrote to Paul about the date, urging him to bring down that morning whatever he might have written by then. I wanted to check his approach. Possibly, too, I'd take him along. It was some two weeks since I had given him the material; in another fortnight I hoped to see the first chapter or two.

Paul generally wrote fast, in longhand, on lined, legal-size yellow pad paper. He almost never rewrote. One draft, and that was it. He couldn't type but relied on Janet, his wife.

Paul was a "natural" writer, an ex-seaman who had driven a milk truck when he was called to my attention some two years before, while I was at Mike Dewell's office. Dewell had then edited *Challenge* and *Man's Magazine*. I had come over to discuss a submission by John A. Keel. As I was leaving, the editor reminded himself of a seemingly forgotten detail:

"By the way," he said, "a fellow was up here with some stuff. Mostly it's short stories and I don't use fiction. He's a good writer. Want to see it?"

"Sure, if you say he's a good writer."

That night at home, where I do all major manuscript reading, I said eagerly to my wife:

"Matilda, I'm reading the work of a *real* writer!"

Paul's first *Journal* story, "Family of Five," attracted TV interest. The issue had been on the stands only two or three days when I received a call from Tom Bohen, then story editor for MCA—Music Corporation of America. Were the TV rights available? They were. "Family of Five" never sold, due only to mechanical-technical difficulties. It was the story of a family of five caught in a flood. What made the story memorable were the fine writing and the deft characterizations of the father, mother, three children. A flood and much rain were needed; TV plays were then mostly confined to a half-hour and a skimpy budget. But the story achieved many translations and was picked by Professor Ruth Strand of Columbia University for inclusion in an anthology of short stories designed for school use. I was sure I had picked the right author.

In addition to being a furrier for twenty-five years, I never had any formal education. This helps explain why, once I became an author's representative, I wanted to be a *good one*. Some thought I was. Aron M. Mathieu had sent me a letter:

Dear Alex: I thought you would like to see this nice letter from one of your clients who got in touch with you through an advertisement in Writer's Digest.

Cordially,
Aron M. Mathieu

It's been about seventeen years since I wrote an article for the Digest, and I would like to try another one, pending your approval. Would like to tentatively title it:

THEN ALONG CAME ALEX
Tribute to an Agent

In 1955 I was after twenty-six years of writing and selling magazine stories ready to toss in the sponge. Then I saw an ad in your magazine for Alex Jackinson. I sent him a collection of forty sports stories that publishers had rejected. He immediately sold the book to Citadel Press. Next he sold my current book, MAN WITH A RACKET, which is the life of the tempestuous tennis star, Pancho Gonzales. Recently he sold MY EYES ARE IN MY HEART, the autobiography of Ted Husing.

In the article I would quote from his letters and telegrams of encouragement and sales; his handing out advances, and the fact that he has assumed almost God-like stature to me—a man I've never seen personally and don't want to, because I have built up a picture that he is not of common flesh and blood.

The article would be rather lightly written and not too long.

Sincerely,
Cy Rice

Cy Rice had a knack for the light-vein biography, especially sports and theatrical figures. I sought assignments for him, and induced Hy Steirman, who had then started Paperback Library, to let Cy do a Liz Taylor biog, Cleopatra in Mink. But I doubted that Cy would have been right for Hughes. Cy knew that he was not a *depth* writer—Fitzsimmons was. I looked forward to seeing what Fitz would turn in.

Howard Hughes died as miserable a death as some Bowery derelict falling unattended in an alley. A Mexican specialist called in just before the end felt that Hughes had died of "neglect." Not so—as "neglect" is understood. It was a circumstance, a deterioration, no one around him could have helped or avoided. Hughes *at all times* had around him his retinue of attendants: male nurse-secretaries, doctors, security men. And his suite of rooms had a fully equipped hospital room. Why, then, was he found emaciated, dehydrated, a skeletal shadow? There is an answer. To understand Hughes, my sketchy portrait will have to emerge in segments.

Power always commands attention, probably because so few are in a position to manipulate people, and people in some extremely high places. Hughes had irritated many; he had *helped* many more, and there are legions who bless his name. He commanded, as though he were some imperial ruler. While there was periodic defiance and some mutinies among his "subjects," mostly he had his way.

That it was a *sick*, tortured way is beside the point. Hughes could no more control most of his actions than a person in a catatonic fit is free to act differently. Many factors combined to condition Hughes, and he isn't apt ever to be captured in any single biography. A spate of new books about him were published, but, without his direct participation, different interpretations only added to the mystery. Hughes was a singular individual among singular individuals—mad, capricious, arrogant, cagey, suspicious, complex, but at all times compelling.

When my article appeard in *Nugget* in 1957, the half-billion had grown to two billion. The wide-soaring 747s made his huge plywood flying ship as outmoded as Galileo's first telescope. But Hughes personally flew the "Flying Lumberyard," proving that the costly disaster *could* soar. He had used plywood because aluminum and other metals were then war-scarce.

In his declining years the interest in women inevitably ebbed. Probing more deeply, I found that nothing basic had changed. A communist very often becomes a strong anti-communist; an ex-alcoholic can become a zealot on the reform side. Hughes was extreme as a roisterer and excessive when he later locked himself into his sanitized isolation. He always professed to "dislike publicity about himself," and calculatedly attracted it in torrents. But back to *then*.

October 3 rolled around. Fitz appeared at my office early—to tell me of another turn-around.

"It's no go," he stated a bit sheepishly, returning all my research material.

I accepted the bulky envelope, stared at him.

"I tried, believe me," he explained, "but feeling as I do about the man, I'd have to force myself, and that's no good."

"It isn't," I agreed, "if you have to force yourself. But why do you have to *force* yourself when the man's life is so highly interesting? The movie making. The women. The aviation, Hughes's genuine contribution to flying, his several crashes, escapes from death."

"You're right, but I can't overcome my prejudice that he's a calculated showoff, a man who'd get absolutely nowhere if it wasn't for the inheritance."

"That's not true," I protested. "Hughes *compels* attention. He's singular, unique. I'd have sworn you'd relish digging into this book. That tussle with the Government—didn't *that* stir you? His three-day flight around the globe?"

"I know all that," Fitz said. "I'd certainly turn out a best-seller, if I felt about him the way you do. But I see him so differently. I see sham where you see heroism."

"Weren't you supposed to tackle this book as a pro? You said a pro should be able to handle *any* theme."

"Yeah, but maybe I'm not a pro. If I was, I'd be batting 'em out for the *Journal*."

I looked inside the envelope, and sorted through the various clipped sheets. I hoped to find something Paul had written. Searching, I said; "Hughes courted Lana Turner, Ginger Rogers, Jean Harlow, Katherine Hepburn, Jane Russell—sizzling material."

"I found those so-called romances staged and phony; Hollywood crap."

I stopped searching—I saw nothing in Paul's handwriting.

"Didn't you get *anything* down on paper?"

"Not a sentence. Each time I thought I was ready to start, subconsciously there'd be a diversion. An idea for a story would come along. Right now I'm trying to shape a play."

"Of course, we'll have to refund the advance," I had to say.

"Certainly."

I wanted it spelled out. "If you had turned in some text, and Beacon did not like it, there would have been no question of a refund."

"I know. Take it out of the next slicks' sale."

There was a "next slicks' sale" and the advance was returned, but when Fitzsimmons confronted me, he was broke. Broke but unbowed. Broke but determined not to tackle a piece of writing simply because it promised to be a gusher. Foolish? Perhaps by commercial standards, but I found myself pleased all over again that I had this gifted maverick.

Fitz could impersonally regard the "Hughes book," a subject about which I felt so intensely. But there was no *immediacy* involved. Back of my mind, an audacious thought circled around: Why don't *I* tackle the overdue book?

Agenting left precious little time for my own writing; indeed, I did no writing to speak of for the first three or four years. Only one poem in my *Confetti for the Hearse* collection was new, and that was written when I was moved by the plight of J. Autherine Lucy—the girl who was barred on color grounds from pursuing a college education. But now, my business more solidly established, there were ways by which I could manage to set aside some weekends for myself. At the editorial end I was determined always to do my own evaluating, but if I still could not employ a secretary, along with my messenger, even a part-time office worker would be of great help. To "do" the Hughes book became an extension of the temptation that had inspired the article.

To go further meant undertaking a formidable job, made the more difficult because I did not possess Fitzsimmons's writing gifts. Fitz would have held attention by sheer brilliant use of words; I would have to rely more on *information*. If the opportunity arose, I'd mention it to Charles McVarish.

The Hughes representative turned out to be Gregson Bautzer, who had just flown in from his Beverly Hills home base. I had first become aware of him from reading Farr's book, and then, alerted, I kept coming across his name in the papers. Hughes employed many sets of lawyers, specialists in various fields—patents, finance, business, aviation—but when it came to personal affairs, he relied mostly on Greg Bautzer, whose law firm was one of the six largest in the country.

Bautzer had other clients besides Hughes, and he had other interests, mostly theatrical. He was a major voice in Joseph M. Schenck Enterprises. On the lighter side, he was good copy for Broadway-Hollywood columns. He attended the major primieres, generally with some outstanding star. He had been linked with Ginger Rogers and had recently married Dana Wynters. I couldn't help thinking that he could be a valuable contact.

Introductions over with, I said to Mr. Bautzer, "I hope Charles McVarish briefed you on the previous time I was at his office, when I learned that Farr had sold all rights to both versions." I opened my briefcase, pulled out the Farr folder. "For the record, glance through some letters from Farr." While Mr. Bautzer studied the letters, I studied him.

If images of all the popular movie (and fictional) heroes were fed into a computer, the composite picture would very much resemble the man I gazed at. In his forties, Bautzer could fasten his belt on the same notch he had probably used in his twenties. He had a full head of wavy hair, just gray enough to be distinguished. A booming voice matched a husky physique. He bristled with an aura of good grooming and achievement.

Done reading, Greg Bautzer said, "I'll say this for Farr—he certainly can write."

"The letters would not have been written, if I was not excluded from the negotiations," I offered. "Why was I?"

"Because there are authors who like to cheat their agents, Mr. Jackinson. You certainly have a case against Farr. The repurchase of the Citadel agreement—with your money—made possible the later sale."

"My lawyer," I said, "also thinks that I have a case against Howard Hughes, in that by his representatives putting pressure on Farr, he interfered with my legitimate pursuit of business. But I at no time felt that I had a quarrel with your client; we all do what we think is best for us. I'd be glad to drop my case upon payment of the two sums to which I am clearly entitled."

The lawyer spoke emphatically, essentially paraphrasing what Charles McVarish had said.

"Mr. Jackinson, Mr. Hughes will under no circumstances settle Farr's obligations. That's definitely out!"

"But," I pressed, "if we go ahead, Farr's letters will have to be made public."

"It will not be the first time that Mr. Hughes will have gotten into the papers."

My lawyer had spoken of suing for $50,000 and felt that there was a good possibility of collecting, though not anything like "quickly." But a successful book could be great compensation. Since I would need to establish a close liaison with those around Hughes, I was prepared to forfeit my sizable retainer.

Mr. McVarish was the next to speak.

"Tell us about that Irish writer you mentioned, Fitzgerald or Fitzgibbons."

"Fitzsimmons," I corrected, "Paul M. Fitzsimmons." I showed Greg Bautzer a book placement list which I had previously shown to Mr. McVarish, and which I saw had remained on his desk.

"You will note that Beacon Press is going to do a collection of short stories by Fitz. That, as you know, is quite a tribute to him, since short story collections proverbially do not sell unless a big name is involved."

"What sort of a publisher is Beacon Press?"

"Don't you know?" I couldn't decide if Bautzer was serious.

"Really, I don't. In publishing I know Simon & Schuster, Doubleday, Random House. A few others."

"Well, I'll brief you. Beacon is not a *large* house, reckoned in numbers of books published annually; in terms of prestige, it is very highly respected. Nominally it is a Boston religious house, the publication arm of the Unitarian Church; under the hard-hitting editorial directorship of Tom Bledsoe, they are issuing a general trade list. A book has to be good to get in, and we thought that Fitzsimmon's book would have been very good. So good that Beacon Press was ready to challenge Hughes. To my regret, and that of Beacon, Fitzsimmons decided that he was not right for the job. After that it was no use appealing to him on grounds that a *good* book would score big."

"There won't be a book?" McVarish asked skeptically.

"No. I don't feel inclined to call in any other writer; they wouldn't do as well. So I have nothing to negotiate." I made a move to leave, but Greg Bautzer held me.

"Have you time, Mr. Jackinson? I must dash to the hotel; I'm at the Warwick, but we can talk while I grab a quick shave and change suits."

I agreed.

In the corridor, waiting for an elevator, I said;

"While I think of it, Farr mentioned you in a letter I received in May of this year." I took the letter out of my folder, handed it to him. He read:

Dear A. J.,

Concerning the $6,000, you are right in assuming that I received a check for that sum, but a great deal went on behind the scenes that I am certain you do not know about, and which I cannot divulge to you in writing at this time. I cannot and have not enjoyed the proceeds of this money, and it is quite likely that it will be returned, as things stand now, and a substantially larger and much more equitable amount obtained. At which time you will receive your just and fair percentage on this book.

Mr. Bautzer returned the sheet without comment, but shook his head sorrowfully, feeling for Farr the same ambivalent emotions I experienced—a defensive desire to ward off blows. There was also a feeling of compassion, for here was a man who clearly obstructed his own progress.

I spoke first. "Did you hear from Farr about this?"

"Not a word."

A "down" car stopped.

When we walked out of the building—a new building at Second Avenue off 42d Street—my mood was a mixture of anger, defeat, and a

feeling of promise. I was annoyed at Fitz for having backed out; it left me
with an empty arsenal. Over the legal route, I was not sanguine about
collecting my out-of-pocket loss without a long wait, perhaps many
years. The *promise* came out of a sense of expectancy—why was I invited
to the hotel? I assumed that some sort of an *offer* would be made; beyond
that bit of speculation I decided not to try to guess.

En route uptown in a chauffeured foreign car put at Mr. Bautzer's
disposal by a client, I again unzippered my briefcase. This time I fin-
gered an advance copy of *Nugget*.

"Did you happen to read my article?"

"Yes. McVarish sent me the tearsheets. It's a good—*Nugget* article."

"I'm thinking of expanding it into a book. To make it as good a book as
possible, I'd like to have Mr. Hughes's cooperation."

"Well, you aren't going to get it, Alex. Why should Mr. Hughes make
available his files to you? Have you ever written a successful biography?"

"No, not a biography, but I've had a good number of stories and
articles published."

"I am one of those who has Mr. Hughes's ear who has urged him to
have a book written, a book by Ben Hecht, say."

"That would be a good choice," I agreed, seeing it as a "typical"
attitude.

If Howard Hughes did not read Farr's book, I did not doubt Greg
Bautzer did, and found it wanting. Especially when he considered the
sort of book a writer like Ben Hecht might turn in. The next step was to
keep the book from being published. And it was a simple deduction that
Farr considered Richard Dorso's $6,000 a good bit of income for a book
he planned to get published despite the agreement.

"If not Ben Hecht," Greg Bautzer went on, "it would have to be
another writer of stature. Howard Hughes is a perfectionist. He'd not
want a bad book about him to appear any more than he'd turn out a bad
airplane. Or missile."

"That figures." I wanted to inquire if Stephen Longstreet would be
acceptable. I was in touch with the author then, but decided to first ask
Longstreet.

"Tell me about some of your other clients."

I was glad to brief him.

"I've a Doubleday novel, *The Winter House*, by George Abbe. The
central character is the son of a minister, one who finds himself in
conflict with the status quo. A gentle love story is woven in. . . . I've a
new novel from Edward Anderson. He's the author of *Hungry Men* and
Thieves Like Us. Paramount made a successful picture of *Thieves—They
Ride By Night.* . . . *Jadoo,* an exciting adventure story, will soon be published by Julian Messner."

Bautzer seemed impressed.

"What are you trying to sell in Hollywood at this time, Alex?"

"Man With a Racket," I said quickly. "That's the Pancho Gonzales story, Greg." It was as easy to adopt a friendly air with this high-placed lawyer as to be formal.

Because his law firm represented some top accounts, he could with becoming ease be the dignified Mr. Gregson Bautzer. Where there was no need for the striped pants approach, he could don metaphoric slacks and a sports shirt, and that fit well, too. I felt myself liking the man, and I sensed intuitively that the feeling was reciprocated. I went on, "Cy Rice is the *With* author. There's movie interest in this story of the boy from the wrong side of the racial tracks who made good in tennis. The trouble is, unknown to us, it turned out that producer Herb Margolis had a prior arrangement with Pancho Gonzales to do a screenplay on his life. Result, a snarl developed which makes a sale impossible."

"What's at the bottom of it?"

"A lot of accusations and counter-accusations; I-came-first-and-you-came-last sort of stuff which now adds up to a lot of personal animosity."

We reached Fifty-fourth Street and Avenue of the Americas. We got out, and the car drove off.

At the hotel we were led to a suite. Mr. Bautzer rang room service for a valet and a pitcher of coffee. Waiting, my host reverted to the Hughes book.

"Farr got into your gut, it's clear. I can understand that. And you want to get back at him by doing the book. It might even be a fairly good book, but you just won't get Mr. Hughes's cooperation."

"His not wanting a *bad* book about him to appear certainly makes sense," I conceded. "I'll admit that Farr's book had holes, but didn't Quentin Reynolds make a try?"

Bautzer gave me a sharp look.

"Is he supposed to be such a fine writer?"

The valet appeared first. For the first time outside the movies, I saw a valet at work. He unpacked the two large bags and laid out on a bed the next change so efficiently, I saw the *time saving* in having a valet around. Soon the coffee came. Between sips, the lawyer prepared to shave. Shaving, he left the bathroom door open, and we conversed. I said, "I can well understand that Hughes does not want his marriage to Ella Rice raked up, perhaps the playboy-eccentric stuff. But it's all on the record. Books do not reach many, but along comes a series in the *Daily News* which circulates in the millions." Privately, I thought that a book was a *book,* something that nominally is meant to have permanent value; newspaper and magazine articles are specks of dust in the wind.

My contemplated book, I had to acknowledge, probably wouldn't be any improvement over Farr's. Fitzsimmons's would have been much better, simply because he was a much finer writer, but for a truly important book, even Fitz would have needed access to the private papers.

And the matter of ethics webbed in. Fitzsimmons knew—and this is something that impressed Bautzer—that he could have started the book and then held out for a payoff not to go further. To him Hughes was an "unworthy" character, and Fitz had a code. I did, too, but in a rather different way.

I had long fought against what might be called the "arrogance of wealth," or rather the arrogance assumed by many in a position of power. Hughes, through his agents, tried to impose his will. I am one of those who liked to resist undue pressure, but I had no blanket policy. It depended mostly on circumstances, the details and dictates of the moment.

In relation to Hughes, I never at any time felt any *anti*-bias, as so many exhibited. He puzzled me *then,* as he puzzled me until the very end. I hoped that he would do a lot more than he did in areas which interested him, pollution-ecology and allied conservation tangents. I saw nothing laudable in his Las Vegas takeover, though he may have rationalized that he would be running a cleaner ship. (Las Vegas had always fascinated Hughes, and he had spent a great deal of time there.) He had plans to make the city of casinos a huge port for supersonic jets like the SST's, with smaller planes shuttling to nearby cities.

It troubled him that Nevada was used for nuclear bomb testing, and he protested vigorously. He considered Nevada "his" state. He was in a strong position to influence decisions. This was by contributing to, or withholding funds, from election campaigns. Hughes had always had high Pentagon links, but the tests continued; he could not have his way. He had trouble with the Nevada Gaming Commission. Hughes packed up and left his adopted state.

Considering the many twists in his life, I continued to hope that Hughes would agree to an authorized book, though not a whitewash. I never changed my mind that his true story would make absorbing reading. In that Clifford Irving and McGraw-Hill made no mistake.

I can recall quite vividly what was said at the Warwick because, just as soon as I returned to my office, I committed to paper the meeting, quite like a doctor will make notes while a patient's visit is fresh on his mind.

Through all the years the "Hughes business" remained important to me, but then it had a fresher, a more pungent, a more immediate grip. I'll never forget feeling that I certainly would not want a distorted book about me to appear. In that light I understood Bautzer's efforts to block Farr-type publications. I also recall saying:

"Let's forget *bad* books—is there any chance of the private files being opened to Ben Hecht, or some other top-echelon writer?"

"Not at this time, but I just can't say for the future."

"As far as my agency is concerned, I'm taking the long view. Looking ahead, I would agree to drop my plans if I could be the one to agent any future book on Hughes."

"How does this appeal to you? We'll pay you twenty-five hundred for what you wrote so far on *Gold-Plated Sneakers,* and you will be the agent on any book Hughes will agree to."

If I am offered two thousand five hundred, the smallest amount of business sense would dictate my asking a higher price. This could have been done easily, but I wanted something more important than immediate cash.

Placing books on the market was more than a business to me; I loved working with authors and editors. A book sanctioned by Hughes would have given me a prize to confront editors with. I never forgot what John Budlong had said: "If you can get Mr. Hughes's consent, come back here and write your own ticket." I would have held the joker as well as four aces.

And twenty-five hundred more than covered my out-of-pocket loss. To wait could be to profit greatly. I brought in a related tangent: "Supposing the eventual author will have an agent? Let it be understood that I will be the agent of record, and that there will be an additional 10 percent."

"Agreed—to the extent that Mr. Hughes will have any control over the matter."

"He no doubt will," I decided hopefully, "since, as you said, a look at those private files will be necessary."

Greg Bautzer extended a hand, which I gladly shook.

"Set. When I get back, I'll draw up a formal agreement."

A few days after Greg Bautzer returned to the Coast, there was an air mail special delivery letter from Cy Rice. Cy wrote jubilantly: "We held a meeting at the Bautzer office on Monday. Everyone came. The Bautzer office regards you like a long lost brother and keeps mentioning, 'We want to do something for Alex.' This is a very healthy state of admiration for you on future deals. Bautzer's fee for this would have been at least ten thousand."

The immediate snarl was resolved, after which Desilu showed purchase interest. In the end, there was no sale, but the legal barriers were removed, and I always appreciated very much the friendly attempt to help.

The formal agreement pertained to Joseph M. Schenck Enterprises buying the material which would have gone into *Gold-Plated Sneakers.*

The lawyer was a stockholder in this enterprising TV–motion picture producing firm. As can be assumed, all acts performed on behalf of Howard Hughes had to be executed in ways which could not be traced to him. (This was long before the formation of Rosemont Enterprises.) Aside from the agreement, there was a supplementary letter. A part of the text reads: "It is understood that in the event Howard Hughes, during his lifetime, approves the publication of a biography of his life and such biography, or publication thereof, is controlled by him, you will be retained as a literary agent to handle the sale of such literary property. It is further understood, of course, that in the event Mr. Hughes has no control over the writing and publication of said biography, or that it is an unauthorized writing or publication, there will be no requirement to retain you as such literary agent."

10

Legal (and Illegal) Shenanigans

Back to 8 December 1971.

Once I reached my office, the first thing I did was to approach a steel cabinet. I pulled out a box stuffed with personal papers. There was the original Bautzer agreement, untouched and unlooked at since 1957. What I had kept for handy reference was a copy. Now I read again the contract and letters. I needed the original to make a few copies.

I could now relax, take off my shoes, and slip into old loafers. Should I get a call from some editor, calling me over to negotiate a contract, or meet for lunch, I have at the office a good suit, some mod shirts, and appropriate ties. For clients, I am the *agent*, the businessman-negotiator; for myself I am a very casual sort of guy. I work in my shirtsleeves and have never been too meticulous about dress.

I like to arrive at the office before eight. Once mail is delivered the routine office work starts, and I shelve personal matters, like a bit of my own writing. Today was an exception. My first act was to write to Mr. Bautzer. When I finished, it was time to call my Xerox people to send a pick-up messenger. For my own messenger service I prepared copies of *Barnum-Cinderella*, in which there was mention of my agreement. The book was to be delivered to McGraw-Hill, Dell, and Life. At each house there was some editor I knew and dealt with. A copy, addressed to Clifford Irving, also went to McGraw-Hill. I was very much *for* his book!

Also that day I made it my business to contact the lawyer I had originally retained. Since my attorney or I would be negotiating with legal departments, I wanted to be prepared. Lawyers invariably prefer to deal with their own kind. Like doctors, they speak a language which is singularly their own. "Logic" and "legal" are totally different words, but they are words on which laymen often trip. What is *logical*, and should seemingly follow, might not be at all *legal*.

While I did not need a lawyer in terms of *proving* my case, I reasoned that, if it was true that Hughes acted independently, then even Bautzer and Chester Davis, a top Hughes executive, might not know about the Irving book. And their employer might not be aware of details of the agreement. If so, once they were called to his attention, I was quite certain that Hughes would say to some aide, "Settle with the man."

Up to 1966, no book had appeared on Howard Hughes—not because no authors tried but because for one reason or another, publications were blocked. The two most prominent book-blockers were Greg Bautzer and Chester Davis. But in 1966 the ice was broken—broken with a flood of acrimony and with a barrage of lawsuits that probably set a record for chicanery, double-dealing, and sheer cupidity. The criss-cross maneuvering was so heated, so complicated, the various ramifications are still not fully resolved.

If no books appeared, articles about Hughes kept popping up steadily. It is difficult to think of a magazine which had not given him coverage. Two in particular later became pivotal. One set of articles by Stephen White appeared in *Look* magazine in 1954; the second feature ran in *Life* in 1962, written by Thomas Thompson, then a *Life* staffer.

At Random House Mr. Thompson was signed to do a full-scale portrait. The publishers and author knew, of course, that there would be "consequences," but Random House was Random House, and they decided to travel the path previously chosen by Citadel and Beacon Press . . . and let the court writs fall where they may. Mr. Thompson did not deliver. In time, John Keats was called in to complete *Howard Hughes: A Biography.*

In another sector of Publisher's Row, Lyle Stuart paid Ezra Goodman a $10,000 advance for a similar book. This was in 1964. The publisher was promised a manuscript by the end of 1965.

Random House officials did not have to wait long. According to *Publishers Weekly* (11 July 1966), "An affidavit submitted by Bennett Cerf, said that in 1965 a lawyer for Mr. Hughes told the then-Random House Chairman that Random would be be recompensed if it withheld the book, and would be in great trouble if it did not." The lawyer was Greg Bautzer.

Here let me sketch in a bit about Rosemont Enterprises, the house firm that then sprang into being. Chester Davis wrote:

> Recognizing that the name and achievement of Mr. Hughes now have commercial value, being willing to make use thereof in a manner consistent with his interests, my client, Rosemont Enterprises, Inc., has obtained the sole and exclusive right to use or publish his name, likeness, personality, life story or incidents therein. The publication of any story about Mr. Hughes would appear to invade such rights, even if the matters therein are assumed to be factually accurate.

Rosemont had previously bought all rights to the prior *Look* articles. The articles were based, it was claimed by Rosemont spokesmen, on eight months of extensive research, including personal conferences between author and subject. In 1954 H. H. was still living in an open society, as willing to give as to receive. Rosemont argued that the Keats book was not "authentic biography." In Greg Bautzer's session with Bennett Cerf, the lawyer held out many glittering promises—that if Random House cooperated, there would later be interviews with Mr. Hughes so that, in time, a *genuine* biography would ensue. Bennett Cerf stood his ground; the Keats book would be published as planned.

The Hughes attorneys won a preliminary injunction, restraining Random House from publishing, distributing, advertising, or selling any copies. Random House in turn charged that Rosemont came to court with "unclean hands," as a tool of Howard Hughes, that the *Look* copyrights were bought for the sole purpose of suppressing a biography, or "buying a lawsuit." This is where "logic" and "legal" can be examined. Rosemont *was* a Hughes offspring, seeded for a specific purpose, and its officers were Hughes Co. people. So logically a judge should pay no mind to Rosemont spokesmen; *legal* is another fish. Chester Davis won this round.

Random House had to put a temporary lock on the seventeen thousand copies. For those interested in the contents, *True* magazine, with a circulation of two and a half million, excerpted the book. It caused this comment inside the Hughes hierarchy: "Chester successfully guarded the mouse hole while the elephant walked by."

The beneficent thing about law is that there is always an adversary side—two sides to a question and often a great many interpretations. The right of privacy is juxtaposed by the right to know. In an appeal, Random House won.

Rosemont also crossed the Lyle Stuart threshold. Ezra Goodman did not deliver—he couldn't, having made a compact with Rosemont. As a counter-move, Lyle Stuart, the correctly-named "independent of independents" sued Hughes and Rosemont for one million. There was also an action against Mr. Goodman, charging that the subsequent agreement between him and Rosemont was based on duplicity.

An action inevitably begets a retaliatory move. In California, where he resides, Ezra Goodman lodged a counter suit, naming as codefendents Mr. Hughes, Rosemont, and Lyle Stuart. *Publishers Weekly* reported: "Sheriff's deputies have combed the California hills to serve papers on Mr. Hughes, who is described as more closely guarded than President Johnson." Martin Sheinman, Stuart's lawyer, tagged the actions as "a three-ring circus, or maybe a four-ring one."

The upshot of all the in-fighting and out-fighting was that Random House proved its case that knowledge about Hughes was open to all. Ezra Goodman was subsequently paid $37,500 not to go further. Lyle Stuart was offered a similar sum to call in the dogs, but he boldly refused. He also rejected the offer to wait—to wait until Hughes was ready to cooperate on a *real* biography. In defiance, Stuart published Albert Gerber's *The Bashful Billionaire,* and then followed up with a second Hughes book, Omar Garrison's *Howard Hughes in Las Vegas.*

In these rounds of legal shenanigans, so much was spent in lawyer's fees, Jack Goodman had certainly called the shots about *costs,* a major consideration for a publisher, during our discussion in 1954.

Standard contracts carry a clause that the author will hold a publisher blameless for any libel or invasion of privacy suits. Often this proves to be utterly meaningless, as publishers become deeply involved. Some carry expensive insurance policies. In many cases there are no royalties due an author from which to deduct legal expenses. In the Random House book, friction ensued between John Keats and the publisher. In the *Wall Street Journal* Keats said: "I haven't seen a dime in royalties. Any money the book made went to pay the lawyers."

I quote from a *Wall Street Journal* feature:

> Mr. Keats maintains he shouldn't be forced to pay legal costs because the court never found he did anything wrong and because Random House was aware all along the book might provoke a suit. The publisher replied that Mr. Keats knew the Hughes book was controversial, was aware beforehand that he must share the cost of any legal action against it, and received an advance against royalties.

Legal fees did not trouble Howard Hughes, but for all the frenzied maneuvering, he could not indefinitely keep books about him from being published. And these three marked only the start.

Again let's pose a compelling question: how could Hughes have died in such a horribly wretched state? By simply not obeying, or being psychologically unable to follow advice, even that of his doctors. Hughes had always been his own commander-in-chief. While he could breathe, there was simply no defying his wishes, even if it meant pushing away a tray of food he needed to stay alive. Only when he was comatose, almost dead, was it decided to risk moving him to a hospital in Houston.

At the top echelon, many Hughes aides were exceedingly loyal, at times tenaciously so, and over long periods of time. This surprised many. Serving Hughes required iron nerves and Herculean fortitude, and *income* was only a partial answer. Something about *that man* cast a fascination.

Loyalty to Hughes, it must be mentioned, was manifest only until there was a break in the orchestration. Then the seemingly built-in clamor for vengeance asserted itself. For Noah Dietrich and Robert Maheu, revenge took the form of books, books designed mostly to sink in the harpoon. Here efforts to negotiate, as with a Robert Farr, would fail. While bank accounts may certainly have counted, income was manifestly secondary.

Robert Farr was able to buy from an ex-secretary a pretty complete dossier. That was in 1954. In 1972, Mrs. Marjel Jean DeLauer of Tucson, Arizona, a public relations woman who once worked for Hughes, said that copies of numerous confidential papers had been spirited from Hughes's headquarters and offered to writers during the previous two years. Even at the Pentagon, or the White House, loyalty ends when an overflow of temper cracks the dike.

In mid-December 1971, I watched McGraw-Hill events surrounding the Clifford Irving book very closely. A person believes what he or she *wants* to believe, and so I accepted the prevailing feeling that the Hughes book was authentic. I simply could not believe that McGraw-Hill, plus *Life,* could possibly be taken in. They checked. There were the affidavits and letters from Hughes. Handwriting experts verified them.

I had a reservation on one score only, Hughes's top lieutenants not being told about the book, but even this could be accepted. It could be *like* Hughes to act on his own initiative on a matter of this sort. Why *should* he confide in all, or some, of his close aides? Had not Noah and Maheu proved to be ungrateful bastards, as Hughes would see it? And didn't Rosemont prove to be a bust?

Once my lawyer studied my agreement, letters went to McGraw-Hill, Life, Dell, putting them on notice. We doubted that matters would ever come to court; we also knew that it would be next to impossible to "catch" Hughes, but money could be attached at the source. I was willing to pay premiums on the huge bond which would have to be posted.

Editors at Dell and *Life* to whom I had written replied quickly that the controlling rights were held by McGraw-Hill. Faustin F. Jehle of McGraw-Hill's legal department wrote that Harold McGraw, to whom I had written, was out of town, and so he was replying. He stressed something I knew, that my claim related to Howard Hughes and Greg Bautzer. This was obvious, but I wanted to be *prepared.*

Greg Bautzer replied very amiably:

> Dear Alex: First of all, Happy new Year. Secondly, I am completely aware of all the commitments which we entered into with you. However, the much publicized, anticipated biography of Mr. Hughes, in so far as any information that Chester Davis and I have, is totally unauthorized.

I began to fear then, early in January 1972, that if I went out and bought myself a new desk, it would not be with "windfall money." But society at large did not know. Hughes was yet to hold his televised phone interview. To almost everybody, the McGraw-Hill-*Life* imprint *assured* authenticity, and so well-wishers continued to think that I was about to cross over into sudden riches. Even after the Bautzer letter arrived, I rationally thought that it was futile to hope—but I hoped.

I called an editor at McGraw-Hill, and we set up an immediate date. That day at five, in my office, which was a few blocks east of the (then) McGraw-Hill building, I showed him Bautzer's letter—he was unmoved. The editor said:

"Personally, I happen to think that Irving is a shit, a blow-hard, and not a particularly good writer. But this is a personal view. The brass has absolutely no doubt that the autobiography is authentic. Plenty of Hughes experts at *Life* claim that there is enough inside stuff which could not have been faked."

So the interview left me a bit less divided, but still puzzled and apprehensive.

11
Literary Hoaxes

Below is the first paragraph of *High Vermillion* (Houghton Mifflin and Bantam Books, 1947), a Western by Luke Short.

> Behind him, the lingering heat from the assay furnace touched his back with a welcome warmth for this high-country September night. Larkin Moffat ceased his writing now. He lifted both big hands from the rough deal table on which he'd been working and, his black brows drawn straight in a frown of concentration, reached past the kerosene lamp and released the catch on the delicate glass-cased set of sample balances beyond.

Here's the first paragraph of *Strike at Cripple Creek* (Lennox Hill press and Belmont-Tower, 1971), a Western by Bob Haning.

> Behind him, the lingering heat from the assay furnace touched his back with a welcome warmth. It tended to get cold in the high country on a September night. Boyd Sinclear ceased his writing, lifted both hands from the rough table on which he'd been working and, his brows drawn in a frown of concentration, reached past the coal-oil lamp and released the catch on the set of sample balances beyond.

The almost word-for-word duplication runs through the entire book. How could such flagrant thievery happen? Let's toss the ball around a bit.

English literature is full of references to literary hoaxes, and more recently it was brought out that Coleridge could have stood a bit of investigating. Unique in the history of literary frauds is the Richardson & Snyder fracas—unique because more than a hoax was involved. The questionable book was *God's Broker* by Antoni Gronowicz, published in April and pronounced dead in July.

This hoax not only killed a promising new firm, it set the two partners into bitter combat. Stewart (Sandy) Richardson had for many years occupied top slots with some leading publishers. He formed a partnership with Julien M. Snyder, founder of *International Moneyline*, a financial newsletter with some twenty thousand subscribers.

I watched this firm very closely, for here was a new house that seemed destined to grow. A highly knowledgeable book person allied with a financial source, E. P. Dutton was to be their distributor. The foundation was solid.

The *New York Times* was the first to announce, about *God's Broker:* PUBLISHER TO WITHDRAW A BOOK ON POPE'S LIFE.

Mr. Snyder called the book "a blatant attempt to do a high-class Clifford Irving hoax, but it was my bank account, or the business bank account, that was being taken advantage of." He added, "It is incredible that a former editor-in-chief of Doubleday would buy it without checking out the obvious details."

Sandy Richardson had an answer *(New York Times)*. "The book was taken on in good faith. I was influenced by the text itself and the endorsement from Cardinal Krol."

Cardinal John Krol of Philadelphia, who had close ties to the Pope, had written a note to Mr. Gronowicz on 27 December 1982, saying: "I am not engaging in flattery when I say that your book is a masterpiece—different and better than anything I have read."

But later Cardinal Krol wrote to Mr. Richardson that he was retracting his endorsement of *God's Broker*. The Cardinal tried to explain: "Toni importuned me to write a brief commendation of his book before I had a chance to read it. In good faith and trust I wrote a note to the effect that his treatment was masterful. Having read selective parts of the book, I must direct you not to use my statement in your publicity."

Sandy Richardson was also impressed by a photo showing Pope John Paul II and Antoni Gronowicz, but the picture, it later was reported, "had been cropped from a group audience with the Pope, to indicate his close personal relationship with the Pope."

Mr. Gronowicz is also the author of that widely disputed Garbo biography which Simon & Schuster contracted to publish only after her death. John Herman, a senior editor, said, "We think we have a wonderful manuscript. As of this moment we plan to publish it energetically." While Mr. Herman did not think that the Garbo book would be affected in any way by the controversy over the Pope book, I had my doubts. I knew that the Garbo manuscript had been offered to Putnam. Bill Targ was not the only editor who smelled some stale caviar. Collectively they said, "Thanks, but no thanks."

The Hitler diaries hoax is of too recent vintage to need repeating. Another somewhat recent embarrassment stands out. It is *In His Image: The Cloning of a Man* by David Rorvik. The publisher was J. B. Lippincott. In his book Mr. Rorvik made the claim that an unnamed American millionaire had financed the birth of a boy who had his genetic makeup. (Cloning is producing a genetically identical duplicate of an organism using the nucleus of a cell.) The book brought in research by J. D. Bromhall, an authority in experimental embryology, for that needed aura of authenticity. Dr. Bromhall sued, claiming that the Rorvik book was a fraud and a hoax, something with which he vehemently wanted no association. There was a jury trial and Dr. Bromhall won.

Lucky Luciano's reported *Last Testament* supposedly was based on numerous taped interviews granted to film producer Martin Gosch. But when it came time to step into the ring, no Luciano tapes were found to exist. Provable errors in previously published books were also picked up in the new work. The author was Richard Hammer, called in after Martin Gosch's untimely death.

While the Clifford Irving bonfire flared, some ashes sparked embers on another set of "memoirs," this time by novelist Robert P. Eaton, who had at one time been married to Lana Turner. Since Ms. Turner had been close to Howard Hughes, she no doubt picked up valuable anecdotes to which her husband could have been privy. *The Ladies' Home Journal* excerpted parts. There was this note, supposedly from *the source:* "Robert—These notes are for your eyes only. I authorize you to edit them and arrange to have them published as my memoirs." Knowing the fierce bias, I did not think the words carried the ring of truth. Nor did a judge, who issued an injunction against the book being distributed. The publishers obeyed.

When he had been the editor of *Smart Set,* Charles Hanson Towne had unwittingly published a story that had appeared three years before in *Atlantic Monthly.* This prompted him to write an essay for *International Book Review,* describing the care an editor must exercise to avoid deception.

Trader Horn, which old-timers will recall fondly, was a palpable fraud, as was Joan Lowell's best-selling "autobiography," *Cradle of the Deep* (Simon & Schuster, 1929). Miss Lowell had turned in a stirring sea epic which covered her early years. She wrote of having been taken to the South Seas before she was a year old. Growing up, she sailed for sixteen years and more than one hundred thousand miles aboard a four-masted ship commanded by her father and manned by a crew of colorful old tars. With exposure, it came out that her childhood was spent tamely in Berkeley, California. The Book-of-the-Month Club offered a refund to its sixty-five thousand subscribers, though few took advantage of the offer.

Louis de Rougemont deserves special mention. He had walked into the offices of *Wide World,* a prestigious London men's magazine distinguished for running *true* "action" stories, which is the exception and not the rule in the men's magazine field. The adventurer regaled the editors with an incredible yarn—or rather a series of astounding yarns. He spoke of having gone on a pearl-fishing expedition. Came a typhoon and the fleet was wrecked. First he swam to a sandbar. There he beach-combed long enough to build a boat that brought him to Australia.

The wary *Wide World* editors called in experts familiar with the Australian bush country, and a lot of questions followed. For de Rougemont claimed that to stop tribal warfare he had erected stilts seven feet high. Seeing this giant god, the enemy panicked. He claimed that he had painted his face in four colors, mounted his hair on strips of whalebone two feet long. Before the story was published, it was properly "authenticated." Once in print, the fantastic narrative was widely republished on a world scale.

Hailed and feted, de Rougemont lectured extensively before scientific academies, and even the experts were taken in. It was some time before exposure caught up, and it happened quite unexpectedly. De Rougemont's deserted wife saw a picture of the "famed explorer" in an Australian newspaper. The imposter was "plain" Henri Louis Grin. "Unfrocked," exposed, the erstwhile "cannibal chief" became a music hall entertainer, billing himself as "The Greatest Liar on Earth."

Lyle Stuart's *Naked Came The Stranger* remains too well known to need much elaboration. The book, as almost all know, originated with Mike McGrady, a columnist for *Newsday,* a prosperous and a long-established Long Island newspaper. It was Mr. McGrady's sister-in-law, Mrs. Billie Young, who impersonated "Penelope Ashe" on television and in interviews. It was she who was supposed to have brought the manuscript to the fire-brand publisher. What is not generally known is that when an unknown appeared at the old Lyle Stuart Manhattan office—the firm had since established itself in Secaucus, New Jersey—he or she was told that the firm was not accepting submissions because the lists were filled for the next two years. This was done to discourage unsolicited submissions, which would invariably fail to meet Lyle Stuart's keenly specialized requirements.

Stranger was a highly felicitous publication for the House of Stuart. And it is very possible that this "sex-in-the-suburbs" pastiche might never have seen the light of day had a literary agent been involved. Agents do submit manuscripts under assorted pseudonyms, but one reason editors overwhelmingly prefer to deal with agents is that the reputable ones privately explain a book's true status. Agreements are not valid unless signed by an author's actual name. Then it is added: "Who writes as. . . ."

An agent might have gone along with the spoof, but the book's true circumstances would have been explained. Forewarned, the Lyle Stuart first reader might well have said the equivalent of: "No, thanks, it sounds too complicated; one never knows how a hoax will turn out." But Lyle Stuart was aware. He later wrote to me: "The girl who came to our window with *Naked Came The Stranger* insisted that she had written a book 'as good as anything done by Jacqueline Susann.' She did not know then or on the subsequent visit that I was aware of the gag from the beginning."

Soon after the heavy promotion started, it was calculatedly exposed that the book was writted by twenty-four co-writers on the *Newsday* staff. But, it should be stressed, all were capable, professional writers—or they would not have been employed by *Newsday*. Exposure did not hurt sales.

Quentin Reynolds was a much-publicized victim. The brazen ripoff, *The Man Who Wouldn't Talk,* stemmed from the bragging of George DuPre, a Canadian intelligence agent who returned safely from World War II. Loquacious, he told exciting stories of his experiences with the French underground. After regaling friends and neighbors, he began to lecture at local church and club meetings. Then for out-of-town audiences. Lecturing became a semi-profession. After six years of it, DuPre's stories began to include accounts of Nazi tortures, which were fanciful. The tales caught the attention of people connected with Reader's Digest. Next, DuPre was teamed with Quentin Reynolds. Random House published the book. After exposure Bennett Cerf reclassified the book as fiction, and commented wryly, "The book should have been called *The Man Who Talked Too Much*."

Hoaxsters can start very young. Consider the exploit of Lloyd Lewis. Lloyd, then a fifteen-year-old farm boy from Plattsburg, Missouri, won a $5,000 prize for an essay about peace. The competition had been keen. The contest, no doubt because it was sponsored by Eddie Cantor, was highly publicized. Lloyd must have glowed before his parents, friends, and especially his teachers. The boy was invited on an expense-paid trip to New York. More fame and hoopla. Exposure followed the discovery that Lloyd had copied an article by Dr. Frank Kingdon, president of the University of Newark. Dr. Kingdon's article *How Can We Stay Out of War?* had been published in the December 1935 issue of *Peace Digest.*

Bouregy & Curl (which became Thomas Bouregy Co.) once received the manuscript of a mystery novel, *The Golden Ballast,* by Anthony Hodgson. They liked the story, contracted for it, paid an advance. Because a published book goes first to reviewers, a copy went to Anthony Boucher, then the *New York Times* reviewer of whodunits. The story seemed very familiar to Boucher, who discovered a verbatim copy of a Doubleday book, *Tender to Danger,* by Eliot Reed (a pseudonym adopted by two British writers, Eric Ambler and Charles Rodda). The two thousand copies that were already distributed had to be called back post haste. The fraud was extensively written up at the time. Tom Bouregy took his loss philosophically. "The publicity helped us sell other books," he said to me.

As previously reported, I had the good fortune to crawl out from under a bomb before the burning fuse reached the detonation point. The hoax would have had classic proportions, inasmuch as it featured a name that is still prominent, Jonas E. Salk, M.D. This is how the book was listed in the Citadel Press Spring 1955 catalog:

The Story Behind the Salk Polio Vaccine

By Dr. Jonas E. Salk

Dr. John F. Enders, Dr. Thomas Francis, Jr.,
Dr. Dorothy M. Horstmann, Dr. Joseph A. Bell,
Dr. David Bodian, Dr. Albert Sabin, Surgeon
General Leonard A. Scheele and others

as told to Robert N. Farr

formerly feature writer for the Scripps-Howard Science Service

Here is the first authentic account of one of the greatest discoveries in medical history—the Salk vaccine for paralytic polio. While it is true that few events in medical history have been more publicized, more widely discussed in newspapers and magazines, and have created more controversy, there has yet to appear the true, full story of how the Salk polio vaccine was discovered, how it is manufactured, and how it is distributed both in the United States, Canada and elsewhere.

Now, in The Story Behind the Salk Polio Vaccine, this need has been met and by the only men and women who could fulfill it—Dr. Jonas E. Salk and all of the other important scientists and public figures directly associated with the discovery, manufacture and distribution of the Salk vaccine. Told in the actual words of these men and women— there are four chapters by Dr. Salk—as related to Robert N. Farr, a distinguished scientific editor who spent months with Dr. Salk and the other contributors, The Story Behind the Salk Polio Vaccine is unquestionably one of the most important books published in the last decade.

Soundly scientific, this book is basically a warm, human story that will bring tears to the eyes of the reader and joy to his heart. For it tells the dramatic story of the emerging triumph over one of the greatest scourges civilization has ever faced. It is a book of hope for all mankind. With 16 photographs.

When Farr's Hughes book collapsed, I also had to seek a new publisher for the polio anthology. Citadel had now lost their zeal for Robert Farr, and also for polio. That year a mild epidemic broke out, and the polio reality continued to be confused, unsatisfactory.

I struck interest in the polio book at Funk & Wagnalls. Strong interest. However, they wanted to publish only Dr. Salk's part of the anthology. Farr was then on a visit to New York, and the two top Funk & Wagnalls editors, Herbert M. Katz and Otto V. St. Whitelock, had Farr and me to lunch. All details were worked out for taking over the Citadel contract. Farr "guaranteed" that he would "deliver Salk"; that is, produce more chapters, provided he was given a free hand. Again my spirits soared.

Otto V. St. Whitelock had strong science connections of his own, and he put through a call directly to Dr. Salk. The Funk & Wagnalls editor then phoned me—to astound me by saying that Dr. Salk knew nothing of the projected new book, or the chapters attributed to him in the old book.

I wrote to Dr. Salk, and drew this reply.

May 4, 1956

Dear Mr. Jackinson,
Would it surprise you to know that I have had but one meeting with Mr. Robert Farr, and not a very encouraging one for him. I have not seen either the chapters attributed to me, nor the book. Nor did we, at that one meeting, discuss such details as agents, etc. You may, therefore, understand that I am at a loss to know how he had made representations such as he seems to have done.
I was especially amazed at the description in the catalogue of the Citadel Press. From your letter you apparently know of my communication with Funk & Wagnalls and can understand that whatever you submitted to them cannot have my approval any more than that which you have at Citadel Press.

Sincerely,
Jonas E. Salk, M.D.

What happened was that Farr had gone to the medical journals and completely rewrote Dr. Salk's scientific papers. In the rewriting, he added liberally his own "popular" touches. If this had been done with proper authorization, everything would have been ale and hale, but that missing consent was very much like forging a check. And there was no insurance for the publishers.

So many years later, the involved editors and I still wonder: *how were we taken in?* The Citadel heads also had had Farr and me to lunch. Farr, a very large, fat man, was gracious and well-mannered. He spoke softly but eloquently and convincingly. He had an ingratiating manner, but we were duped because Farr offered what seemed to be valid arguments. Dr. Salk, he insisted, disliked dealing with "merchants"—publishers and agents—but that he, a fellow scientist, always had an open door. So the contract should be with him, and he, he explained, had private arrangements on royalties with Dr. Salk and other contributors. An echo can be found in Clifford Irving's insistence that he had Howard Hughes's full confidence, but that it would "blow the whole ball game" if McGraw-Hill violated Hughes's wish for secrecy until *he* was ready to spring the news.

Until the floodgates opened, Clifford Irving's fame, such as it had then been, rested mostly on his litigation-loaded art book, *Fake!* His first novel, *On A Darkling Plain,* was published in 1956 by Putnam's. It had had eight previous rejections. *The Losers, The Valley, Spy,* and *Battle For Jerusalem,* a story of the Six-Day War, came next. The books must have done well, or he would not have been consistently published by McGraw-Hill, but one would have to go to the *mystiques* of publishing to understand why the McGraw-Hill contract guaranteed Irving total advances of $150,000 for his next three books.

It is well-known that *Fake!* told the story of the Hungarian artist, Elmyr de Hory, called "the most successful art forger of modern times." On the CBS show "Sixty Minutes" (6 February 1972), Irving described how he personally had brought "Matisses" and "Modiglianis" to reputable art dealers, fibbed about having inherited the paintings from a rich aunt in Paris, and had his words taken at face value. De Hory, who ought to know, said, "The more outrageous a hoaxster's behavior, the more easily he was believed."

Irving hoodwinked the Museum of Modern Art. Other prestigious museums and top-level dealers eagerly bought de Hory's fakes. Prompted by Mike Wallace, Irving stated: "All the world loves to see the experts and the Establishment made a fool of. And everyone likes to feel that those who set themselves up as experts are really as gullible as anyone else. And so, Elmyr as the great art faker of the twentieth century becomes a modern folk hero for the rest of us."

It was not de Hory who had sued Clifford Irving, but Farnard Legros, the art dealer who claimed that he had been defamed. He sued for a modest $55 million and he won a judgment. For a descriptive tag to *Fake!,* the author came up with a twelfth-century French proverb: "If fools did not go to market, cracked pots and false wares would not be sold."

Fake! tempts many to think that it had probably been the seed, the inspiration point for the rupture between Howard Hughes and another of his general staff, Robert Maheu.

For McGraw-Hill, hoax-scandals ran tandem-fashion. While Irving was still claiming attention, it was brought out that *The Memoirs Of Chief Red Fox,* a best-seller here and abroad, was deemed questionable. The so-styled 101-year-old Sioux Chief, William Red Fox, was accused of lifting many of his recollections from James H. McGregor's *The Wounded Knee Mission,* published some thirty years before. McGraw-Hill acknowledged its error and settled with the McGregor heirs. Chief Red Fox's veracity began to be questioned by his own peers.

It is interesting to note how some alert individual can catch these frauds. The Luke Short swindle surfaced in September 1975, over this letter sent to Belmont-Tower books:

Yesterday, I purchased a copy of *Strike At Cripple Creek* by Bob Haning. This is an exact copy of the novel, *High Vermillion*, by Luke Short, first published in 1947. The only thing that has been changed in the book is the characters' names. Everything else is the same, word for word.

I am very much annoyed. I think this is illegal because it is called "plagiarism." If the copyright laws have expired and it is legal to do this, not only do I think it is in very poor taste but Frederick Gliddens, who used the pen name "Luke Short" has recently died of cancer, and I don't really think this is fair to him.

Yours truly,
Rodney L. Gigone

I replied:

Dear Mr. Gigone:
Your September 8th letter to Belmont-Tower was passed on to me because I am Bob Haning's literary agent, or rather I *was* until the swindle surfaced. It was I who placed the book—first with Lenox Hill Press, the hardcover publisher, then with Belmont-Tower.

Everyone involved in Publishing is aware of a wide assortment of deceits, plagiarisms, hoaxes. When it is brought to light, we, the victims, are hurt. Haning's is a swindle of the vilest sort, for it breaches the very core of an agent-author relationship. An agent has faith in a client; editors, in turn, lean on an agent's dependability. . . ."

For Bob Haning I had placed seven gun-and-hoof sagas. Six were with Lenox Hill Press, a division of Crown Publishers. All six were published. At the paperback end, I worked out a six-book deal with Belmont-Tower. Two paperbacks were issued: a third was on the presses when the lid blew off. The remaining three were quickly pulled out of the printers' paws. The published book was out less than a month when Mr. Gigone's attention was snared.

Houghton Mifflin had published Luke Short in hardcover; Bantam, in paperback. An exchange of letters followed from the various publishers and their lawyers. I quote part of a letter Nat Wartels of Crown wrote to Victor Temkin (then) of Bantam:

. . . I am confident that you, Houghton Mifflin and any other people involved in the book business will understand that except for the "author" of *Strike At Cripple Creek,* we, Jackinson and Tower acted in good faith and were victims of this kind of trick which occasionally happens and which it is almost, if not entirely, impossible to avoid.

Publishing is a many-winged romance, with cupid at times getting shot with his own arrow.

12
Greed

Farr's polio hoax died aborning, so there was no publicity. The Hughes book was also buried alive in anonymity. I have not again heard from Farr. I have been trying to locate him ever since my first book began to take shape. That was back in 1963. I wrote to Farr. All letters were returned, "Address Unknown." I wrote to Farr's mother, Wanda Farr; the reply came from her lawyer, and it said briefly that, if I was able to locate Robert, to please let the worried mother know.

While I was dealing with Citadel, and then with Funk & Wagnalls, Farr kept pressing me for additional advances. "Since you collected a Hundred Thousand on your cigarette patent," I questioned, "why do you claim to be broke?" He replied glibly that the money was in a trust fund, and that he could touch only the interest. It seemed believable. For his spendthrift tastes, it simply was not enough. The most lavish box of candy Matilda or I ever saw was a "gift" to her from Farr.

In submitting manuscripts to Fleet Publishing Co., I got to know Nancy Hunter. It turned out that, for a short time, the editor had been married to Farr. Nancy and I began to compare Bob's fantasies. The hundred thousand tobacco income was a fabrication, as were most of his grandiose "plans." We agreed that he could write well and certainly knew science. He might have succeeded in either field, but some unfathomable impulse compelled him to traverse rather devious byways.

I long nursed a sneaking hunch that Farr was too egotistical to adopt a pseudonym and that, sooner or later, a book of his would appear. So I kept watching for his name. My vigilance was finally rewarded: in an April 1975 issue of *Publishers Weekly,* there was an advance review of *The Electronic Criminals.*

I phoned a senior editor at McGraw-Hill. What could she tell me about Robert Farr? She did not know very much, save that he resided in London. I explained why I asked. She did not know of *Barnum-Cinderella,* where Farr is conspicuous. I said that a copy of my book would go over by messenger, plus some old letters from the author, so that Farr's signature on the contract might be compared.

In conversation a week later we established that we were speaking of the same person. The editor had learned that Farr was considered a "big man," and that the book had previously been published in England. It says on the jacket: "A close-up look at criminal capers in a technological age. Based on the author's own experiences as an expert in the field of computer fraud and industrial criminology, the book's cast of characters includes fakes, forgers, swindlers, embezzlers, con men. . . . Mr. Farr details Ponzi schemes, computer rip-offs, international heists and a host of hoaxes and frauds." The London wife, Betty Farr, and Nancy Hunter, could exchange some interesting notes!

After the break, Farr had undertaken a biography of Edna St. Vincent Millay. He then moved to Maine, close to the town where the poet was born. Crown was to have been the publisher. A sizable advance was paid; there was considerable press converage. Later I proposed buying the contract for an idea I had about publishing the book under Impact Press. Nat Wartels replied that the book was totally unpublishable, though it read well. He said that sections were lifted from a book published in England, parts were fabricated.

Farr, whom I had gotten to know quite well, was calculatedly clever, glib, a delight to listen to. I also met Haning. His conversation was flat, colorless, a reflection of the man. How do hoaxsters reason? Unless we are dealing with an advanced mental case, a person who undertakes a fraud must weigh chances of exposure. How could Haning have reasoned? Luke Short was very widely ready so chances of discovery would seem to be too great.

Farr could speak convincingly on almost all topics. He was especially well-versed in science and law. Rationally, he had to know that he was taking horrible risks. Before the contracted-for polio book appeared, someone might contact Dr. Salk directly, as eventually happened. Or, when published, it was a certainty that much publicity would follow. Highly unpleasant repercussions were inevitable. The book would certainly have to be withdrawn and royalties, if any, held up. Farr would have to face me. Others. Laws against fraud and misrepresentation. Was he too deeply in the delusional fog to reason? Or did he look ahead with some perverse relish to the inevitable fuss . . . even though future books might have to written under a pseudonym?

How could Clifford Irving have reasoned? That Hughes was sick, incapacitated, and perhaps might conveniently die? Or that Hughes's behavior was so erratic, his disclaimers could not amount to much, either way?

Irving claims to have long been fascinated by Howard Hughes. The author stated that his father, Jay Irving, a cartoonist, had known Hughes personally, and that Jay's sister had dated Hughes. The basic idea for the Hoax of Hoaxes must have been deeply rooted, but Irving's plans began to take concrete shape in the fall of 1970, when news erupted of a violent split at the very top of the Hughes organization. This was the firing of Robert Maheu, which pitted Maheu into conflict with Chester Davis and Bill Gay, another high-slot Hughes executive. Hughes accused Maheu, of "robbing mc blind." Maheu promptly sued for defamation. The break received very wide publicity.

Time and then *Life* carried follow-up features, and reproduced Hughes's signature on the "Dear Chester," "Dear Bill" letters that authorized them to take full control. There was the signature—H. R. Hughes—for Irving to study, copy, perfect and later use—so effectively, even experts were fooled.

The idea seeded, Irving carefully nurtured the embryonic plant, gave it the right amount of sun, shade, water. He did not at once produce a manuscript. The start was low-key. First there was a series of letters supposedly from Hughes to him. This led to the book proposal. Irving spoon-fed intriguing letters to Beverly Jane Loo. Would McGraw-Hill like an authorized biography of Howard Hughes? It was like asking if a publisher would like Nancy Reagan's unvarnished memoirs. Miss Loo ferried the proposal to the top. All were enthused. This again makes me recall what John P. R. Budlong had said years back.

Miss Loo, let it be quickly stressed, was no naive, dewey-eyed recent lit grad who entered publishing with a lot of romantic notions about writers and publishers. Beverly Loo was a war-scarred veteran. As *McCall's* fiction editor, she could spot and spit into the eye of a phony. But Irving had been a McGraw-Hill author for twelve years; she had immense faith in him, and they had become personal friends. She had been a house guest at Ibiza. *Any* editor in a similar spot would have been sucked in.

Many felt about Hughes as did Fitzsimmons. Not only after the gigantic exposure; the difference was manifest long before. But an infinitely greater number found the *old* Hughes an intriguing, sphinx-like character, fascinating precisely because he stood alone atop a mountain. And there was that wishful-thinking. *What I would do if I had a tenth of his money!*

Irving's manuscript grew and grew, and so did McGraw-Hill's confidence that they had a great scoop—so great that Beverly Loo had no difficulty in pinning down the following subsidiary rights prices: Dell, for the reprint, $400,000; Book-of-the-Month Club, $325,000; *Life,* for some excerpts, $250,000. The outlay of $750,000 in advances was more than covered. What if the Man of Mystery was cash-minded and demanded more and more? Book buyers always responded to the ballyhooed book, and there was all the subsidiary rights loot. Just about every country in the world would pay heavily for translation rights.

Irving, it seemed, went about it very cleverly. First, he pledged McGraw-Hill to utter secrecy—and it seemed plausible. Hughes was an unstable man to deal with, and had to be handled with the care of one stepping on nails. Irving was well aware of the Hughes Tool Co., and of Rosemont. So he wrote into the agreement that he, Hughes, was acting *independently*, and thus in this instance bypassed his closest associates. This, too, carried a certain built-in acceptance.

Checks should be made out to H. R. Hughes. One large check was drawn in the name of Howard R. Hughes, and Irving asked that a new check be issued. Later it became obvious why; at the time it was chalked up to another of Hughes's idiosyncracies.

When Edith Irving started an account at a Swiss Bank under the name of H. R. Hughes, it was a thoroughly routine transaction. Hughes is a fairly common name. The first Hughes check passed without incident. She, too, had learned how to simulate the signature. Swiss banks were very secretive about Swiss accounts—unless fraud and forgery were involved.

Clifford Irving had to take some calculated, or miscalculated, risks. If Howard Hughes *agreed*, why couldn't he, Irving, simply appear at the hotel in Nassau? Hughes *didn't* agree, and so the taping sessions had to be held elsewhere. Irving invented trysts in Mexico, Puerto Rico, Florida. He was not alone, only instead of Hughes, he was resuming a long-standing on-and-off affair with Baroness Nina, and then starting a new romance with Anne Baxter, the scuba-diver teacher.

In California, Irving renewed some old friendships, with Irving Wallace, and especially with Stanley Meyer, the man who made possible the transformation of Hughes's biography into an *auto*biography. This had much more cash value. Here might be a good time to bring in Noah Dietrich and James Phelan, the ace investigative reporter who, being a prime Howard Hughes watcher, is responsible for having given the mystery its final solution.

As history recorded events, the first effective thrust to the hoax's jugular was Howard Hughes's elaborate phone interview with the seven preselected reporters, picked because each of them had known Hughes and had interviewed him. The taping was done on 7 January and was offered to the public two days later. The death rattle started then.

While almost any sort of erratic behavior can be expected from the unpredictable "shadow in the public glare," as I once called Hughes, there are many things which it is a certainty that he would *not* have done—he would emphatically not deny granting an author interviews if he had actually done so. So I knew then that I no longer had a case, but tangents about the affair continued to be mystifying. Since McGraw-Hill insisted that the story they had was *authentic* Hughes "inside stuff," how did it get to Irving?

Before the open break, Noah Dietrich had had a long and a very intimate connection with Hughes. For thirty-two years he had been a sort of proxy father, first to young Hughes, and then to the adult. Dietrich, an astute accountant-business man, was an executive of the Hughes Tool Co., also of TransWorld Airlines. The main reason for the eventual rupture was Dietrich's claim that his substantial salary (half a million a year) was eaten away by state and federal taxes, but that the Hughes empire kept growing—thanks, he stressed, to his acumen. He wanted stock options in the Hughes Tool Co. Howard Hughes was prepared to give his closest aide-de-camp *anything*—anything save an indirect partnership. That would "dilute" his sole ownership, a matter about which the autocratic Hughes felt very strongly.

After Mr. Dietrich packed up his private papers, he filed suit for compensation. The action was settled out of court in 1959. Two agreements were reached, mostly dealing with large additional payments. In exchange, the ex-Hughes official agreed not to disclose any information about Howard Hughes or the Tool Company, or Hughes Aircraft, TransWorld Airlines or other Hughes business activities. But in recapitulating events for print, the old preceptor offered some revealing insights into the Howard Hughes when he was a roisterer. They had worked well together, Dietrich playing the role of attendant, adviser, and hatchetman when heads had to roll, which was frequently. They fit like a lock and key.

What is forgotten is that Dietrich could be a witness only up to 1957. After that his utterances to the press and on TV talk shows were extremely unreliable. He too patently exhibited an accumulated hostility, and he knew Hughes after 1957 primarily by tuning in on public information.

Those who, for one reason or another, had their telescopic sights set on Howard Hughes, had known for some time that this highly placed subaltern had done a hatchet job on his ex-boss. It was a book that had trouble landing a front-rank publisher. Editors were not afraid of *sales* so much as they were dubious about the quality of the book. There were enough nasty tidbits about Hughes to arouse interest, and that meant sales, but corollary problems stirred second thoughts. Publishers feared litigation. On a book considered really worthwhile, and which critics might praise, risks would sooner be taken. But Noah Dietrich's exposé was considered a notch or two below first-class entertainment, and thus not worth the involved risks.

James Phelan is a salty character who likes to dress as though he were racing through a time machine to have drinks with Daniel Boone or Davy Crockett. There is a frontiersman tang and honesty about the reporter, who had long made a specialty of writing about Hughes. Or Phelan could be pictured dropping out of a chopper to interview Hemingway in the midst of a tiger hunt. Phelan was Noah Dietrich's first collaborator. And it seemed to be an ideal mating. For a while the marriage worked fine.

Both lived in California, close to the Hollywood orbit. In the Beverly Hills set, great stock is placed in the "contact," in someone knowing someone who knew someone else. That is how a copy of the Phelan-Dietrich manuscript got to Stanley Meyer, and through him to Paul Gitlin; and also, surreptitiously, to Clifford Irving.

Paul Gitlin, of Ernst, Cane, Berner & Gitlin, is a combination New York lawyer and literary agent, or rather literary entrepreneur. Gitlin has a reputation of being a top, tough "businessman-agent," representing mostly giants like Harold Robbins and Irving Wallace. Philip Roth entered the gilded portals, and there was a lot of publicity about it. Quality writers, too?

It is argued that the multi-million-dollar deals raise legal and tax problems which are over the heads of most agents. Hollywood contracts have long been handled by lawyers. Many stars use their lawyer's office as a clearinghouse for sundry activities, which include the acquisition of properties. (I have submitted many stories to attorney Louis C. Blau meant for Richard Widmark.) In effect, the lawyers also serve as the star's agent. The practice has spilled over into publishing.

Paul Gitlin auctioned off Irving Wallace's next three books. The auction, which was held in a Manhattan hotel suite, took five hours. Bids came and went from publishers' representatives. Simon & Schuster and Bantam emerged as the "winners." Quotes are used deliberately, for this sort of stock-exchanging carries seeds of disaster. Rivalry being what it is, the six-foot writer will want what the seven-foot giant received, and so on up the line.

An Irving Wallace might privately wish to be left alone to complete a book and bring it to his agent or publisher, but he could point to "pressures," to an ego-wish to be one of the pack's heads. We glory that in our competitive society the loudest homage is paid to one who bangs the cash register the hardest. Good, but not always. Those next in line are also spurred to prod their agents or to seek a lawyer. Too many books are not *written* so much as they are prefabricated to meet a deadline set long in advance.

Viewed one way, McGraw-Hill would have come out ahead, and in that sense the heavy outlays were justified. The Irving Wallace books would assuredly make money, even if critics were displeased. The point is, once the big houses allow the super property to become dominant, they will individually rue something they could not do collectively: set a standard of self-regulation.

Paul Gitlin was not called in to sell Howard Hughes but Noah Dietrich. It was thought all he had to do was to make a few phone calls. How could book people say No to *him*? But this time even Gitlin failed to haul in the big fish.

Stanley Meyer was at one time a co-producer with Jack Webb of *Dragnet,* and he took part in many other TV-movie deals. Meyer had married the daughter of Nate Blumberg, once the top banana at Universal Pictures. Meyer had "contacts," including some in publishing. The *New York Times* of 16 February 1972 reported that Stanley Meyer was "a friend who had advised Mr. Dietrich on marketing his memoirs." The producer also knows Greg Bautzer. I quote from the *Times* story: "Gregory Bautzer, a lawyer in Los Angeles who has represented Mr. Hughes, said Mr. Meyer had left chapters of one version of the Dietrich memoirs with him in a series of meetings that began on Nov. 23, 1970. Mr. Bautzer said he could not explain why Mr. Meyer brought him the chapters."

More than one guess is needed!

The *Times* writer should have gotten Mr. Bautzer's first name right, Gregson, but something much more significant was involved. Bautzer was in Howard Hughes's corner; by 1970 Noah Dietrich stood snarling at the other end of the ring. So why, indeed, was Mr. Bautzer shown the text?

One theory has it that deliberate sabotage was at work to "kill" the publication of the Phelan manuscript. Word got to the elderly and crochety Mr. Dietrich that the manuscript wasn't very well done, and that another collaborator was indicated. Mr. Dietrich was impressed. After a lot of searching, the job fell to Robert Thomas, Hollywood correspondent for Associated Press, and author of many books.

In that *Times* report, Stanley Meyer denied sharply having transmitted the Dietrich memoirs to Clifford Irving, but when he was subpoenaed before a grand jury, his story changed. Others also learned that it was one thing to toss out statements to reporters, and something else when an indictment for perjury hung overhead.

Stanley Meyer claimed that he showed Irving the chapters simply to induce him to come in as Dietrich's collaborator, but this leaves some unanswered questions. If the producer was working in the best interests of the Dietrich story, why did he go to Greg Bautzer? It might also be that Irving made his own Xerox copy surreptitiously. It is reasonable to assume that if Irving's friends knew that he was doing a Hughes book, they would automatically want to see his book published first. Once James Phelan learned of the similarities, he exclaimed to his wife: "I've got it! That bastard Irving has stolen my manuscript!"

Mr. Dietrich went down one publishing road, James Phelan took another. Warner Books published with much success Phelan's own book, *Howard Hughes: The Hidden Years.* It was the best of the many Hughes books issued at that time.

13
The Tide Ran Out

This book, originally called *Twenty-five Years with Authors and Editors,* was long in the making. It was about to go to the typesetter in 1976 when Howard Hughes died, which necessitated important changes. I now had to write of him in the past tense. And agency matters were taking shape that I wanted to write about; a few movie sales could be called pending, and Peter H. Engel, then the president of Helena Rubenstein, was coming through with his first book. The horizon was so full of promising events, I decided to wait to publish the book, which could now be called Thirty Years.

In that early version I had a chapter called, "Will Hughes Ever Agree?" It appears below in its original form.

Reports from London (spring 1973) indicate that Hughes is gradually emerging from his fog of isolation. He had been to a night club. Possibly the Nicaragua earthquake shook him up in more ways than one. How intricately ironic that this morose manipulator of kings and men was so helpless (and so lucky!) in escaping a catastrophe he could not control. A severe earthquake. But, being Howard Hughes, he was able to command escape routes that would have been closed even to kingpins of the highest rank.

Hughes had evaded death's clutches several times before. Back in 1946 he had test-piloted an experimental plane for the U.S. Army, the X-F-11. He had been in the air eighty minutes when, in a flash, malfunction set in. The plane crashed into the bedroom of actress Rosemary De Camp. He was badly hurt, his chest crushed, and it was touch and go for several weeks. Having survived the earthshaking might well have mellowed the reedy recluse. I know that some in his entourage are trying to induce Hughes to agree to a book. The time is ripe. If this is still to happen, my personal involvement will have that proverbial "happy ending," but I remain cautiously skeptical. Hughes is too deeply steeped in secrets to open up. But it *could* happen!

Between 1957, when our agreement was drawn up, and 1966, when the book prohibition barrier was broken, it could be said that I was on the Hughes side. This is not because I "sold out." Partly, of course, I wanted to have an outstanding acquisition, and partly I felt passion for a man who is basically a Hamlet-like figure, tragic in that he was pulverized by forces within himself—his phobias and strange psychic makeup—and by forces from society, such as greed and excessive curiosity about public figures.

Hughes is not apt to return to America. As he stated in that telephone interview, he did not want to spend the rest of his life in courtrooms, or dodging subpoenas. but to whatever country Hughes migrates, it is never as an *individual.* Always the top floor of a large hotel has to be isolated. Once his private compartment is sealed off, provisions must be made for his large staff: security people, personal attendants, chef, doctor. Aides see to the logistics involved, but Hughes keeps tabs on the considerable expenditures, and on returns from his vast holdings.

One of the certainties on which we can all make book is that a scramble in the marketplace will start on any event which will strongly capture public interest. Or on any individual.

Interest is always heightened where a colorful personality is at the hub. Until Clifford Irving stood abject in court, confessing and pleading for mercy, the perpetrator was so pleasant-looking a person, and he made such an art of lying with a straight face, he came through with charismatic force. Americans have always had a weakness for glamorizing, even idolizing, the super bandit, the super swindler, the supersuccessful con man.

McGraw-Hill was an institution, and Irving an individual. Attention shifted to him just as soon as the James Bond ramifications began to unfold. Such colossal *chutzpah!* The interest sharpened magnetically when sex opened its indelicate bosom. Nina. Anne. Secret love trips. A wife and kids sidetracked. Scandal. Intrigue. Swiss bank accounts. Forgery. Handwriting experts proven wrong.

Cashing in on the publicity, Baroness Nina Van Pallandt, a small-talent folk singer, hurried to America. Media could not have made a bigger fuss over her had some miracle-pill restored Cleopatra to life and she came bounding off a jet. In a very short time there were two appearances on the Dick Cavett show, two with David Frost, two with Mike Douglas, and once with Johnny Carson. *Life* had her on the cover. Night club engagements followed. A movie offer. There were press conferences. Inevitably, this created a rush order for a book.

The continuing twists and turns of the scenario attracted attention on the widest possible level. One day when I was riding in a cab, the cabbie turned his head during a red light, and asked unexpectedly, "What's with the Irving deal? Did his wife pocket all that dough?"

"A great story," I commented, almost tempted to mention my own involvement.

"I think Howard Hughes himself is dead."

I had heard that expressed by so many that it made me wonder about *gullibility.* When David Frost had Robert Maheu on his show, he posed the same question: "Is there any truth to rumors that Howard Hughes is dead?" I chafed at the fact that such a ridiculous question could even be contemplated. One can assume that the impossible is possible in our miracles-to-order world, but the death of Howard Hughes could not be suppressed for more than an hour or so, if that long.

In what was called the "Palace Guard" or the "Mormon Mafia," as Jim Phelan had dubbed it, there might be divided loyalties. Some might dislike Chester Davis; others might not like Bill Gay, or Richard Hannah, two top Hughes executives, but each would have to be notified.

Regardless of how airtight a will Hughes might leave, tangents might never be resolved—disposition of the casinos, disposition of numerous lawsuits, management of his various companies. With the ultimate headline, all sorts of power-jockeying would inevitably ensue. Hughes might not want to appear physically even before close associates, but everything he does is known to *some,* and they couldn't keep quiet about his death even if they wished to. And the press has ways of finding out things!

Matilda's prime interest was art. She followed art exhibits, diligently saved the most impressive catalogues. She showed me a gray-white brochure whose front cover featured a picture of a puckish-looking girl with tousled hair. She was holding a placard that announced: *Selected Artists Galleries: Oct. 21 to Nov. 1, 1969.* And in red letters—*E. Sommer.*

Matilda showed me the booklet and smiled. I betrayed no immediate recognition.

"Don't you know who this is?"

"No," I said.

"Look inside."

I turned some pages, noticing first a stunningly colorful painting called "Fairy Tree Eruption." I then noticed *Clifford Irving.* I smiled, and read what he had written:

More nonsense is written about modern painting than about any other art form. A painting is the result of physical labor fired by a vision, and it communicates a visual experience. Why a painting and its creator should so often be victimized—and with so little protest—by so much metaphysical, multisyllabic and quasi-analytical jargon, is something I

have never understood. . . . Edith Sommer's paintings are not representative of pop art, op art, kinetic art, minimal art, modern German
painting, hard-edge painting, naturalism or even surrealism. No convenient label or temporarily fashionable ism will do; she has never run
with any pack. So I am spared the dreary task of comparison, so
degrading to any serious artist who must remain a prickly individual
or dissolve into the mass and perish with last year's fads. . . .

Much more follows, but this sampling is enough. Not many knew then
that was a husband writing in praise of wife, praise which, for her art,
was fully justified. And not even the brightest of soothsayers foresaw that
this couple was slated for elevation to head roles in another gallery, one
reserved for famous rogues.

Once events led *Time* magazine to call Clifford Irving "Con Man of the
Year," the hoaxer began to slip off his pedestal. At one point, when
question marks began to befuddle McGraw-Hill editors and executives,
Clifford Irving exclaimed heatedly, "It's my integrity at stake!"

The posture was pulverized, but "integrity" remains a good word to
ponder over. How highly does society value it?

In a world of diminishing standards, an easy answer would be, "not
very much," but this would be only a partial truth. America lives (at times
dies a bit) by the profit motive. It is the winning lottery number from the
making of a book to selling dope. Not always equitable, but until a better
mousetrap comes along, we'll make do. The profit motive does not have
to spell *greed,* but greed is a part of the tapestry.

Integrity and publishing. Let's compare this with other industries and
professions—law, for instance. Book for case or case for fee, publishing
would come off wearing a white gown. Ditto for the medical profession.
Advertising is another catch-all which would not stack up well. Nor
Manhattan real estate manipulations. Movie making and television have
a lot of dirt under their rugs. The record business is saturated with
payola and drug trafficking. Banks and loan societies with their great
stress on credit-buying, might be the worst offenders of all. Loan-buying
might add a dash of prosperity to a lagging economy, but the need to pay
back piles up great stress on the debt-harassed individual. And that's a
great many Americans. Admittedly, Ralph Naders are needed in many
nooks and crannies, including publishing, but there is that matter of
degree and perspective. Isolating the word "integrity," there is a provable honesty on the part of most publishers, editors, writers. Even agents,
the breed which is by definition the most entrepreneurial-minded.

At the tail-end of events, almost as if to prove that trouble tends to
come double, it was disclosed that a highly placed McGraw-Hill editor

had accepted a loan from two co-authors of a book that McGraw-Hill was publishing, and on which the editor was working. The loan, hastily repaid, was in the amount of 10 percent of the advance. The implication was clear that the loan bore a very close resemblance to a gift. The story would not have been made public had not one of the authors become dissatisfied and complained. It did not take three days for a woman in Connecticut to send me the *Times* story, and she suggested that I offer some editor a fifty-fifty deal. I replied quickly, and quite angrily, that this was *not* done. To be sure, if one scrapes the entire huge vat, a few grams of dirt will be picked up.

When *the case* was at its peak, many books about *that book* started to be written, even though the dust was far from being ready to settle. Speaking to Roz Magzis, an editor who knew that I was gathering material for a new book, I said, "I don't plan my book to be about Hughes, though my personal involvement will certainly be featured. My main emphasis will be on what I call The Blunders And Wonders Of Publishing."

Albert Leventhal, the McGraw-Hill official most involved, and probably the most embarrassed, was at that time supposed to be racing the deadlines. Subsequently he left McGraw-Hill and started his own company, Vineyard Books.

James J. Sherwood was quoted in a *Times* story as having said:

> A month ago I couldn't find a water-cooler at any publishing house. Suddenly I was swamped with requests from Doubleday, Random House, Simon & Schuster and Houghton Mifflin—not to talk of the magazines. I've known Clifford fourteen years. I've known all his wives and I know stuff about him he probably doesn't know himself. It's a real inside job, if you know what I mean. Wow!

A Hollywood agent, Fred Field, reported at that moment in history to be offering Irving's own story for one million, two hundred and fifty thousand.

That was Barnumized press agentry, but in the heat of the headlines, Lyle Stuart offered Irving an advance of one hundred thousand. Even Rosemont Enterprises announced that they were hiring writers to do a book on Clifford Irving.

That Fawcett paperback publication, *Howard, the Amazing Mr. Hughes* by Noah Dietrich, offers a classic example of the importance of *timing*. It bears mentioning that when a general trade book appears as a paperback original, it either means that a hardcover publisher declined to go along, or else the time element dictated some short cuts. The heavy sales invariably do come from the paperback end—on known properties mostly, but prior hardcover publication gives a book that valued sendoff.

Here additional Barnum-Cinderella touches apply, with "beating the market" coming first. Originally, NAL—New American Library—was to have done the Dietrich book. The advance was $7,500, which seems just about right. The sum was dwarfed by Fawcett's offer of $65,000— $40,000 for the paperback end; $25,000 for use in *True*. What carried a nominal price tag one month, greatly increased in value in the heat of the publicity. With ballyhoo drums creating a climate for greater sales, many hardcover houses would have overcome original reservations, but now leaping ahead of the competition came first, and paperbacks have a sharp edge on rush jobs. Indeed, they learned how to move very fast on the topical number.

From one perspective it could be said that NAL had needed a crystal ball, but when it comes to the final tabulation, regrets might not be necessary. Aside from other considerations, legal costs might be close to sky-level even for Fawcett. Hughes emissaries moved quickly with attachments, claiming for Rosemont a share of the profits.

"Howard must need money, poor boy," said the (then) eighty-three-year-old Mr. Dietrich. "Don't laugh, he may be getting hard up. The casinos are losing more money than the Hughes Tool Co. is making."

The Hughes suit was not just a lark.

Chester Davis once said to a reporter: "Look at it this way. If you are going to bring out a bat and put Joe DiMaggio's name on it, then you have to pay DiMaggio a royalty." The Davis viewpoint, of course, is easily challenged.

Viking Press was determined to beat the market with its contracted-for book. They won with their *Hoax—"The Inside Story of the Howard Hughes-Clifford Irving Affair."* This journalistic feat was done by three crack newspapermen from the London Sunday Times: Stephen Fay, Magnus Linklater, and Lewis Chester.

Three skilled and hard-working journalist-writers, especially with newsroom facilities at their disposal, could obviously produce three times as much copy as a sole writer, but that is only a token explanation. This journalistic triumvirate worked so well together that the book was published on schedule, and they turned in a coherent, highly readable collage of events which were seeded a long time ago, but which became known to the public with that McGraw-Hill release.

It was mid-March when Mr. Linklater was in my office, interviewing me, and the book was scheduled for mid-May publication. The deadline on copy was the end of the month. The basic facts were then in, but there lingered the fear that some new turn might bob up. And it almost did! I reproduce the last two pages from *Hoax*.

Postscript
In writing this book we were always confronted by a basic problem.

Our estimate of Clifford Irving was that he had a certain glib talent but that he was incapable of formulating by himself an idea as original as the hoaxing of Howard Hughes.

Twenty-four hours before going to press we uncovered evidence that goes some way toward resolving this contradiction. It suggests that Irving's confession of guilt, as revealed in the indictments, does not tell the whole truth.

The evidence is contained in a conversation which took place during a dinner party in late November 1970, in New York. Present: Clifford and Edith Irving, Mike Hamilburg. During the course of the dinner Edith revealed that Clifford was contemplating "a proposition" that could be worth upward of $500,000. It would, she said, be a dangerous one to undertake, since it concerned people "who would stop at nothing to achieve their own ends—even murder." She did not elaborate on the nature of the project, but she suggested that because of the risks involved they might well turn it down. It is interesting that the phrase she used about the men "who stop at nothing" is almost identical to that used by the Irvings more than a year later to describe the Hughes organization. But it is rather more significant that the conversation predates by one month the official birth of the hoax as outlined in Clifford Irving's testimony to the grand jury. It suggests that the idea of writing a Hughes biography was prompted by more than the chance reading of a magazine article.

The Manhattan publishing world is a small gossipy one, with which Clifford Irving is familiar. It now seems evident that in November 1970 he picked up intimations of the fact that the first part of Noah Dietrich's memoirs was becoming a "literary property." He may also have learned of the basic marketing problem it presented: too much Noah Dietrich and not enough Howard Hughes.

This, of course, was precisely the problem that he was able to resolve.

This leaves more unexplained than it suggests.

Granted that Clifford Irving knew in 1970 that he could get a copy of the Dietrich manuscript, he could *not* have known what ultimately would become of it. As it turned out, it was Jim Phelan who had made the sale to Fawcett. At a lesser price, he might have done this a year before. He was paid to step aside for the second collaborator, Robert Thomas, but Phelan still had a stake in the publication. And supposing Gitlin had been successful? Prior publication would have severely crippled *Project Octavio,* as the Hughes book was called at McGraw-Hill.

The three authors end their book by saying:

In the end the striking thing about the hoaxer and the hoaxed is not the gulf which separates them, but the similarities between them. Both are egocentric men, deeply absorbed in their personae; both are manipulators, using other people for the cultivation of an image of themselves; both are willing to sacrifice friends and acquaintances in a crisis. Hughes would never have been hoaxed if he had not, during the upheavals in Las Vegas, behaved with such imperious disregard for other people's lives. For his part Irving used his friends so ruthlessly to make his hoax work that when he really needed their support he found that it was spent.

It is difficult to avoid the conclusion that Howard Hughes and Clifford Irving deserved each other.

This is a catchy tag which seemed fitting, and so it was frequently quoted in reviews. I find the comparison inaccurate, even loathesome. It might be said that Howard Hughes and Noah Dietrich deserved each other. If, to Hollywoodize events a bit more, Irving had left his wife and flew into the beyond with folksinger Nina, they would have deserved each other.

Irving lied to his friends, violated confidences. Ultimately, no matter how one views it, he stood exposed as a thief and a manipulator. One who lost. Howard Hughes certainly took baronial liberties with other people's rights, but that might be the legitimate prerogative of autocratic rulers. Who gave him the right to play king? The power of money was the basic architect. He quickly moved into a position of command. If he did not want books about him to appear, he "commanded" that they not appear. If he had to pay a price—who cared? But note how often power becomes powerless. And take inventory of what happens to the most despotic. In his own twisted way, Hughes was in many ways *moral*, where Irving was *a*moral. At the very least, Hughes deserved a biographer who would take writing too seriously to reduce a book to a swindle.

When I encountered the name "Mike Hamilburg," I wondered if it was the Mike Hamilburg whom I knew? I checked with Stephen Fay, who said, "Hamilburg is a literary agent." That was all I needed to hear. Mike is the son of Mitch Hamilburg, a long-established literary agent in Hollywood. I wrote to Mike, with whom I had co-agented some books when he and Sylva Romano had run Allied Literary Co. Mike's reply came from Maine, where he was vacationing. Yes, he was indeed Clifford's cousin. Ah, I thought, here I would get the lowdown!

In that period, there was this *New York Times* news item:

Mr. and Mrs. Clifford Irving brought a $1.5-million law suit against Mr. Irving's former publishers, McGraw-Hill, charging a conspiracy to prevent them from publishing an account of how they hoodwinked McGraw-Hill with a bogus "autobiography" of Howard Hughes.

The Irvings, who have pleaded guilty in state and Federal courts to charges of conspiracy, mail fraud and grand larceny in connection with the Hughes hoax, said they were preparing "a new manuscript" describing the creation of the spurious autobiography.

But, they said, McGraw-Hill and its editors "have deliberately conspired among themselves and their friends in other publishing
houses . . . to convey to members of the hardcover and paperback
industries that the plaintiff (McGraw-Hill) will view the publishing and
distribution of the new manuscript as an unfriendly act."

The actions, the Irvings charged, have created an "illegal boycott"
that "stifles competition."

For undiluted gall, this probably set a record. It was good publicity
fodder, but the charge simply does not wash.

"Publishers" breaks up like an ice floe into many divisions. The industry is too fragmented and too rival-conscious for one house not to desire
to cop an edge over another. A friend might here and there show signs
of fealty, but that would be an individual act. If one probes beyond the
surface, the real reason for publishers' resistance to Irving was that a
countertide had set in. While the anvil was still fairly hot, Irving's new
lawyer, Maurice Nessen, undertook a Paul Gitlin turn. First, the original
asking price was scaled down considerably, and feelers began to go out.
Soon it was announced that Grove Press would do Irving's book.

Stanley Leeds phoned me at once.

"I'm not surprised that it's Grove," he said. "For some time it's been
known that Barney Rosset was wearing a very tight shoe, and this is a
desperate gamble to relieve the pinch. However, I'm afraid Grove will
lose."

"Why?" I asked. "Because no one would *believe* Irving?"

"That's part of it," Stan replied. "If Irving again repeated that his
father had known Howard Hughes, and Hughes denied it, I would fully
believe Hughes and totally disbelieve the hoaxer. This might be called
prejudging the book, but it is more a post-judging of some shabby stalls
in our market place." Then Stan added:

"Clifford Irving and Edith are now Public Figures, capital P and F.
Everything they will do from here on in will rate press coverage, but on
this book, the tide simply ran out. As I read it, publicity will not help."

This proved to be true. Grove Press was not helped out of its crisis,
and loud (but familiar) grunts began to be heard from the author's side.

Julian Bach, the literary agent called in to give the transaction a tone
of respectability, felt that Irving could not contradict grand jury testimony. True enough. The indictment parts were *fixed,* and Irving could
not deviate from what he had told two grand juries without inviting
further legal complications. What reputedly happened is, and was, too
well known, and voluminously indexed for posterity. What would have
been of interest is what really happened in terms of the unseen—how
Edith *really* felt about her role as the highly regarded and grossly dis-
regarded wife. Some interesting revelations could be made, but there

wasn't time for the grapes to ferment. This had to be a rush job. The "truth" about the "truth" might have to be saved for a post-jail de profundis.

Edith Sommer's own "true story" could be a tempting prize, and the human mechanism is such that in time she may well commit her post-awakening agonies to paper—not anything done in haste, and not in the shadow of her over-towering husband, and also not in partnership with the third conspirator, Richard Raphael Susskind.

Edith Irving's role was sustained, extended. She also lied, connived, deceived on a grand scale, but it is easy to feel that she was the victim of a husband's elaborate loquaciousness. Irving must have painted the enterprise in some gay colors—screwing the Establishment! And in a way that they would emerge as three very clever manipulators. And didn't the corrupt publishing world deserve a grand-scale rooking? At the worst, if someone or other should blow the whistle, they might be indicted, but de Hory served only two months in an Ibiza jail. Wouldn't they be abroad? Safe, with money stashed away no one could touch? If they returned to America, America so loved its de Rougemonts, it might even be to a ticker tape parade! If not along lower Broadway, then it would be on mythical Publishers' Row, where the soft wings of the artist were mutilated by some dollar-clawed fingers.

Edith Irving was in a major sense *the* key figure. Only she could have carried off the Swiss bank account with such initial success. It meant practicing endlessly the copying of H. R. Hughes, but wasn't she a gifted artist? It meant forging a passport. In order to foil a possible investigation, transferring the loot to another account became imperative. For this she traveled to the home of her ex-husband, Dieter Rosenkranz, a nonliterary German business man. There Edith "borrowed" the passport of Hanne Rosenkranz, the new wife, and then posed as Frau Hanne.

What was an artist doing in an Agatha Christie characterization? Only Edith could tell why she allowed her innate good sense to become so totally submerged. Was it that she had so long lived in a world of fake art, fake values, that the harlequin began to take on flesh-and-blood aspects? Aside from being a co-conspirator, she was also a *woman* as well as the openly loyal wife. What should make her story truly poignant would be insights when word came of her husband's trysts with her friend Nina, and then Anne Baxter.

Where lay Clifford Irving's major miscalculation? I would guess that it was in disregarding, or not analyzing sufficiently, the reactions of the numerous Hughes aides. Those around Hughes, and on whom he relied, were exceedingly alert individuals. As was seen, they sprang quickly into action—the lawyers, the Carl Byoir people, the security agents. All believed that involved were the machinations of Bob Maheu or Noah Dietrich, or perhaps both. Hughes let it be known quickly that he would not pay taxes on money he had not received. He was critical of Chester Davis for not having tracked down the source quickly. The postal authorities, the IRS, grand juries all started probes. Actually, it was Hughes's security people who first appeared at the Swiss bank. Mister Hughes? They were told, but there is no *Mister* Hughes. That started the downward slide.

Before Clifford Irving began serving his sentence, the convict-to-be had taped a series of TV interviews meant for synchronized release with publication of his book. Irving was an abject figure, berating himself for his "stupidity" in embarking on that "lunatic thing." The glamorized aspect had long muddied, and yet the aura of braggadocio still lingered.

Inevitably, there are many with the whitewash claim that, after all, no machine gun blasts went off, so where was the *crime?* A peccadillo, yes. Literary hoaxes were always treated lightly, and almost no hoaxer ever went to jail despite sums of money having been pocketed.

At an auction of Edith Irving's paintings, Arthur C. Clarke bought one. The *National Observer* quoted him as having said: "I think Cliff did a rather remarkable job of writing. I don't think anyone suffered much. Also, they've done a good deal to add some enjoyment to our rather dull world."

Others will be less forgiving. To some in the inner circle it will be remembered that Irving had tricked many who had had inordinate faith in his basic integrity. Outsiders will feel simply that he did *not* get away with it. Fallen heroes arouse no envy. He alienated close and distant friends, abused confidences.

I had planned to meet with Mike Hamilburg after his vacation. But I never wrote to him again; there was no longer any need for clarification. The "hero" was off stage center. There had been so much to-do, the saturation was reached and surpassed.

Bob Maheu's contribution to the Hughes sweepstakes was slated to be published in cloth by Quadrangle Books, long a *New York Times* subsidiary. And in softcover by Manor Books. Nobody was in a rush to get the books out; quite the reverse was true. None of the published books did well; many in the developing stage were dropped—even the one with Baroness Nina, which was to have been published by the conservative Walker Co.

C. David Heymann carries a unique distinction. He is linked directly with Ezra Pound, and indirectly with Howard Hughes/Clifford Irving. One publisher was victimized by a hoax, the other by an author's gross carelessness. By his own admission, Heymann had hired "five or six" researchers to help him gather data for his aborted Random House book. Fine. Authors do hire researchers, but it remains an author's obligation to check facts. *All* the facts before a book is made ready for the typesetters.

Once publicity erupted, Rosalind Magzis phoned me and asked, "Didn't you once represent Heymann?" I gave her a brief rundown. Agents losing clients is a constant merry-go-round with author A going to agent Z and Z's client moving to A. But in this instance I would like to detail *why* it happened. Heymann had once written:

> I look back on that novel now as a learning/teaching experience, an experience of great, great suffering for me, but something I had to get through. I now have 3 contracts for books with major publishing houses and have written for the likes of *Saturday Review, The Nation, Village Voice, Now, New York Times, The New Leader, Esquire,* etc. That's not half bad considering the shit of *Inside Out,* that first miserable outpour, which you, out of kindness, were good enough to send around.

If the author's new estimate of his early effort was a valid one, I would appear to be quite stupid to send out a "miserable outpour" and "out of kindness." Going back to *then,* this talented but immature author came to me on the recommendation of Harry Smith—poet, publisher, editor of *The Smith* and that lively trade news sheet, *The Newsletter.*

Heymann's *Inside Out* was certainly no commercial entity which I could bring as such to Doubleday, Putnam, or any publisher on that level. Then why did I go to John Day? Publishing can be likened to a long railroad journey. Beyond Grand Central there are many wayside stations. And even the top commercial houses were ready to spring an occasional surprise.

Heymann was a facile, inventive writer who at that time "couldn't write just to sell." His novel was well-written, which was my justification for trying. An explosive vitality about the prose captured attention. It was an offbeat, experimental work, totally devoid of a coherent story line. The ending had no connection with the start. I pointed out this to the author, and suggested a conclusion that would tie the end to the beginning. Then he'd have a more unified novel rather than a disjointed ramble. Heymann disagreed. At that time he wasn't ready for the commercial mold. I had a choice—rejecting the manuscript or trying openings where a fair acceptance chance existed. I opted for pulling the cart up the rough hill.

I considered the novel "submittable," submittable to the limited number of editors who favored stories that were closer to Kafka than to *Peyton Place.* Winter House (a small quality publisher) was then seeking novels where a disjointed ramble had an advantage over something neatly plotted. Follett's Round Table Books was a possibility. A few other portals could be tried. The mass-circulation paperbacks became aware of the college readership. Of course, I hoped that a hardcover editor would be impressed by this clear talent. Revision could follow. Heymann rejected my suggestions, but he'd be apt to follow the guidance of an editor. With some revision, the novel could be a possible contender for the Liveright or Knopf First Novel series. I also hoped that the author would come along with something less avant-garde. The maturity came, as I was sure it would.

I could not profit because of Heymann's own definition of his work. Why continue with an agent who submitted something he so passionately denigrated? I did not *place* the novel, so the author could stick to his evaluation. When he began veering into commercial channels, he wanted an agent who was not linked with "growing pain" rejection. My "compensation" lies in not having erred in evaluating a promising potential.

I quoted at length from Farr's letters because there is utterly no way that he could make a case for libel, invasion of privacy, or a breach of ethics on my part. Mr. Heymann *could* object, but he would have to prove that he was in some way *hurt*. I clearly had something to explain in my own behalf. *The right to know* is a legal counterpoint.

Aware of Howard Hughes's fierce stand against books about him, I knew very quickly that Robert Eaton's quote was a phony and it caused the publishers, Hippocrene Books, a heavy loss. Could I *prove* it was a phony? I could not. But based on my long experience with frauds, I developed a hound's gift for sniffing out.

Let us again go back to Howard Hughes and competitive *greed*. The profit motive, per se, is behind all endeavor, and needs no apologies. The greed part can be debated. If it was visible with Hughes, it certainly applied to *Poor Little Rich Girl: The Life and Legend of Barbara Hutton*.

Hughes and Hutton!

Heaven couldn't have arranged a more classic combination!

Each had those symbolic silk sheets, but each, in effect, might have slept on spiked pallets. And each, when books about them were written, brought consternation to the publishers.

Random House was big enough to recall the first printing, 58,000 copies. A certain best-seller strangled at birth! But a few questions remained open. Once the acknowledged errors were corrected, who would re-publish the book?

It was a foregone conclusion that none of the main-line publishers would compete. Whatever the possible profit, it was deemed too much a headache book, with new problems apt to arise. But publishing has its quota of Peck's Bad Boys, of whom Lyle Stuart is surely one. After much negotiating and renegotiating, he emerged as the new publisher.

The additional problems that I suspected might arise were not long in surfacing. They are described in a *Publishers Weekly* (27 April 1984) news item, "Forgery and Deception Charged in Hutton Book." It is best to read that report, written by John Mutter:

A letter from the late Barbara Hutton encouraging C. David Heymann to write her biography and samples of notes about her life that form a part of Heymann's book *Poor Little Rich Girl* are forgeries, Charles Hamilton, the handwriting expert, has charged.

Hamilton said that after "a careful examination that didn't take too long" he found that handprinted notes supposedly written by Hutton "were written by Heymann." Hamilton also said that the letters were not written by Hutton, but did not say that Heymann had written them. The key letter purportedly from Hutton asked Heymann to write "the real story" about her and gave him permission to use her notes, letters and other material and to dispose of them as he saw fit.

In a related development, Karen Davison, an American freelancer for West Germany's *Bunte* magazine who paid Hamilton to look at the material, has charged that she has found no proof that Heymann ever visited and interviewed Hutton during the period in 1978 when he said he had. At the time, Hutton was under constant medical care in her suite at the Beverly Wilshire Hotel, and Davison said: "I went to her chief nurse, her best friends, saw the medical logs that recorded visitors, and I haven't found anyone who had seen Heymann with her." She also claims that no one ever knew Hutton to keep notes or diaries other than in the mid-1930s, and that those diaries were later burned.

Heymann called the accusations "ludicrous," and Lyle Stuart, who will publish a corrected version of *Poor Little Rich Girl* in October, said that he would probably sue Hamilton.

Random House published *Poor Little Rich Girl* last year and recalled the book when Dr. Edward A. Kantor, a Beverly Hills physician, threatened to sue over a number of erroneous statements about him. Other inaccuracies cropped up, and there were charges that Heymann used material from a Ned Rorem diary without credit.

"I am willing to swear my entire reputation on this," Heymann said. "I'm willing to do anything—take lie detector tests or submit the material to neutral handwriting experts. Hutton had unique handwriting. It was impossible to forge her handwriting."

Heymann added that he blamed Random House. "I think they're trying to prevent my book from coming out since it will embarrass them."

Stuart said that the material was "checked out," and continued, "There's no question in my mind that Hamilton—who's known to be a publicity seeker—thought he could make these charges and get away with it."

Hamilton confirmed to *PW* that he was paid a fee of $1,000 to look at the material by *Bunte*. According to Davison, *Bunte* has been investigating allegations made by a West Berlin paper that the magazine Stern, publisher of the forged Hitler diaries, had "messed up again" in a series on Barbara Hutton that borrowed heavily from *Poor Little Rich Girl*. As part of the investigation Davison requested copies of the Hutton letters and notes from Random House, which, she said, gave them up "reluctantly." A Random House spokesperson, who declined further comment, said only that one letter in particular was submitted by Heymann as Hutton's "authorization."

Hamilton said he based his charges of forgery on various factors beyond mere handwriting. Some of the charges were apparently borrowed from Davison's research. Concerning the "authorization" letter, for example, he said that it was typed and bore the initials of a typist "no one knew" and who was not listed in the medical log. Also, the letter was not on personal stationery, which he said Hutton regularly used, and the title Hutton used at the end was not the one she customarily used for business letters.

I was not at the McGraw-Hill meeting when Irving proclaimed, "It's my integrity at stake," but I have it on the authority of someone present that Irving was totally convincing. I was present at two separate dinners where Robert Farr spoke of his contacts with Dr. Salk. It was difficult *not* to believe him. When Farr spoke to bank executives and large loans were involved, he obviously had to appear trustworthy. With exposure, Farr was "most disturbed that his reputation was ruined." A book could be written about authors who become so adept that *Lying with a Straight Face* could be the title.

Robert P. Eaton: "These notes are for your eyes only."

Barbara Hutton asking Heymann to "write 'the real story' about her and gave him permission to use her notes, letters and other material and to dispose of them as he saw fit."

When Howard Hughes was ready to make a major statement, he was very selective about picking reporters. All highly publicized individuals, when ready for a book, pick writers they feel comfortable with.

In a somewhat related issue, *Publishers Weekly* had reported:

Mr. Heymann yesterday also blamed academic jealousy and scholarly infighting for an earlier accusation by two scholars that he borrowed heavily, without attributing it, from other authors for his 1976 book, "Ezra Pound, The Last Rower."

One of those scholars, Hugh Kenner, Andrew W. Mellon Professor of the Humanities at the Johns Hopkins University and a leading Pound scholar, wrote in a review that he had doubts that a 1971 Heymann interview with Pound included in the book ever occurred.

At the time that we had been in correspondence, Mr. Heymann had written: "I met with Pound a number of times in Venice in the last years of his life and became, like others before me, inspired." I never questioned the interviews, but I did think that *The Last Rower* should have been offered as a novel. Utterances attributed to Pound somehow did not ring true to me.

Again from *Publishers Weekly* (16 November 1984):

> *Poor Little Rich Girl,* C. David Heymann's biography of Barbara Hutton, published by Lyle Stuart after being scratched by Random House, has gone for the floor bid in an auction. Pocket Books got it for $50,000.

Part Three
THE ROMANCE OF PUBLISHING

14
The Agent in a Classroom:
How to Become a Better Writer
Than You Are

Each writer is unique, sovereign, and although it is hazardous to lump writers into an "average," it has to be done. If the *average* unpublished writer is not going to be helped by a union, what will help? Many things, especially the ability to learn.

Many phases of writing can be learned. Not that every tyro can evolve to a Danielle Steel or a Stephen King. Individual gifts cannot be successfully copied, but each writer who leans toward commercial goals can become *better* by simply avoiding many mistakes writers make. Oversimplification? Not really. Not to one who sees those errors firsthand.

Too many writers are prone to say, "I do not know the least thing about markets." Well, they *should* know the rudiments. It should be a vital part of their preparation—preparation for stepping from amateur to professional. Those who do learn the essential first steps find the going a lot easier.

Even the least likely to succeed as authors are led by some inner radar to the writers' magazines. Chief of these are *The Writer* and *Writer's Digest*. Some of the agents listed in the *Digest* are not agents so much as they are literary counselors. A few are operators of fee-traps. These are to be avoided. One way or another, the novice becomes aware that there are authors' representatives. Some consult market guides where agents are listed. The authors feel that their problems would be solved if only they could interest an agent. So I receive incredibly naive and stupid letters. (Some will be quoted in the chapter called "Authors Who Defeat Themselves.")

The late Ernest Tidyman, white, was the creator of the successful *Shaft* books. When asked how he could understand black sensitivity so well, Tidyman had a very good rejoinder: "The writer is the most rejected person in the world." Until the solid breakthrough comes.

This part of my book is about unlocking those gates. Some will make it, some not, depending on their ability to learn. Yes, *learn*. Touching stars and the total and near-total zeroes are committed by *people*. Individuals write; individuals accept or reject.

I stressed more than once that to survive in the mercurial world of writing-publishing, it helped to have high doses of perseverance, hope, and the ability to *wait*. Some careers seem to zoom; others take a long time to blossom. I receive plaintive letters from authors who have written a novel saying that they simply cannot start a second work until the first sees publication. This is giving up before the first salvo is fired. Without a shift in attitude, there isn't apt to be any progress.

Numerous authors cannot write other than *their* way, whether publication results or not. Long before I became an agent, I knew that I could not possibly please a client before I first pleased an editor. My first priority was to win the confidence of those who do the picking.

I am focusing on the talented tyro (beginner at any age), the writer who could attain some degree of success if he or she recognized that possession of a talent is not enough. Talent is only a component of the publishable or producible manuscript, whatever form the production or publication might ultimately take.

Purists will argue that *true* talent will find recognition, and that no guidelines or lessons are needed. It could even be stressed that lessons and guidelines could ruin the genuine gift. That certainly could apply to *some*, but the overwhelming majority of authors have to go through an extended learning-winnowing period before they have anything to offer an editor, either directly or through an agent.

Despite an extremely active schedule, I allocated the time to teach some classes at The New York Institute of Technology, a growing college which is heavily involved in all phases of communications. I was on the adjunct faculty, which made it possible for me to teach despite my lack of formal credits. Years back I was also offered a teaching post at Tahoe Paradise college—a small, private institution on Lake Tahoe. They did not want me to give up my agency simply to move it west. I was to have a unique title, Agent-in-Residence.

I did not seek the post at the Institute; in a sense the job found me. Charles Wigutow, a longtime friend, had switched careers. In maturity he traded the cable television business for teaching. He advanced to head the English Department of the Institute. He once phoned me and said that he would like me to speak to his students on marketing. I readily agreed and returned several times in the same capacity. I spoke at the Manhattan branch, which was then on 57th Street, within walking distance of my office, and at the main campus, in Westbury, Long Island. My talks were well received; the students appreciated the direct, behind-the-scenes insights about how novels were placed and at times optioned. There was a letter I welcomed:

Dear Mr. Jackinson:
   Allow me to express my appreciation for the fine lectures you presented as a guest of Professor Wigutow in his Seminars in Mass Communications Problems.
                                        Cordially yours,
                                        Lee Morrison, Chairman
                                        Communication Arts Dept.

Subsequently Charles called again—would I take on some classes? My duties would essentially be an extension of my office work, and what I had been doing at the many writers' seminars of which I was a part. I agreed to put in some overtime. My Institute courses were called Writing For Film/Television, and they extended over a three-year period.

That first day before a class I took inventory. It was a class of eighteen. All but three aspired to be writers of one sort or another. The three hoped to work in radio or television, but not primarily as writers. They felt that knowing the fundamentals would help.

Seven pupils turned in half-hour scripts, all tailored to fit running hit shows. Three were sitcoms, four delved into crime. Two students were concerned with documentaries. Two favored the short story. The rest were interested in writing, but in a broad sense, the interest ranging from poetry to essays to shaping pilots for a TV series.

We soon got down to business.

"Each of you," I stressed the next time we met, "will have to remember an important word, *preparing*. The class will be called PREPARING to write for film or television." I continued, "The Screen Writers Guild, both East and West, runs a pretty tight closed shop. The established producers can hire only Guild members. None of you qualify for membership—yet." I put a heavy emphasis on *yet*.

"My policy on submitting to running hit shows is first to establish whether it is an open market. Most producers rely solely on their staff writers. Where slots are open, I like to ask for assignments. Obviously, it has to be for an author who could qualify. None of the scripts I read come remotely close. All of you have a goal—to become a better writer than you are. By the end of the term possibly I will have something to market. A number of you show some real promise."

From week to week I hammered away that writing for the tube or screen was emphatically *not* for the amateur. I stressed that one could view any number of hit sitcoms and correctly conclude that the writing was "elementary" and the plotting shoddy. I also stressed that no story editor was going to be impressed by tasteless copies of previously done shows. While it hardly takes "genius" to become a published writer or write for radio, cable, or home screen, it does take a considerable amount of professionalism. It takes knowing what fits where. This has to be learned. And it *can* be learned.

To accelerate the learning process I turned the classroom into a workshop. Students who had not yet turned in some form of writing had to do so. It could be whatever they felt closest to: short story, article, the start of a book, novel or nonfiction; documentary, juvenile, a film script. I primarily stressed not writing that was "good" in an academic sense, but writing that was good for the market at which it was aimed.

I watched the steady progress, as did the students. And there *was* progress. They read their work; there was general discussion and criticism. The students, eager to learn—at least anxious to get good grades—cooperated.

As an agent, I receive numerous screenplays, but invariably the submissions have to go back. In the mid-1980s, days of heavily curtailed production, writers submit material that would have been called dated and derivative twenty years before. This is a pitfall writers can learn to avoid.

Many writers believe that where they have a weak, unoriginal plot, too weak to make the basis of a novel, they can turn it into an original screenplay. The rationale is that the various descriptions, elaborate stage directions, and angle shots will fill the empty story gap. It does not work that way.

The technical aspects of a script—medium shot, exterior, pan to, etc., etc., are extremely important, but not at *the first stage*. To repeat, all pieces of writing develop by *stages*. Whether we are dealing with a book or a film script, interest must first be gripped by some novel setting, by the creation of some vital and original characters, and then by a dramatic situation between two central characters. What forms a dramatic situation is difficult to pinpoint. Let's invoke that classic definition: A person *wants* something. There are hurdles to be crossed before the goal is reached.

Fine writing helps, but it is not a prime requirement; making the reader or viewer *care* about the people introduced and about what is going on—*that* is crucial. This is a knack the page-turners learned to do well, and we can all profit from it.

Once the first stage is traversed, the next stage would usually be revisions, such as tightening up. (Contracts come later.) Then the writing has to impress a story editor, which cannot be done by bad writing and hackneyed situations. A shooting script is cardinal to success, but this generally takes shape in the final stage.

In the "Zebra" chapter I mentioned that CBS had successfully aired a feature called "The Last of the Good Guys." This grew out of what I had called a book/screen story outline. The title was *16 Days* by Clark Howard. Clark had a considerable track record, so I could be sure he would deliver once I interested either a book editor or a producer. I approached both. I never submit treatments or story outlines unless I am *sure* of an author.

Clark's story was based on a newspaper item. A cop died of leukemia. If he had been able to hold out sixteen days more, his widow would have been in line for a special pension. In his dramatization, Clark invented a story—how fellow officers at the precinct conspired to make it appear that the cop was on duty when actually he was too ill to check in. It was a very *human,* touching situation—fellow cops eager to see the wife receive the pension. Sympathy was on their side. Opposition came from a tough sergeant who went by the book and strictly by the book. It became a war of wits between him and the conspirators.

Because the situation was so novel, it aroused immediate interest at Columbia Pictures. From Bob Gilbert the story proposal moved upward to Christine Foster, and then further up the ladder to Renée Valente, with whom I concluded the purchase. Ms. Valente also hired Clark to write the screenplay, something he was eager to do.

Columbia, in turn, interested CBS, but the journey to the screen was a very rough one.

Renée Valente liked the script Clark turned in, but CBS did not. They bowed out. Peter Frankovich, program executive, wrote to my client.

Dear Clark,
    In the event you haven't heard, we've decided not to go forward with SIXTEEN DAYS. The decision was a difficult one to make for we all appreciated your cooperation and diligence on this assignment.
    Our primary concern (for better or worse) is ratings, and we felt unsure about this story's film potential in that regard. I know this comes as a disappointment to you, but I hope we can find something else to develop together.

Before Columbia could interest another network, CBS reconsidered. They wanted the time element cut to ten days. They wanted a totally new script, and hired new writers, one of whom was Clark. In the end, all involved were happy. The ratings were excellent, and there were reruns.

I also receive letters from producers asking to see original screenplays only. Almost without exception, these are budget-conscious, often fly-by-night entrepreneurs who hope to strike a sleeper without a large initial investment. At times it works out, but submitting to these unknowns is a risky business. I do not submit to them before the script has already gone the route, but even then I am wary about anyone whose credentials I have reason to question. Established producers overwhelmingly prefer to base a film on a published book or a produced play.

Writers submit a skimpy half-hour sitcom script which they hope will form the basis of a *series*. This may have worked at one time, but writers who keep abreast of times know that producing a pilot is currently so expensive, a series results as a spinoff from a successful feature. Today a possible pilot must be meaty enough in terms of story values to form a two-hour film. Corn is acceptable, but it has to be simonized to shine like gold.

When a possible series starts to get off the ground, and work finally ends on the master script, ideas for follow-up stories are discussed and outlined. It used to be that thirty-nine stories comprised the season, with thirteen repeats. This has been scaled down to twenty-six, with half going into reruns. Authors called in to do the scripting are without exception veteran TV writers. They have to be, since a huge investment is at stake. Many of the veteran writers are also producers. Later, should the networks renew, assignments go to writers who know how to tailor a script for a specific market, and to fit the special acting needs of the cast. The writers are pros doing a job of work. They might privately lament the collective *taste,* but this is veering into a different area. The writers have agents who keep on top of the assignment dispensers. Is it possible for a newcomer to break through? Very much so—once that needed professionalism is attained by the newcomer.

That first term at the Institute nothing turned up for me to market, but each student *learned.* That was the important thing. Each became a better writer, and mostly because he or she learned that there was a professional side to writing. Two students took writing so seriously, they continued to see me at my office.

Carol Muniz was a Hispanic young woman who could not speak English very well, and her spelling was pretty bad. But she wrote with originality and considerable inventiveness. She was working on a short story, a murder mystery. I admired her drive and earnestness and took special interest in her. I helped her with the plotting, at which she was weak. After she made several revisions, I sold the story to *Mike Shayne Mystery Magazine.* The pay was minimal, but Carol's joy could not be measured. She'd be able to boast, *I had a story published!*

Publication of Carol's story happened a year after the class had disbanded, but when the issue appeared, my new students felt a collective glow. It was great incentive.

The second and third years were a repetition of the first. The students were different, but not the goals. Similar were the strivings, the failures, and the successes.

For my fourth year, my friend Charles Wigutow called and asked me to jot down the schedule for the next term. I did. Two classes. Then Charles said, "Alex, how old are you? I've a form I have to fill out."

"Seventy," I said.

"Oh, spit!" he exclaimed sharply. "Unless one has tenure, we have an automatic cut-off date, seventy."

I urged him not to feel too badly.

That ended my connection with the school, but not with the students. Many stayed in contact. Carol Muniz turned to a full-length novel, a sexy mystery. That published short story was a tremendous springboard. Despite the responsibilities of a household and a job, Carol continued to write. And rewrite. She "made" the time, as all do who have that needed strong commitment. My former partner, Dr. Lin, told me that she used to get up at 5:00 a.m. to do three or four hours of writing.

Carol's novel never became "submittable" as a hardcover possibility or for the top paperbacks. That might have been too big a leap. But I was able to place the story with Major Books. Major was a salvage market, but for Carol, as for many other authors, a salvage market could mean salvation.

15
More on Hollywood

There is a saying in our trade that the way to make money in publishing is not to publish books. But if publishing books is akin to jumping from a plane with a ripped parachute, movie making is infinitely more risky. A picture will cost millions; it could feature an all-star cast, boast a top director; it might even have been made from a best-selling novel—and be pronounced dead on the accounting table. On the balancing side there will be the low-budget sleeper which will coin enough revenue to produce several new millionaires. This happens less often, but it happens. What is certain is that most moviegoers are young and constantly getting younger. *Young* used to designate the 20–35 group. Citizens of this "open" generation liked frankness, so the films in that era were almost disgustingly explicit in their "realism." But a teen and preteen audience developed for science fiction adventure (which displaced the traditional Western), and films featuring rock, outlandish forms of dancing, and teenage romance. Film after film caters to this *kid* audience.

Violence on TV has been a popular debate topic for a long, long time. Does TV simply reflect the crime lived on city streets, or do criminals, especially the *young* criminals, act out what they learn from crime-wise TV writers? It is a combination of both. Because of pressures from all sorts of concerned citizens, and congressional investigations, TV has opted to tone down the machine gun blasts, but with results where the cure was worse than the disease. TV also exhibited sex in forms never before seen on the tube—incest, deviant behavior, homosexuality in its multiple guises.

The public does not know this, but in TV there are the three absolute monarchs, the heads of CBS, ABC, and NBC, who decide what will be produced. An agent can submit properties to a score of independents, but the producers rarely move without prior approval from one of the networks. The networks, in turn, live or die by ratings. So advertising people have to be catered to.

Television and movie making can be called a marriage between Snow White and Dracula. For sheer survival, each has learned to live with, cater to the other. The arsenic and hatchet each might like to use has to be concealed or buried. Executives in both sectors have a common foe to fight, mechanical incursions.

Roughly, three types of pictures are currently manufactured for theatre showing exclusively. The producers know that these films will not get on the tube, and they take this as a mixed blessing. Greater liberties can be taken, which may or may not help at the box office. There used to be the nominally "clean" picture produced exclusively for a Movie of the Week. Here dramatic sequences were neatly tailored to accommodate commercial breaks every nine minutes. In the old films such breaks were artificially imposed, coming at the wrong times, which spoiled the flow and the enjoyment. But the stay-at-homes were in no position to complain.

Aside from the MOW, there is the film meant for both TV and the big screen. These are "cleaner" pictures, with touches of the risqué only suggested. These are few and far between. Then, too, there is the third category, the rank (or rankly) nudity film, very popular on cable.

I again turn to ads in the trades which could be somewhat misleading:

U.S. BOXOFFICE GROSS: $9,000,000
Cinema Arts Production Presents James Whitmore—Tippi Hedren—
THE HARRAD EXPERIMENT
A Dennis F. Stevens Cinema Arts Production

Since successful pictures beget a sequel, there was this:

HARRAD SUMMER
Uninhibited Youth Liberate Their Parents During A Provocative And Free-Spirited Summer Holiday
A Dennis F. Stevens Cinema Arts Production

I covered Bob Rimmer and his novels in my two previous books, but since no pictures had then been made, here is a brief recap.

The Harrad Experiment had piled up its quota of rejections before Sherbourne Press did it in hardcovers, and Bantam in paperback. The softcover editions sold "close to two million copies," putting the book on several best-seller lists.

Harrad, a mythical college, dormed male and female students without regard to sex. A dozen years ago this was innovative pioneering. Rimmer's first novel, *That Girl From Boston,* had already been published when he became a client. Jayne Mansfield had shown interest in the story, which her husband, Matt Cimber, undertook to produce. The film was made, but, up to the time of this writing (December, 1984) never released. In Hollywood, hundreds, probably thousands, of films are "in the can," completed, but cannot find *distribution*. Rimmer wrote:

Dear Alex,
   First THAT GIRL FROM BOSTON—the movie is the biggest mystery in my writing career. The last time I saw Matt Cimber was 1975. He had huge blowups of Mamie Van Doren as Princess Tassle, and the movie was presumably going for editing and would be released in six months. He provided stills to NAL and they brought out a small first printing of a movie edition—copy enclosed. Then—nothing. None of my phone calls were returned and both Moonstone Films and Matt Cimber vanished and I've never heard from him since.
   In the meantime obviously NAL wasn't very happy with me or Cimber and they have finally let THAT GIRL go out of print, and the rights were reverted to me about a month ago.

Another letter, this one referred to HARRAD.

   The whole episode on *The Harrad Experiment* continues to be as messy as described by Paul Nathan. At the first, I have never seen an actual signed contract on the movie. I did have a rough contract that was submitted to me for approval and then that was completely changed and when it was finally signed, I have not been able to get a copy of the signed contract.
   For quite a considerable period of time, Mel Sokolow put his own money into the Cinema Arts Production and then lost faith in it and somehow managed to get out. The movie right so far as the author was concerned called for a $50,000 payment, which, of course, would be divided with Sherbourne Press. However, the fact is that Cinema Art started to make the movie, as I understand it, about a year ago this April, and they only had $300,000 to go ahead. Before they finished they had run up close to a million dollars production cost on the movie and in the meantime Subsidiary agreements were signed with Sherbourne Press, so that there would be no payment to anybody except off the top—after the release of the movie. As a consequence, I was at a point about four months ago, when I heard this (and I did not hear it except through the grapevine) to put an injunction against the distribution of the movie, but was dissuaded from doing that.
   As it now stands, the movie has been, as you know, produced and is being distributed by Cinerama and if the movie makes something over a million and a quarter, I may get paid. Obviously, any payments that I do receive won't be for sometime because there are many, many standing in line in front of me.

And a letter from Dennis F. Stevens. It was written to Andy Bonime, a co-producer on *Harrad*.

   I think HARRAD SUMMER will be my last project, at least for a while. The motion picture business has lost a good deal of its enchant-

ment for me, and right now I'm bored with it. . . . HARRAD SUM-
MER opened Wednesday, August 7, and Joseph Sugar said the
opening day grosses were "encouraging." I asked Richard Zanuck
what the true meaning of "encouraging" was and was informed it
meant "the theatre wasn't empty."

Much has changed in the Hollywood writing arena, but not the way to
attract the attention of screen and TV directors of development, or story
editors. This is done by having something published, preferably a novel.
Next best would be a short story in one of the major magazines. Recall
how MCA responded to the *Ladies' Home Journal* story, "Family of Five,"
by Paul M. Fitzsimmons. Producers cover published material in magazines as well as books.

I once sold to Coronet "The Man Who Sank the Royal Oak" by Dana
G. Prescott, and it attracted TV and movie interest. This was one of a
number of True Sea Sagas that made up Prescott's collection *Rough
Passage* published by Caxton. The story was based on the sinking early in
World War II of the British battleship Royal Oak, which was a major
naval disaster for England and a tremendous triumph for Hitler's Admiral Canaris. The feat was engineered by the German spy, Wehring, who
sixteen years before established himself on an off-shore island as a Swiss
jeweler. He made friends, especially with British naval personnel.
Wehring became a British subject and a respected member of the community. His hobbies were yachting and fishing. He especially liked to sail
his craft around Scapa Flow, a major British naval base. Learning that
certain obstructions at the eastern entrance to Scapa Flow were off-
limits, Wehring remembered what he was there for. His sixteen-year
vigil paid off. He wired by code a German U-Boat. Headlines the world
over blazed forth to a stunned world: BRITISH BATTLESHIP SUNK IN HOME
WATERS. U-BOAT SCORES HIT!

The Prescott feature caught the attention of Julian Lesser, then the
producer of *Bold Journey*. A short time later he was in my office and we
concluded a deal for the TV-movie rights for "Royal Oak." Lesser envi-
sioned a major film based on the story of a man dedicated to a single
mission. A trial run would be a "sample" TV production. Lesser renewed
his option three years in a row. In the end, no picture materialized
because releases were needed, especially from Rear Admiral W. G. Benn,
at that time Captain of the Royal Oak. The Captain vehemently declined,
and continued to decline. It killed the project.

16
Insights into Paperbacks

Ruth Calif wrote me: "The publisher made a beautiful job of THE WORLD ON WHEELS, and even though it will cost the purchaser $25.00, I think that it will sell. Thanks again for selling my book. Even my grandchildren are impressed by this one."

And well they might be. The book is informative, nostalgic, and a paean to American business inventiveness.

When Ruth Calif became a client, she had had a paperback original published by Major Books, *Garden of Evil*. I am a great believer in an author climbing upward.

Jacket text describes *The World on Wheels*. "This is an illustrated history of the bicycle and its relatives. Here is the story of the bicycle and related "contraptions" from 1869 to World War 1. These are exciting tales of the invention and development of the tricycle, roller skates, the unicycle, the ice cycle, and the king of them all, the bicycle. Produced in an oversized format, with over 200 illustrations, this book will be of interest to every bicycling enthusiast." The publisher is Cornwall Books.

1981–82 were heavy down years for publishers. Seemingly solid firms either went under, merged, or went into that familiar Chapter Eleven. 1983–84 saw an impressive upturn. Still, some eight million remain unemployed. It cuts into book-buying. But this must also be said; if many Americans cannot afford to buy *any* book, even paperbacks, a greater number is well-off. For the affluent, price is no deterrent when it comes to selecting a wanted book.

An editor whom I'll call Deborah Elkin has long been with Doubleday's The Literary Guild. When books from my agency were in galley proof, I submitted to her what I thought were Guild possibilities. (*Zebra* was one such book.) She had recommended to me Frederic Young, a very fine poet and prose writer who had Deep South roots. In both prose and poetry, he was an innovator, an avant-garde original. So he was hard to place in commercial markets, but I had no doubt that he would make his mark, since all quality writers achieve recognition in time. I especially had faith in *Many Ingenious Lovely Things,* a first novel. The title is from Yeats's "Nineteen Hundred and Nineteen":

> Many ingenious lovely things are gone
> That seemed sheer miracle to the multitude,
> Protected from the circle of the moon
> That pitches common things about.

Deborah was a friend of Cathy Camhy then an editor at Bantam, and she showed Cathy a copy of Fred's book. Before long Cathy called to say that Bantam was ready to contract. I was pleased; we were dealing with a *first novel.* But I also had some strong reservations.

"Fred's novel," I said, "went to Random House. That means that I hold it in very high regard."

"So do I. That's why we want it for Bantam."

"The four thousand advance is fine, but I want to see the book in hardcover first. I'd like that written in under Special Clauses."

"Management will not agree. But I'm in favor of hardback first, and I'll do what I can to see to it."

"Let me also say this," I added, "I would prefer that some other publisher do the hardback, Bantam the reprint."

"This may work out. First, some revisions are needed. Let's cross that bridge first."

I went along. I also acted. As soon as contracts were signed, I notified Pat Golbitz of William Morrow. Ms. Golbitz replied:

"Thanks for the tip on MANY INGENIOUS LOVELY THINGS. Cathy Camhy will send it to me when ready."

Her letter is dated 14 July 1980. Bantam published the book as a paperback original in 1984.

Things is a big novel, close to a thousand typed pages. It is a Deep South saga of some decaying families. There are licit and illicit loves, some vivid characterizations. The story has a four-generation sweep, so popular with many readers.

Any Paperback Original can properly be capitalized. But large case or small, it has grown from a dwarf to a twelve-foot giant. Authors who miss at hardback publication are ready and eager to accept soft covers, but softcover houses come in as many varieties as birds. The vast Romance market is almost totally paperback. And many bodice rippers which go beyond the sanitized Harlequin-Silhouette formula achieve vast distribution. So authors are happy. Still, at best, paperbacks are second-best.

Hardcover books spell *prestige.* They are noticed by key people: reviewers, paperback editors, librarians, the TV-movie people. Hardcover publication is vital in launching an author towards greater glory. This was my prime concern because it was a question of Fred's career, not just this one book. The advantages of hardback publication were as obvious to the Bantam heads as to the author and to me, but Bantam is a huge setup. There were other influences at work.

Bantam did do a few novels in hardcover, but not with any real success. They were too deeply rooted in the paperback mold. Subsequently Cathy Camhy left the firm. The editor who took over liked Fred's book; there was never any question of Bantam not going ahead, but there were questions about prior hardback publication. Other editors were consulted. Each had changes to suggest. Fred cooperated, but ultimately Lou Aronica, the Bantam editor who took over for Cathy Camhy, wrote:

Dear Fred:
    I know how hard you worked on this manuscript and how much it means to you. I also know that, were mass-market publishing less speculative these days, we would be pushing out enormous quantities of this book after a very successful hardcover publication. It was jarring to realize that a book as fine as yours did not have the kind of blockbuster mass appeal necessary for a Bantam hardcover publication.
    Things became a selection of The Literary Guild—their edition was in hardcover, but it went only to subscribers, not to reviewers. While *some* paperback originals are reviewed, the number is lamentably small.

Marilyn Gilman's story can properly be called a success story, though it is a story that is still unfolding. She wrote three novels; all were published by Zebra Books as paperback originals. Her first letter to me was a desperate appeal for help.

Because of her inexperience, she had fallen into the hands of a fraudulent publisher—in Pittsburgh, where Marilyn lives. To snare a sizable sum for publishing her book, the publisher was overly lavish with praise.

Marilyn was married to an M.D. I had met her husband's father in the years that I had been a furrier, and we continued to meet at the home of a mutual friend. When the father-in-law heard of Marilyn's plight, he recalled that I had become a literary agent. So Marilyn wrote to me. Did I know anything about the publisher. Yes. Would I read her manuscript? Indeed I would.

The story, nonfiction, revolved around her recovery from a mastectomy. The material was exceedingly dramatic, but she told her story in such an amateurish way, it fell flat. I quickly urged her to get out of the contract even if she had to lose the sum she had already paid. I explained why she was not ready for publication, and I doubted that she would suffer any financial loss. I also sent her evidence that the publisher was running a bucketshop operation. I recommended that she file charges with the Better Business Bureau and asked her to show my letter to her attorney. Marilyn won her case. That ended phase one, but for her it meant a new start.

Uppermost in her mind was a question she had to struggle with: did she possess sufficient talent to develop as a writer? I assured her that she did but stressed that she was still too close to her personal ordeal to handle it successfully. Meanwhile, she was married to a doctor, she had a sister and brother-in-law who were doctors, and she knew a great deal about medicine. Medical books had a ready market.

Marilyn worked hard at her writing. This meant destroying several early drafts, but improving after each revision. It wasn't too long before I had a novel to market. The central character was an attractive young woman, an M.D. A doctor at the hospital was very much in love with her. The crisis occurs when she is faced with something she had never anticipated—a hard lump in her breast. The story moved convincingly to a dramatic climax.

I went first to publishers on a Pocket Books level. "Not quite" was the consensus. After several rejects, I approached Zebra. Contracts followed.

Zebra may offer their "money" writers a contract comparable to those of Avon, Berkley, and such. I was sent a bad contract, bad in that we would be paid a year and a half after most of the established paperback houses paid. In effect, they would be using authors' money to finance their operation. But since everything is relative, the Zebra contract appeared gold-edged compared to the one Marilyn had escaped from. At least there was an advance, however modest. Her story was published under a title Zebra concocted, *Diary of a Woman Doctor*. Note the professional exploitation in the jacket copy:

Dr. Ruth Simson was independent, dedicated and somewhat unconventional. She really cared about her patients and she was willing to lay her life on the line for what she believed in. Ruth was more aggressive and more competent than most of her male colleagues at Memorial Hospital. Many found her a threat to their positions, power and egos—especially Dr. Alvin Donovan.

He might be Chief of Staff but as a physician, Ruth thought he was incompetent, inhuman and uncaring. To her, the essence of medicine was involvement. She believed in treating the patient as a whole—the mind as well as the body.

Then suddenly, without warning, Ruth was faced with a life-threatening disease. Her colleagues thought of her as a woman first, then as a doctor. Now she was a patient—and instead of fighting for her career, she was forced to fight for her life!

Several years after publication, the novel is still selling.

Marilyn's second and third books, *Doctors' Wives* and *Doctor's Hospital,* also had medical settings. And they also gathered some rejects before I submitted both to Zebra. Both were accepted simultaneously. The advances were bigger than the first advance, but not that delayed payment clause. And I was not in a position to insist. If rebuffed, I simply had nowhere else to turn.

In writing to Roberta Grossman, the publisher, I once said that Zebra grew out of the ashes of Lancer Books. Ms. Grossman took strong exception; Zebra, she insisted, was a totally new enterprise even though she and Walter Zacharius, chairman of the board, had been key Lancer figures.

In my long tenure as an agent, I have seen many publishers dissolve, merge, fade totally from the scene. Many went into bankruptcy. At Lancer I had several contracts, signed and pending. I had a few submissions out. Unexpectedly, a friendly Lancer editor called and said, "We are going into a Chapter Eleven. The news was unexpectedly announced at a Board meeting last night. If you want your manuscripts back, send a messenger immediately." Lancer was on 47th Street, close enough for me to run over personally.

More recently, several "name" paperback houses found themselves on shaky foundations: Playboy Press, Fawcett/Gold Medal, Popular Library, and Ace Books. Because each had a valuable backlist, the imprints were absorbed by other houses. Zebra is flourishing. The situation was similar even during the Depression. Where some firms found the road rocky, others picked up gold nuggets. A write-up in *Publishers Weekly* stated:

ZEBRA BOOKS: A SHARP EYE FOR THE BOTTOM LINE

The current spate of jokebooks in admittedly bad taste has generated a furor both inside and outside the publishing industry. It has also generated interest in one publishing house in particular, Zebra Books. The publisher of *Gross Jokes* recently rushed into print a sequel, *Totally Gross Jokes.* Although you won't find Zebra Books reviewed in the New York Times, you will find them selling on mass market racks around the country. Zebra Books is bottom-line publishing. Selling is what the company does best.

Trends in publishing do not change as often as Christian Dior styles, but they change frequently enough. Shortly after publishing felt (and reflected) the effects of the black movement in the late sixties and early seventies, the women's market exploded. One offshoot was that a woman lead became more important in a novel than the traditional male hero. Women had always been major readers, but many were unaware that they were an exploited species. Once it was pointed out, they demanded redress. Zebra cashed in on the trend, which is still very much in vogue. Joke books aside, Zebra's main focus is on the distaff side. All of Marilyn's novels were women-romance oriented; she herself is a strong feminist.

For Marilyn's fourth novel she moved from medicine to the world of art. Before bitten by the writing bug, art had been her main preoccupation—aside, that is, from being a wife and mother. Now she paints *and* writes. The art background all but eliminates Zebra as a possible publisher. The book is apt to be regarded as too arty for their readership. But Marilyn's goal is continued growth. Each published novel was better than the preceding one. We both feel that for her Zebra was a valuable launching pad.

At the top paperback level are Avon, Bantam, NAL, Pocket Books, Warner Books, and almost a dozen more. There is a medium shelf, of which Pinnacle was a good example. I could name others. Then there is that "last throw of the dice" market, which become acceptable when other, better choices have been eliminated. Three old-line firms, Tower Books and Manor Books in Manhattan, and Major Books out in Chatsworth, California, were ideal "second trench" firms. I could go to them with rejects from the top. All three simply closed their doors. Ceased to exist.

Writing by Carolyn Forbes (and writing of mine) appeared in the very fine poetry journal, *The Poetry Book Magazine,* sponsored by Alan Swallow, who died in 1966, and who ran Alan Swallow Press, which specialized in the noncommercial novel and books of poetry. This press had published a literary novel by Carolyn; she published another with John Day.

Carolyn was impressed by two collections of religious-devotional poems by Stanton A. Coblentz that I had been able to place. (Mr. Coblentz, a pioneer in science fiction, had published a very fine, traditionalist poetry magazine, *Wings,* for almost thirty years. It was strictly traditionalist. I appeared in it, though my stand on poetry was neither traditionalist nor innovative. I liked the best of both schools.) Carolyn asked if I would handle a collection for her, and I volunteered.

My first appeal as an agent was to my fellow (and sister) members of The Poetry Society of America. What I sought was their prose. Stanton Coblentz responded favorably. So did George Abbe, who then had novels published by Coward-McCann and Henry Holt.

As Carolyn and I corresponded, I learned that she wasn't particularly religious, but that her husband Jeff was. He held a prominent post in a large Christian organization. This was before the Moral Majority came to prominence. The husband would have been a leader in the movement and would not have found a paperback as garish as *Garden of Evil* proper to leave on a coffee table.

But then Carolyn's husband died at a young age of a cerebral hemorrhage; Carolyn was left with three small children. She sent me a desperate letter. "Of all my choices," she wrote, "job, full or part-time, I prefer to leave things as they are. I now have to sell. Is there anything I can turn to? Please tell me what I must do." I replied that there were two wide-open markets, both within reach, if she could make an adjustment. These were the confession group and the "sexy novel." I pointed to my own writing, which I had always divided into two spheres, "my" writing and the writing slanted for a market. Could she do something similar? Her published novels were beautifully written, but were almost totally ignored. They brought in no income to speak of. What income there was was more than obliterated by the expenses an author endures: mailing out manuscripts, often paying a typist. Poetry was an economic drain, to Carolyn, to me, and to most who send out poems. For Carolyn income now became the immediate and dominant need.

As with many other writers, learning meant stumbling and rising, tearing up early drafts, but improving. Soon Carolyn was able to please the editors of both groups. What made this possible was Carolyn's ability to adopt a totally *professional* attitude. Not all writers are able to make such a turn-around.

Carolyn remarried four years later. Now she no longer *had* to sell, but she had gotten into a pattern of work. She had begun to *like* doing both the confessions and those ribald romances. And her husband encouraged her to continue, which she did.

I must also say that, at the vital start, Carolyn had the help of two highly cooperative editors, Yvonne MacManus at Brandon and Beatrice Cole at the confessions.

For the first four crucial years Carolyn, like Carol Muniz, would have considered salvation a proper synonym for salvage.

Today someone in Carolyn's position would find it a lot more difficult to survive. Also, paradoxically, a lot easier. Confession magazines still decorate newsstands, but rates are half of what they used to be. The market fell out from under the sort of mildly erotic novel published by Tower and Major Books, then called Brandon House. And Tower was also Norden, Leisure Books, Midwood, and other in-house imprints. Hard-core pornography became the norm for Greenwood Classics. Holloway House had their special "specialty books." At the other extreme there were the Fab-laundered Harlequin Romances, which began to skyrocket in popularity.

Carolyn did not care to write for either group; sheer taste eliminated the porno market, and Carolyn considered the Harlequin "cleanliness" too patently faked. Other writers who ply the Romance trade, however, find the genre gratifying and rewarding.

17

More First-Book Breakthroughs

A letter from the Reece Halsey Agency arrived long before our contact over *The Zoo*.

Dear Alex:

Still can't get over your admirable perseverance in the case of Jere Cunningham. Because, obviously you never give up, would like to ask whether you would be willing to take on co-presentation of a much-traveled manuscript entitled THE DOCTOR GAME by Howard Olgin, M.D.

As writers, Jere Cunningham and Dr. Olgin are completely different. But they share the Halsey connection and that difficult first-novel breakthrough.

Jere's first submissions, short stories and novelettes, were on the "art" side. Some stories went to Gordon Lish, then of *Esquire*. No sale, but the fiction editor showed great interest in the author. Jere's longer works were unplotted, offbeat, avant-garde. The appropriate markets would have been the mushrooming Little Presses. Like Paul Fitzsimmons, Jere wanted popular success. I pointed out the alternatives. Jere opted for trying to please commercially minded editors rather than go the long way around. This would mean appearances in the literary journals until some sort of a reputation was achieved. Jere turned in a few chapters and an outline of a novel ultimately published by Gold Medal as *Hunter's Blood*.

In the novel five men set out to hunt deer in a rather remote region of Tennessee. Jere, like Raboo Rodgers, who came to me on Jere's recommendation, hails from the Deep South. (Memphis for Jere, Arkansas for Raboo.) The holiday-bent hunters encounter some murderous rednecks, and then poachers who would as soon kill men as deer. Very well written, editors said, but they declined on grounds that it was "too much like *Deliverance*," which was then a best-seller. It was a fairly accurate comparison.

I thought that *Hunter's Blood* would make a perfect Gold Medal number. The partial went to Martin Asher at Fawcett (who has risen high in the editorial orbit since then). Yes, he was strongly interested. Mr. Asher did not want to make a contract commitment; after all, the author had no track record, but the editor wanted to see the story completed. I asked Jere to be obliging. I liked the finished book, but Asher had some reservations. He felt that Cunningham did not follow the original outline. This was true enough. Outlines are invariably changed in the conversion. Finally, I had to write Jere that it was a turndown, and I had to look elsewhere. A letter from David McDowell (then) of Crown is worth quoting.

> Dear Alex:
> Your Mr. Cunningham has a good deal of talent, but I'm afraid that HUNTER'S BLOOD is just not for us. At the moment it is almost impossible to get a first novel through here.
> Best regards

Not too long after, Martin Asher left Fawcett to go over to Grossett & Dunlap, a stepping stone to Pocket Books. I saw an opportunity to resubmit. Because records are kept, I picked a different title. I approached Clover Swann, one of several Gold Medal editors to whom I submitted. I especially wanted a woman's reaction. Half the readership of the old *True* were women. Ms. Swann rejected. I continued the hunt.

Determined to make it, Jere kept turning out new partials. Some I submitted, some not. I picked editors who had previously praised Jere's writing. A number of months passed. Subsequently I received a call from Frank Coffey, whom I had gotten to know at Prentice-Hall. He had left P-H and invited me to submit at Gold Medal. Just then *Hunter's Blood* came back from Pyramid. It went over. Soon after Frank reported that he liked the story. He especially liked the fine writing. The story was somewhat like *Deliverance,* but that did not bother him.

"Is it a contract?" I asked.

"Not yet," Frank replied. He was recommending the story for purchase, but approval would have to come from Richard Hutner, then the editor-in-chief, and from Leona Nevler, the publisher.

Their approval came speedily. The book was not only contracted for, it was accepted with great enthusiasm. It was the third submission to Gold Medal. In all, portions of the book had been sent out thirty times.

How do thirty rejections translate into terms that authors can understand? It means, to begin with, a lot of self-cursing for the insanity to dare hope. And for the bigger insanity to have become a writer. Rejection. Trying to please some abstract editor, and piling up more rejection. And for the agent? Will vindication ever come? If not, is there a burden of guilt for having prodded, encouraged? Is it all worth the candle? The building of an edifice means the laying of a foundation. Once completed, for the viewer there is only a passing thought of the groundwork involved; only appearance counts. "What a beautiful building," it could be said. Letters from Jere Cunningham and his wife are testimonials for writers to learn from. The husband first:

> Whenever I get up to New York, I owe you a super dinner! The rest that I owe you I could never repay. Except maybe in turning out books, which, boy-oh-boy, I'm going to do! Now back to the sober mature writer-author frame of mind. Maybe I'll grow a beard and take up pipe-smoking now that I'm a genuine published sage and misfit.

From the wife:

> Dearest Alex,
> Your phone call came at one of those moments similar to the timing of that old television program, "The Millionaire." I had realized that Jere could not plot, which makes writing for a living somewhat ludicrous, and had begun to push his paintings and inventions. He seems to work best when given an assignment, as you did with *Hunter's Blood.* If you hadn't called his bluff about doing a straight story, I believe he would still be turning out reams of beautifully written but totally disjoined pages. However, at last it looks like he's learning to plot on his own—he's got a good one going, and should have about three chapters and an outline in to you within a week.
> My fondest wish is that this coming year will see your patience, guidance, xerox copies, messenger services and ad infinitum returned to you multifold in commissions with our blessings. . . . Love, Madelyn.

What ultimately counts is not the piling up of the foundation bricks, but the finished edifice. Jere had known that the road to acceptance would be hard. He persisted. He kept plugging on. He learned how to plot and came to grips with the occult/supernatural themes he successfully used in subsequent books. And he had a helpful mate. Soon there was that vital second Gold Medal acceptance, *The Legacy.*

Dr. Olgin's book interested me very much. Essentially that was because *medicine* in its various ramifications is such a vital part of our lives. I am among the lucky ones who never had any sort of surgery, and there had hardly been a day in the past fifty years that I could not have gone to work. I spend very little on doctors. I have had a mild arthritis for the past thirty-odd years, but it is not the crippling sort. I take no medication. I still say, "If it doesn't get worse, I'll live with it." I live with it. But death and illness invaded my family, friends, and my broader "family of clients."

Medicine means some miraculous cures and some major advances, especially in surgery and microbiology. It also means a lot of *needless* surgery, greed, Medicaid and Medicare ripoffs, staggering hospital bills, justified and unjustified malpractice suits. There are mistakes in diagnosis from sheer carelessness. Dr. Olgin dug his scalpel into all these themes. The book was classified as fiction, a first novel, but it was originally written as nonfiction, a book based on Dr. Olgin's experiences as a Los Angeles surgeon.

Once I read the manuscript, I understood why it had received many previous rejections. That did not bother me. The material was exciting, and the writing was basically good. The faults were structural and could be fixed.

I have long drawn a line between what I call a "submittable" manuscript and one that is publishable. I explained to Dr. Olgin and to Reece why changes would have to be made *before* the book could go out again. And I recommended an editor to do the surgery. They went along. The revised manuscript went to market.

To repeat, all books are placed by *stages*, especially when it comes to the unknown writer. An editor must see the promise of a successful publication. Once that is established, other steps follow—how to make that promise even more promising. This generally means the editor's suggested changes. Once an acceptable manuscript shapes up, contracts go out.

I drew a few rejections on the new version, but Peg Cameron, then with Lippincott, showed strong interest. She became the purchasing editor. She had wanted a few changes, and Dr. Olgin again cooperated. Before long there was another letter from Reece, my co-agent:

Dear Alex:
Our thanks, and sincere congratulations. We were in Palm Springs, where Howard called us with the great news about Lippincott's offer for THE DOCTOR GAME. He was, of course, on Cloud #9.

Reece had written that Dr. Olgin was prepared to put twenty thousand into promotion. I knew that this would appeal to *any* publisher, but I made no mention of the offer until the book was accepted. At the editorial end editors tend to look unfavorably at *pressures*. Once the sales-promotion people took over, they were exceedingly glad to have Dr. Olgin pay for some expensive ads.

An old rejection letter from William Goyen (McGraw-Hill) offers another insight into the complex slide we have under the microscope.

Dear Alex:
   I agree with you that there is a cast of very unusual characters here
and this is a story well-told. I'm sorry I'll have to return it to you, our
fiction list being pretty well closed to unknown writers unless they've
produced a stunner. I wish you luck with *The House on Sweet Hill*
elsewhere.

Cordially,
Bill

Ken Edgar, the author, broke through, as practically all good writers
do eventually, but far too many talented writers throw in the towel too
easily.

Ken had started out as a novelist, and he had a juvenile book published by Boxwood Press. Boxwood does no fiction; *The Stardust,* a
Juvenile, was an experiment that did not pan out. Ken's adult fiction did
not do well among established publishers. Thoroughly discouraged, he
turned to plays, which seemed to be a good move because he had a flair
for dialogue and an uncanny gift of understanding people and motivation. This is not surprising; formally, Ken is Dr. Kenneth Edgar, a
professor of psychology at Indiana University of Pennsylvania. He was
cited for a major award in teaching, and he runs a clinical guidance
center; he also counsels students. And he writes. Despite an extraor-
dinarily busy schedule, he manages to produce steadily.

His first submissions to me were two lengthy three-act plays. I was
impressed, but I urged him to return to the novel, since producing a
serious play on Broadway was far more difficult than breaking through
with a first novel, tough as that was. He agreed. *My Father's House* became
End and Beginning. I had both a play *and* a novel to market.

As I had anticipated, the book found a home first, a very hospitable
home, but it took considerable searching. The rejects depressed Edgar.
Aware that he needed the assurance of publication, I assured him that I
guaranteed it. He wondered, how could I *guarantee* anything so mercurial? I mailed him Impact Press contracts. He returned them signed.
Like *Zebra,* the book was one that my associates and I would have been
very proud to sponsor. It was a distinguished work. But I continued the
search for a publisher with greater resources. The novel was published
by Prentice-Hall. Soon after publication, it drew an interesting letter:

Dear Mr. Edgar:
   What a fine book you have written in END AND BEGINNING! On
the one hand, congratulations, and on the other, thank you for
providing me with a rare emotional catharsis and one of the best
reading experiences of this past year.
   You have truly put it all together: current topicality, insight into
characters who are universal, and a novel which holds together so that
its whole is better than any of its parts.

I finished reading your book a few minutes ago with one question uppermost in my mind: Why haven't I heard of this book before? Being in the world of books myself, I can only suspect your book has not been reviewed widely nor has it sold particularly well—or, it was published late in '72 and has not yet risen to its proper level.

I would be most interested to know how the book fares in the marketplace and in reviews, if you are so disposed to write me. I hope for the best, of course, for I do believe books, like people, get what they deserve. If your book does not, then it will be one of the exceptions (in my opinion) and I would like to know about it. In any event, in writing on, do not despair. Your writing, your insight and your good sense should shine through and be most welcome in the sea of books published each year.

Yours sincerely,
Alvin Moscow

My reply:

Dear Alvin Moscow:

Thank you very much for your Feb 21st letter to Ken Edgar. Ken passed on a copy for the good reason that I am his agent. To me, you showed something laudable, something we see too little of—one author showing concern about another, especially a *known* author writing to an unknown.

END AND BEGINNING was published in the fall of '72. It was Ken's luck (and mine) that we struck a perceptive editor at Prentice-Hall, Bram Cavin. Bram went to bat for a *first novel,* feeling quite sure that Edgar was a "real" writer, one who would come through with many books. And the editor was right; another Edgar novel will be published this coming fall, AS IF.

I placed AS IF on the strength of two chapters, and I hoped that the book could be made ready for publication this year. It was. A second novel invariably commands more attention. Not only with reviewers, with movie people and reprint houses. Second novels very often pull the first.

Prentice-Hall launches most books with some initial advertising. END AND BEGINNING was one of four novels lumped in one ad. After that, each individual title has to make its own way. Mostly, we are banking on word-of-mouth recommendation. That is how a book starts to *move,* and where publishers discern movement, more ads follow. Reactions like yours help a lot, and may I have your permission to send copies of your letter to some key people?

In *my* book *The Barnum-Cinderella World of Publishing* (description attached) I write of Dr. Edgar. My book was in production when the contracts came through. I also write of Gilbert A. Ralston. He is that high-placed Hollywood scenarist and TV writer who possesses some extensive credits. He authorized many successful screen and TV scripts, including WILLARD and then the sequel, BEN. He had co-authored with Richard Newhafer *The Frightful Sin of Cisco Newman,* a novel which I had placed with Prentice-Hall. Ralston likes *End and Beginning* very much, and he will do the screenplay once a "package" is

put together. As you know, that is how it works these days. Once a
movie will be in the offing, it will just about assure a good paperback
deal. *End and Beginning* was reviewed, and I'm glad to show you a flyer
I put together.
    Again, thanks for your interest.
Cordially,

No statistics are available on how many unpublished novels are buried
away in trunks, but it is universally agreed that an incredible number of
people write. Most write on an amateur level, but a high percentage take
writing seriously. They keep many writing schools happy—as well as
agents and publishers who exploit the beginner. There is also a vast
number of competent writers—writers who, over the years, have had a
book or two published or enjoyed some good magazine appearances.
Midlist describes them; they are not *known* authors, and this is a handicap, but their work commands some attention.
    If editors—those who read manuscripts submitted to them by
agents—must daily do battle with a frightening pile, they must of necessity do a lot of quick eliminating. Unless the start is gripping, the reading
will end quickly. Almost no attention at all is paid to the possibility that
the full manuscript might warrant an extensive time-investment on
revisions. "Let another house gamble," is the consensus. But where a
start *is* gripping, generated by style or tension, then the manuscript will
be read in full. As I stressed previously, it truly excites an editor or first
reader to pick a shiny nugget out of the dross.
    Ken Edgar had previously aroused editorial interest, most notably on
the part of Eleanor Rawson, then of David McKay. Because of fear of
insufficient sales, the interest didn't go quite far enough. Bram Cavin
also had to weigh and think, but finally he was able to win over the
Prentice-Hall chiefs. For Ken it was vindication—and also for me. It
proved that neither agent nor author should be overwhelmed by odds.
End and Beginning had rolled up at least twenty previous rejections. A
William Morrow editor had this to say:

    Judging by this manuscript, Dr. Ken Edgar has great talent and zest
for life. I found the story unusually interesting and it has some
important things to say. I wish we could do it, but I don't need to tell
you that fiction is giving us a very bad time right now. In final form,
I'm sure this novel would get good reviews, but would it sell? If Dr.
Edgar had a reputation as a writer and a following, I think it might be
a different story.

But would it sell?
This is such an important question that it needs to be explored in more
detail. While *End and Beginning* was making the rounds, Ken completed

The House on Sweet Hill. This was at McGraw-Hill, when the first Prentice-Hall contract came through. So I would have brought it to Bram Cavin save that Ken had started *As If.* This one was so timely (some of the characters fight in Vietnam), and Ken created such vivid and compelling characters, I felt that the book should be published next. I rushed off the start. Prentice-Hall agreed. It would follow the first by a year—if Ken would have it ready in time. Spurred by the encouragement, the novel was completed, and it was published in September 1973, just a year after the first. It was *then* that I brought *The House on Sweet Hill* to Bram. There was a long silence. In conversation with me about another matter, Bram finally said, "Aren't you curious about Ken's novel?"

"No," I said. "I know exactly what will happen. If the first two do well, it will be an automatic acceptance. If the books miss, it will be rejection."

"That's exactly the way it will be," Bram confirmed.

As If also attracted some interesting letters, and a good review in *Library Journal.*

> Despite the weird title, this is a damned good read. Before Tom Welland leaves for a special mission in Vietnam, he must visit his father, his ex-wife, and his grown-up children. There is also the matter of young Holly, whom he suspects he loves. Holly is also the target of young Kramer, the pilot assigned to Tom. Kramer and Tom crash in North Vietnam and are captured. After a series of narrow escapes, Tom returns to decide between Holly and his ex-wife. Basically, this is a love story and an effective one. The reader comes to care about the characters and becomes involved with the many family relationships. There is real warmth generated in the love scenes and in the scenes with Tom and his father. Although the POW sequences would seem better suited to a separate book, the novel does hold together via smooth writing and sprightly dialogue and without explicit sex. Public library patrons will love this.—Robert H. Donahugh, Youngstown Public Library, Ohio.

As a title, *As If* needs some explaining. It is taken from the following dialogue between Tom and Holly:

> She smiled at him, shyly. "Maybe you love me," she said. "That's a strange feeling in this as-if world we live in. People acting as if they're in love when in fact they're only interested in the other person as a commodity to be used up. As-if lovers, as-if friends, as-if preachers, teachers, lawyers, doctors." She sighed. "I'm so tired of as-if people."

The review just about exhausted the first printing of 3,000. But there was no advertising, and the book failed to score.

An author generally builds a reputation *cumulatively,* book by book, and that is what Ken is doing. I still think there will be movie sales and reprint interest, but at that time the books failed to score, so Bram was reluctant to propose *The House on Sweet Hill.*

Ken and I agreed that there was one good way to force Prentice-Hall off dead center, by a novel which would attract movie and reprint attention. That would be a psychological thriller, the easiest type of book to sell. There would be no "Vietnam angle," manifest in the first two novels, and that was a very severe handicap. The few exceptions are known to me, but while the war raged, Vietnam inspired shrugs in both publishing and the film sector. That was because readers and viewers turned away from the subject. A change has come, but for Ken it came too late.

Ken's next novel was *Frogs at the Bottom of the Well.* This one Bram Cavin did *not* like, but Playboy Press contracted. The novel dealt with women revolutionaries. After the book was accepted, Lynette Fromme and Sara Jane Moore burst into prominence. Patty Hearst was captured. All three, and scores more, might have sprung from the pages of Ken's story. A copy went to Universal Pictures. Their story department issued this report:

> This scarily contemporary thriller offers good possibilities for a highly unusual exploitation project.
>
> Timely, suspenseful, with lots of action, a good strong plot, and lots of sex (of several varieties and all a fundamental part of the story, not dragged in), the novel tells the story of Molly, an attractive young policewoman who agrees to work with the FBI and infiltrate a group of lesbian terrorists in New York City. Her task: to find out—in time— when they plan to blow up New York's newly built Trade Center with a miniature atom bomb.
>
> As the young policewoman becomes the lover of the head of the woman's group, she learns the atom bomb is being brought to New York in pieces by the California male activist who built it. Sun, the activist, finally arrives. He, too, has his sexual hangups, which Molly makes use of as she gains his confidence. The conclusion is an exciting mix of suspense and action as Molly and the FBI inspector manage to pull the teeth of the atom bomb at the last minute. There's a happy ending for Molly personally, too—with the FBI man.
>
> Throughout this absorbing suspense melodrama, as Molly shares the lives of the women terrorists—and the bed of one—we are given a terrifying look into the world of these twisted, sick-souled women— how they think, what made them what they are, their plans. The author, a psychologist at Indiana University of Pennsylvania, has given his novel an extraordinary ring of authenticity.
>
> A very good prospect.

A very bad turn for writers.

Dear Alex,

As you may have read recently in *Publishers Weekly,* our Trade and Spectrum Divisions have just merged. This means that in future, I'll not be interested in fiction, biography, autobiography, or anything with a narrative. What we're looking for now is what I can best term "layman's textbooks"—how-to and self-help volumes written by professionals (ideally, college instructors) in every subject—math, science, computer science, economics, finance, psychology, and so on. If you have anyone who's currently teaching and can write a "Complete Guide To . . . ," I'd like to hear about it.
Cordially,

Tam Mossman
General Publishing Division
Prentice-Hall

A later bit of book news:

GULF & WESTERN TO ACQUIRE
PRENTICE-HALL FOR $71 A SHARE

The Over-Achievers, Peter H. Engel's first book, was placed before the author became president of Helena Rubinstein, but inasmuch as *promoting* a book is so all-important, Dial Press and I were delighted that the dynamic and attractive-looking Mr. Engel was moved into that high slot (which he no longer holds).

Talk Shows might not have hesitated about inviting the author, for he is an eloquent spokesman for the achiever, the under- and over-achiever, and this hits some universal notes. Who doesn't relish success? What *makes* an over-achiever? Is it a laudable trait? Is it something America could do with less of? The fact that the energetic Mr. Engel was right *in* Big Business made him more attractive to place before large audiences, and books are often accepted or rejected on an author's ability to plug effectively.

Mr. Engel was one of the bright stars in the Colgate-Palmolive galaxy. Because the huge soap-detergents-cosmetics makers spend so much on advertising, they are a tremendous voice in television and radio. And being international cartels, the multinational giants cast some strong global shadows. The Engel book was not meant to be a searing, exposé-type publication, although there was plenty to expose in these all-powerful corporations, from bribes for contracts to bypassing pollution controls. With a career to safeguard, Peter Engel wasn't throwing rocks; rather his is a very friendly, anecdotal, "inside" story of how products are conceived, developed, packaged, and finally merchandized. And such a book could also be interesting. This one *is.* Popular Library did the mass audience paperback; Crain Books of Chicago published a limited edition aimed at their special market, the business community. The McGraw-Hill Business Book Club bought a block of copies.

Peter Engel had first contacted me from Canada. This was some twenty years ago, when he had been a striving (and probably starving) author. Then a recent college graduate, he had sent me a campus-background novel. I explained why it could not meet professional competition. Next, I rejected a short story. Once again, a talent was apparent, and, because of it, I took the time to point out some clear and unmistakable market pitfalls. After that, silence. But I had an instinctive feeling that I should keep the file open.

Many years passed before I did hear from him again. He had meanwhile moved to the States and began to do exceedingly well as a young business administrator. He proposed a book about American executives living abroad, an area he knew first hand. I approached editors with several chapters and a precis. The project, *The Expatriates,* did not place, but it did come close a few times. Success in his *established* field Peter Engel had in spades, but there nestled that unsatisfied *urge,* which other writers will recognize. The wish to have a book out prompted Engel to begin a new effort, a proposed book on noise pollution. I again showed a partial. He wrote:

Dear Alex:
The City of Boston is suing airline companies for over ten million dollars on noise pollution.
A few days ago there was a prime-time television special on noise pollution. Dupont has invented a new plastic to stop metal from sounding so noisy. And a garbage can which doesn't clank is already in production. A garbage can that doesn't clank!
So you see, noise pollution is just on the verge of becoming glamorous. People are beginning to talk about it and care about it—and they'll want to buy books about it. I'm scared, however, that other writers will cover the subject, and prempt us if we don't get a move on.
Is there anything you or I are not now doing which we could be doing to get *The Din Around Us* moving foreward?

We *were* beaten to market; a book did appear on noise pollution, but it created no waves. Rachel Carson's *Silent Spring* stood in a class apart. The potential market for *Din* was deemed too limited, as it was for *Expatriates.* Noise pollution concerns a limited segment. Most citizens accept noise as they accept poisoned streams and dead wildlife—as penalties for living in a vinyl chloride age. Plastic bags displaced clattering trash cans, with what overall results? Eventually plastics are incinerated, and where air is watchfully cleaner, waste is hauled to the ocean and later returns to beaches as sludge. No pollution control has been effective.

When Helena Rubinstein died, the House she had built began to founder, which is not unusual when a charismatic superstar leaves the stage. (It also happened with Elizabeth Arden and the Charles Revson firm.) Colgate-Palmolive absorbed Helena Rubinstein, and Mr. Engel was sent in as the chief executive officer.

That he was an exceedingly busy man goes without saying, but it is always the *busy people* who somehow "make" the time to do everything they want to do. Laugh when someone says: "I'd write a book if I had the time."

As a writer, Peter Engel is clearly not of the avant-garde "artist" breed. He wants to *sell*. This means that he accepted the prevailing norms and tried to please editors. And now that the rocky road was properly cemented, he is back at his original springboard—the novel. Very little invites more success than success itself.

18

Authors Who Defeat Themselves

In August 1977, the press and television gave wide coverage to a spectacular exploit by Dan Cameron Rodill, and in that desperate bid for publicity lies an important lesson for countless writers; mainly, that certain acts are self-defeating. A second lesson is the vast difference between *promotion* and getting by at the editorial level.

The New York Times headline was: FRUSTRATED WRITER LEAPS OFF BROOKLYN BRIDGE AS STUNT. This is part of the story: "In an apparent publicity stunt for his latest literary effort, an aspiring playwright clad in a wetsuit and floatation gear, placed his unpublished manuscript on a railing of the Brooklyn Bridge yesterday afternoon and plunged 130 feet into the East River. He was critically injured.

"The victim, 37-year-old Dan Cameron Rodill, a former freelance journalist in Indochina, had tried unsuccessfully for months to market his play, *The Dry Season,* a work drawn from his experiences in Vietnam and Cambodia . . ."

Some months before the near-fatal plunge, I received several letters from the author. In one he wrote:

Dear Alex:
   The Indochina play I mentioned to you in December, is still at about eight theatres for consideration, tho it's been turned down by three others. So, still having to write in a vacuum, and encountering some unusually bad luck during a recent Latin American trip, I now find it necessary to consider the ultimate gamble.
   Let me come swiftly and clearly to the point. I'm in the early stages of planning a "spectacular" which is not, strictly speaking, a literary endeavor. I won't be any more specific about it except to say that it's not a criminal act, although it requires frowns from social hypocrisy. My chances of survival are about 50% (this is only my own rough estimate). I know how to put it in social context so that it is seen as more than just a wild, semi-suicidal stunt. Despite the obvious risk of death, my goal is to survive the exploit and profit by it. In proof of this

point, I will go through with the exploit only after assigning exclusive rights (probably but not necessarily news media rights) in exchange for a financial guarantee. . . .

When I read "semi-suicidal stunt" and "in exchange for a financial guarantee," I was so certain that the author was on the wrong track, a memo quickly went off: "I am exclusively a literary agent, not a promoter. Whatever you might undertake, I wish you Good Luck, but I must emphatically stand aside from any involvement."

There were previous letters. I'll quote parts because it contains a lot of self-delusion shared by other aspiring writers:

"Dear Sir:

Regarding the current Hollywood interest in Indochina material, I've spent this year constructing a full-length play with a S.E. Asian setting. We'll just call it INDOCHINA STORY. Altho written for the stage, this drama contains plenty of story, action and characterization for motion picture adaptation.

INDOCHINA STORY, copyrighted November 1976, is currently under consideration for production at leading theatres here and across the country. Its characters include Americans, Asians and a Frenchman. In addition to the male leads, there is an important role for an American female. If your agency is among those interested, please advise. . ." He offered a capsule bio:

"9-year background in Asia. War correspondent, columnist in Saigon; first hand accounts of life behind the lines with the Vietcong and sailing with Mekong Convoy appeared in Newsday, the Chicago Sun-Times, Chicago Tribune, etc. Press Liaison for World Airways President Ed Daly in March–April 1975 during the controversial Babylift and Last Flight to Danang; Acting Bureau Chief at CBS Bureau in Saigon after regular staff personnel had been evacuated as the North Vietnamese Army surrounded the capital." Rodill offered a list of References, and added a Postscript. "Current interest in Indochina material was confirmed by the William Morris Agency. They told me they had four such scripts at the moment. WMA has not seen my script."

I replied, in part:

Every published and produced writer was once a novice waiting outside the gates. Writers break through in different ways. You write that INDOCHINA STORY is "currently under consideration for production at leading theatres here and across the country," and so I wish you well. If you contact other agents, be aware that agents are interested only in the product the author has to sell, and in professional credits. Personal references are of no interest at all . . . As far as I know, the theme least appealing to the TV/movie people, is "Indochina material." Story Editors would consider an Indochina story, providing there was something very special about it. As a *theme,* such stories go to bat with 2½ strikes against them.

I never got to read Mr. Rodill's play, but it is his faulty reasoning which concerned me. Getting a play read is easily done. Plays *are* read. At least, a reading *begins.* If it terminates by page ten, it is more the author's fault.

Authors who aspire to become playwrights should know what the chances are of a Broadway producer showing interest in a *serious* play. Unless it is superbly written, and has a small cast, even previously produced playwrights will be turned down. Plays are almost totally at the mercy of critics. For sheer survival, plays on Broadway depend on Theatre Parties and out-of-town buyers. So musicals are favored. The keynote is *entertainment,* and this applies also to the serious play.

Off-Broadway, and lanes stretching from it, will welcome something offbeat. A play about Vietnam would be acceptable, but unless the theatre is subsidized, the size of the cast and other costs must be carefully measured.

Regional theatres? The same applies. Dinner Theatre and Summer Stock do mostly revivals.

In Publishing, as at the movie end, the most hated single word was Vietnam. The subject carried a plague-like flavor. By 1976 the bias eased. Novels, plays and movie scripts which could make no headway before, began to surface. The theme was no longer tabu, but each submission had to *force* attention.

Mr. Rodill's problem was not to get his play *read,* but to go further as a writer. Unless a NAME is involved, or something very special, plays are not *published.*

If, at the time of his exploit, the author had a book in the stores, or a play on the boards, *then* publicity would have helped greatly. The fact that Mr. Rodill became momentarily newsworthy was not going to change the established *modus operandi.*

Men now and then risk their lives for that one burst of notoriety. That was clearly Rodill's motivation, but if he aspired to make it as a writer, a number of other options were open to him. He might have converted his story to a novel. He should have known that most playwrights (or novelists) make it with the second or third try. While "waiting," they learn—learn that producers and publishers also face problems.

Fantasy, daydreams of success, are vital parts of an author's equipment, and it is all to the good. But a line should be drawn between wishful thinking and self-delusion. It does an author no good to mistake myth for fact or fact for myth. It happens all too often, and it blocks progress.

Ladies and Gentlemen:

Did you ever close your eyes and see real beauty? The beauty of perfect patterns, the rainbow in your mind? Thoughts are more beautiful than sunsets because they represent true feelings.
Nothing is more beautiful than the truth; The crimes of our lives are only in our distortions.

You are in business to make money. I am an unknown author who has written his first novel, "REBIRTH." In today's society, we have become worlds apart. IF I sign this letter Richard M. Nixon, you'd all be rushing to the phone. Unfortunately, I am not a frightened paranoid, nor an indirect murderer (all in the name of national security).
    So what am I trying to say? I am trying to determine if there is any feeling left in our robotized society. I am trying to get my goddamned book published!
    I can bullshit and tell you wonderful things about my book, or I can say nothing. Since this is my letter, I choose to say nothing. Wait a minute, I'll give you a brief outline:

    love, evil, guilt, adultery, children, love, marriage, love, GOD

In all sinceriosity, I believe that my book is a money maker for the profit taker; that's you. If you really want to piss me off, send me back a form letter signed ROBOT (I'm sure I'll get a couple of those). Just don't sit on your assive and be passive. Say things like; no, I'm not interested, yes, I am interested, yes, I'd love to read your book, wow, are you a shnook.
    I end now with my strongest feeling,
                                        LOVE
                                        George Aegen

I had an intuitive feeling that this shriek of despair was designed to cover up deficiencies in the manuscript itself, but I like to be shown. I replied:

You want to see your "goddamned book published." Okay. I'd guess that 95% of fiction is sold by NAME, but you are *you,* and you will have to make it in *your* terms . . . All recognized authors were once unknown. They *became* known. So will you, if, on the one hand, you have "saleable merchandise," or, on the other, a high literary quality. Yes, I'll risk a time-investment to call your hand. Before I comment on REBIRTH, allow me a personal note . . . When I read the manuscript of THE SEXUAL KEY TO THE TAROT, I personally thought that it was pure (or impure) garbage. But my function as an agent is to form *professional* judgments. Acting as the *agent,* I felt that there was a market for the book, and it went out. The book achieved soft and hardcover publication, and it is still selling, a dozen years after publication. At some future date I may write how REBIRTH struck me *personally.* I will then comment on what I thought of your blend of

170   THE ROMANCE OF PUBLISHING

biblical allegory and current realism; your using poetry and those four
letter words; I will comment on the characterizations and the intereac-
tions between the different characters. Now I want to reply strictly
professionally. As the *agent*, I doubt that I could interest any publisher
on a Dutton-Doubleday level. What other *levels* are there? Well, New
Directions (and a few more such), place the emphasis on Art, Literature. REBIRTH does not qualify as such. *Parts* have a Kafka-like
quality, but other parts are pure pulp-paperback-sex. . . .

There are the many "Small Press" publishers. You probably know
that the sponsors of THE PUBLISH-IT-YOURSELF HANDBOOK
(where I have a chapter) are coming out with a new book, one which is
all about the small press publishers. These you could try on your own.

A letter from Avon Books:

Dear Alex:
Thank you for sending me Vane Vinnie's STATE HOSPITAL. I'm
afraid I saw the same story last week under the title THE TUNNEL,
under the representation of the H. N. Swanson Agency.
It's hard to tell which of you actually represents the work, but I know
it's not for us.
I appreciate your thinking of us for Mr. Vinnie's work.

Yours sincerely,

Robert B. Wyatt
Editorial Director

No comment needed.

Writer Chuck Ross likes to play a game which could aptly be called:
Testing and Tricking Publishers and Agents.

PUBLISHERS NIX KOSINSKI NOVEL

IF YOU'VE got a schlocky novel, we've got a publisher for you.
Fourteen publishers, in fact, each of whom rejected an award-winning
novel by the eminent Jerzy Kosinski. In the current New West, Chuck
Ross made an experiment to prove the difficulties of getting first
novels published. He took Kosinski's 1969 *Steps*, winner of the National Book Award, typed out the entire book, and sent it to 14 houses.
Among them: Random House (original publisher of *Steps*), Doubleday, Houghton Mifflin and Harcourt Brace—all of which have published Kosinski works. He put a fictitious name on the manuscript.
The upshot: several houses refused to read any unsolicited material,
the rest rejected it, with most of them doing so by form letters.
Harcourt Brace wrote that "the content didn't inspire (enough) enthusiasm." From Houghton Mifflin: "Some very impressive moments, but
gives the impression of sketchiness and incompleteness." Undaunted,
Ross tried to get an agent, sending the book to 26 of them. Big-time

Julian Bach responded: "It jumped about so much that it did not hold interest." And from Candida Donadio: "lacked that all important dramatic tension." Everyone else turned down the book or said they were full up on clients. Top agent Gloria Safier refused even to read it unless Ross sent $25. This he did. Then Safier rejected it.

This appeared in the New York *Post* 1/29/79. The bit was mailed to me by a writer, who added; "Whatta racket, Alex, whata racket!"

So that writers might *learn*, let's examine the salient parts:

"The difficulty of getting first novels published."

This is an old and a well-established fact. Yet first novels are still published. More likely than not, they are not the first novel *written*. Writers need time to mature. Each does it a bit differently. Those who are serious about their craft stay with it. The amateur who stays an amateur never breaks through.

"Several houses refused to read unsolicited material; the rest rejected it, with most of them doing it by form letter."

If publishers refuse to accept unsolicited submissions, the fault lies with the huge cadre of authors who submit long before they learn to write anything worth submitting. Going back to the days of the old Saturday Evening Post, Gwen Lysaught had presided over the slushpile submissions. She and her staff tried very diligently to sort out the occasional nugget. When the Post came upon lean days, the department, expensive to maintain, was dropped. It had been nurtured essentially as a public relations good-will gesture. In our day, Simon & Schuster was the first of the large houses to put up barriers. It was a time-wasting luxury they found it expedient to drop. Submissions still arrive; they are returned with a list of agents culled from Bowker's Literary Market Place.

As stressed previously, at the brand-name publishers, no over-the-transom submission gets to a senior editor unless recommended by whoever might pick up the manuscript for evaluation. It could be said that only a dunce could miss a best-seller like *Steps*, but that's murky reasoning. So far, no book has yet been written, including the Bible, which could please all readers, be they assistant editors, editors, or agents. Someone at Random House had gone to bat for *Steps*, and the gamble won. Unless one had read the book, it simply would not be familiar. The same trick-game could be played with any current best-seller. Robert Ludlum is diamonds-and-sapphire. Yet send any of his published novels around surreptitiously and it is likely to be rejected. Comments could read, "Too many clichés." "Implausible situations." "Drastic cutting is needed." In rejection, the sheer volume of submissions makes a form letter inevitable.

Candida Donadio and Julian Bach are known to me as excellent agents, and they have the clients who will swear by them. I have the clients who will take an oath on me. That does not mean that I have not made my quota of mistakes. No agent is right for all writers. Writers learn this as they grope towards professionalism.

"Not taking on new clients."

This is a convenient dodge many agents employ as the easiest way out. Every agent seeks new clients, providing the client is already an established asset, or shows some genuine potential. Otherwise, why bother? Agents have to cope with a tangent very few authors consider, an everrising Overhead.

Highly trained psychiatrists will shake their heads at human foibles.

With their own health at stake, men and women will withhold vital information from their physicians. And some writers will not be truthful when they approach an agent.

There is no reason to expect authors to be more honest than bankers, doctors, firemen, lawyers, or what-have-you, but I would expect authors not to act as self-defeatingly as many do. I am speaking of actions and motivations which clearly act against their own best self-interests. A letter stated:

> Dear Mr. Jackinson;
> Please allow me to present my manuscript for your consideration. My previous agent is no longer in the business.
> Thank you for your attention.
>
> Ziley Whitestone

Since the novel came in cold, and was a Xerox copy, I had some questions to pose: "Have you copies with other agents? Who was your former agent? Has he or she sold anything for you?"

Her reply:

> I was formerly represented by the Paul R. Reynolds agency. No sales were ever made. As I understand it, both Stein & Day and George Brazillier (her spelling), were interested in another of my properties, but both times the deals fell through.
> I currently have no representation. I hope this information is sufficient.

I began to read the novel. I did not have to turn many pages to decide that there was utterly no possibility of the Paul R. Reynolds Agency offering such a dud. I phoned, and drew this reply: "We have no record in our files of any correspondence with a Ziley Whitestone." Well, records can get lost, or misfiled, but there are the author's own words: "My previous agent is no longer in the business." Since the Paul R. Reynolds Agency, one of the very best, is very much *in* business, the author's word became her tombstone. She had phoned me, and so I knew that I was dealing with a woman.

Another letter, from a teacher in Dubach, Louisiana.

Dear Sir:
   I am doing graduate research on Harmon S. Blake for a course in English at Louisiana Tech University at Ruston, La. Mr. Blake told me by phone that he had a "Magellan Series" and a "Detective and Adventure Series"—so far I have not been able to find anything on either. Could you supply me information on these series, or an annotated bibliography of his complete works. I could also use any biographical information or information concerning the Walt Disney movie of Swamp Lad. I would appreciate any help you could give me on this. Thank you.

Harmon S. Blake (a made-up name) came to me after he had had a number of low-grade "sexy paperbacks" published by Novel Books. His problem was this: how could he "grow" as a writer? I suggested that he turn to the Juvenile field, since he had an aptitude for writing about young people. He followed my suggestion. I was able to place his novels with John Day and with Follett. He also tried the crime-detective story. None, I felt, could be submitted to the higher-level paperbacks. On his own, he later placed two rejects with Tower Books. That was it—two paperbacks of dubious quality. Three juveniles one could be proud of. The two "series" never materialized. An "annotated bibliography"?
   I had to send a copy of the letter to the author. He quickly phoned me from Louisiana. "Ignore the letter," he said. Clearly, the author had done a bit of bragging. Harmless fantasy? I regarded it as an act of sheer stupidity. He should have known that the woman might take it upon herself to contact me.
   There was also self-delusion on the author's part that the plot of a Walt Disney movie was lifted from one of his Juveniles. I did, indeed, show the book to Paul Nathan, then the Disney New York Story Editor, but there was utterly no plagiarism involved. I explained this to the author. For reasons known only to him, he preferred to believe that his story was "stolen." Many authors share "like" delusions.
   Since the Kosinski "exposé," Chuck Ross tried a new ruse.

Casablanca may be a Hollywood classic, but it wouldn't stand much of a chance in today's Tinseltown, according to an investigation by a Los Angeles writer.
   Chuck Ross sent the script of the 1942 picture to the 217 agents suggested by the Writers Guild of America as go-betweens with the

major studios, which won't read independently submitted projects. He called the work *Everybody Comes to Rick's,* the title of the play on which Casablanca was based. Ross explains in a story that will appear in next month's issue of Film Comment.

"Only 33 agents recognized what they were reading, and another 41 rejected it outright," he told *New York.* The Trejos Literary Agency, for instance, said, "Try for a script that has audience identification and one that can be filmed in the U.S.," while the Larry Karlin Agency said the project didn't "grab" it. Three agents told an astonished Ross that they'd represent him, but most of the others said they didn't handle unsolicited material.

"Hollywood agents don't know what's good. It's the same as with publishers," said Ross. Indeed, when he typed out Jerzy Kosinski's *Steps* and sent it to fourteen houses—in a widely publicized 1979 experiment—they all rejected it, including Random House, the publisher that had brought out the National Book Award-winning novel.

I was one of those who received the script, which came to me from Erik Demos of Santa Monica. The covering letter was brief: "Dear Alex Jackinson Literary Agency. Enclosed please find a screenplay for a full-length feature film for your consideration. I would appreciate any comments you may have."

The script was obviously going to other agents as well. When this happens, I generally give the author ample time to play the field. Several letters passed between myself and Demos. In one I wrote: "You are very close to the 'Hollywood scene' and so you can check this out for yourself. When it comes to a 'Casablanca-type' story, a post-War-two setting, German spies, desert intrigue, a huge expenditure is involved. And so 48 out of 50 producers would want the prior backing of a published book."

On the carbon copy of my first letter, I made this note: "Wait till he hears from other agents, and write again. The basic material could make a good adventure yarn."

I had seen *Casablanca* when it had first appeared, some forty years ago. Of course, I had never read the original screenplay. I knew that the script I received would be an expensive film, and so I thought primarily of a novel. Not that it has to be one or the other; it could be *both,* with a book coming first.

"Hollywood agents don't know what's good."

There is some truth in that. At least Ross-Demos knows how to put over a gag. I will now look for his name where he will impress editors without resorting to gimmicks.

19

Three Portraits in Black

In our world of belles lettres, divine and comic, stories are legion of authors and editors who drank excessively. Here I will confine myself to three very gifted, highly unique individuals. Each died differently; in no case was the root cause attributed to alcoholism, but drink was the ghastly and ghostly skein which tied together Tom Bledsoe, Gil Orlovitz, Edward Anderson.

Excessive drinking is invariably caused by a mix of personal, emotional, family problems. But here, in each case, the "publishing scene" was the hammer that drove in the nail.

When Tom Bledsoe had become editorial director at Beacon Press, he put together a little brochure he called "Reflections on a List of New Writers." I quote in full because the message is even more "immediate" today.

> One of the things about the book trade that gets pretty clear to anyone who had been around for a while is that this is a business where nobody is exactly sure of anything. Publishing houses have been made by a single best seller, and most of our ways of book selection, manufacture, promotion, and distribution are in some way geared to this wayward pot of gold. And yet nobody knows what makes a best seller or why a particular book becomes one—not even by hindsight.

> For a small industry, we spend, all things considered, a disproportionately large percentage of our income on advertising and promotion. But no competent advertising manager in an honest frame of mind would claim that he knew exactly how to get a book rolling or that he was really certain what helped most to keep it going once, somehow, it got under way. Our evidence is general and contradictory, and too often the thing that's clearest is that the kind of campaign that sold one book successfully was a flop with a similar one. And yet we advertise and advertise, and I do not believe that any of us—publishers, booksellers, wholesalers, agents, admen, critics and reviewers—doubt its necessity. We just aren't sure how or why.

> It is no wonder then—publishing being at once a business, an art,

and a world of practical and verbal uncertainties—that our trade is characterized by slogans which we quote, live by, but believe only at our peril. One of these, especially current, is that fiction is in a bad way. Another is that the best way to lose your shirt is with first novels.

I don't believe it. I wonder if we haven't sold ourselves an even bigger bill of goods than the one most of us are uneasily conscious of. It stretches no imagination to speculate on the reception today of Hemingway's Torrents of Spring. Faulkner's Soldier's Pay or Mosquitoes, or Fitzgerald's This Side of Paradise, were they offered to publishers or to the trade as first or second novels.

"First novel, heh? Promising young writer?" says the President.

"Most promising manuscript I've seen in my three years, four months, two weeks, and one day at Elephant and Whale, Inc., sir," replies the editor. "But he has a second in the works, and he has published stories in Infinity, Inevitability, Insecurity, and Instability. We have marvelous quotes from Tristran Evergood and Isolde von Braunschweiger."

Or:

"No, second. He had one published two years ago by Scriveler and Birdbrain, Ltd. But the most promising . . . one day . . . Whale, Inc. He's published . . . marvelous . . . Braunschweiger."

"Hmm. Interesting. But how about Walter Oakhead of the Preview Syndicate? Will he push it? How about Shoebooks, Inc.? Low-hat Editions? And obviously Scriveler and Birdbrain . . ."

"Well, you know . . . No obvious . . . But in the long run . . . And I'll stake . . ."

"Will it sell 7500 copies first printing?"

At this point we mercifully lower the curtain. Only the foolhardy, the irresponsible, or the wise would go out on this limb, and the respectable habits now prevailing in our industry do not encourage these undesirable types to long endure. The curtain rises on the improbable chance of the book's having been published, and we find Norman Humson, salesman, closeted with Joseph Eiderdown, buyer and part owner at Ream, Eiderdown and Skate, sellers of books, records, stationery, fountain pens, office equipment, stuffed dogs and pennants (there's a university eight blocks away), greeting cards, tranquilizers, and a select line of table specialties.

Joe, who is speculating on ways of expanding to include wines and liquors (political problems with the state liquor commission), a cafeteria, and a high quality line of lipsticks and hairsets featured on the 32½ Million Dollar Question, is preoccupied.

"Secondary fiction, hey Norm?"

"Well, sure, Joe, but this kid's got it. Look, I'm telling you, I read it, and have I ever let you down? You do what I ask, take twenty-five and put them up front, and you'll never regret it."

"Okay, Normie, seeing as it's you, tell you what I'll do. You know I trust you, but I don't have to tell you how Ream is about secondary novels. Put me down for five, and I'll explain it someway."

Or,

more probably, George Lowband and Joe Eiderdown, same time, same situation:

"Secondary fiction, hey, George?"

"Sure, Joe, I know how you feel. Maybe later if . . . But here's one you've got to make it up on: Grace Ellwood's My Five Years in a Tibetan Monastery. Movie . . . digest . . . prepub."

Curtain.

This parody would be less painful if it were less true, and I have of course made only two stops along the line that runs from A for Author to R for Remainder, and these stops not entirely respectful. But it is easy to show, at any point in our industry, how easy it is to forget the unique qualities of what we are making and selling, and the individual attention our books, even the most slavishly imitative, demand.

It is on these grounds that Beacon takes a stand for new fiction and young writers. Obviously the Hemingways of tomorrow will develop only if they are published today, and while we claim no monopoly on discovery, we are willing to invest substantially in books by new young writers of first-quality fiction in the belief that, in cooperation with book-sellers and, deo volente, with serious consideration from critics and reviewers, we can develop a number of writers who will be both saleable and artistically imporant.

Accordingly, we are putting together a fiction list made up, at this writing, entirely of first novels or first book publications. The character and methods of these writers vary widely; we insist on no single literary line. We do believe that each of these writers reflects a genuine talent, and that each of them has something to say which reaches well beyond any clique, and which is potentially interesting to a wide circle of readers.

These circles will vary from book to book, and we will be disappointed if readers who most like some of our books do not dislike others with almost equal enthusiasm. But we will be surprised if they do not recognize quality and originality even in what they dislike, and if, in the next few years, Beacon does not come to be recognized as a place where first-rate new writers are to be found.

The book which leads off this list, on March 15, is Willa Thompson's Garden Without Flowers. This tautly written novel of a woman's inability to love, set in the beauty and terror of a Swiss skiing resort and hospital, has the intensity and inevitability of Sagan but, despite its tragic ending, a more positive theme. Our experience has been that our readers have either liked it enormously, as I did, or have been disturbed by it, and critical. It is in essence a dramatization of one of the recurrent problems of American women, and we hope it will find many readers. This book, incidentally, will be backed by a considerably higher advertising appropriation than most first novels, and will be promoted in some unusual media which may be of real interest to the trade.

This fall we are publishing three new writers. Michelle Lorraine is a young Frenchwoman whose Castle in the Sea won the Grand Prix des Ecrivains de la Quest and was enthusiastically reviewed in both France and England. A sensitive and beautifully written book about a group of children who discover the meaning of tragedy, it is certain to touch the responsive and to charm those who are interested in first-rate writing. Miss Lorraine's second novel, The Schoolboy, has been even more warmly reviewed in France and is now being translated into English. Beacon will published it in 1958.

Daniel Curley is a young American writer whose stories have appeared in Accent, The Kenyon Review, Perspective, The Atlantic Monthly, Harper's Bazaar, Best American Short Stories of 1955, and other publications. His stories have been highly praised by Katherine Anne Porter, John Crowe Ransom, and many others. That Marriage Bed of Procrustes and Other Short Stories introduces Mr. Curley's varied talents for the first time to a wider audience. He is now finishing revisions on a novel, How Many Angels, which we will publish next year as a major book.

Daniel Doan, who lives in Vermont, has written, in Amos Jackman, a novel about Vermont in the 1930's and the breakdown of the family farm which is at once deceptively quiet and intensely passionate—a paradox which only a reading of the novel can explain. It is an adaptation of the methods of the great tradition of the nineteenth-century novel to the Depression era, and is quite unlike anything I know in contemporary fiction, as well as being a fine and saleable book. Dr. Doan is also at work on a second novel.

Under contract for future seasons are, for example, Short Stories by Michelle Maurois (daughter of André Maurois), who is also working on a novel; The Paradise Garden, by Michael Swan, a young Englishman who writes in the tradition of Waugh and Isherwood. Black As Night, an intensely moving novel about a young Negro and his family which is as gripping, as violent, and as significant as anything I have read in years, and which has the potentialities of another Native Son; The Sleep of the Just by Mouloud Mammeri, a novel about changing cultures and interrelationships in North Africa among the old Algerians, and the French, which provides remarkable insights into this troubled area and is the first mature evidence of a developing Algerian-French literary tradition.

Other books are in process and are steadily being added to the list, but this is enough to suggest what we mean by an expanding and varied program of interesting new writers, supported by a lively promotion program. To revert to the theme of the first paragraph of these reflections, we won't swear to any one thing in this uncertain and fascinating business; but we are willing to bet that in this fiction list and in Beacon titles in other areas such as, this spring, Ilse Stanley's The Unforgotten, Kenneth Underwood's Protestant and Catholic, Michael Burn's Mr. Lyward's Answer, Geddes MacGregor's The Vatican Revolution, and others, you will find a list which is alive, growing, and which will continually increase in influence.

Thomas A. Bledsoe

I responded with warmth and began submitting. When Tom came to New York, we met and eventually became close friends. He was a big man physically, one strong enough to carry a vision, and we had common goals. Before long I had five Beacon Press contracts—*Black as Night* (Dan Nern); *Poet on a Scooter* (Harry Roskolenko); *Operators & Things* (Barbara O'Brien); *Under the Stars* (Iris Wells); *Short Stories* (Paul M.

Fitzsimmons). Two more contracts were pending, one for Edward Anderson's *Seven Hundred Wives*. As could happen only in publishing, all the contracts were abruptly cancelled. *Black as Night* was then at the binder's, but it escaped the axe only technically. Beacon Press preferred to lose the advances paid on each book.

Bledsoe had looked forward to entrenched stay at Beacon. He thought that he had the funds and the time to experiment. He didn't. Not too long after the wagon started rolling, there was an unexpected call from Reverend Walter Kring, president of the Unitarian Church, whose publication arm was Beacon Press.

"Tom's policies," Dr. Kring explained chokingly, "all but put us out of business. Once our accountants went over the books, we were shocked at the losses." Tom had no choice but to resign. Beacon Press went back to its old policy of sticking to books that had strong sociological significance. No more fiction; no more experimenting with general trade books.

Barring *the* end, agenting is a business of links that stretch on and on. Now I might sell to the movies a book originally designated for Beacon Press. It is *Operators & Things*. Barbara O'Brien is a pseudonym; the story supposedly is not. It is the account of a young woman who had a six-month siege of schizophrenia—and pulled out of it. Balance restored, she decided to write up her bizarre experiences.

A very good editor, Tom had no difficulty in finding jobs; his problem was staying put. He was too independent-minded to follow house policies; he always wanted to steer the ship. His post-Beacon move was to form his own firm, Arlington Books (not to be confused with the later Arlington House). In my many meetings with Tom, he never said it in so many words, but I knew that there was an intense desire on his part to prove that he had picked sound titles for Beacon. Once set, he inquired if *Operators & Things* was still available; it was. Tom contracted for it and published the book. And he took over other titles cut-rate from Beacon. Before too much time elapsed, Arlington raised the distress flag.

Tom had long nourished the ambition many editors share—to turn author. Tom failed utterly—failed in *his* terms, which was to make some sort of a dent in the sphere of the creative, noncommercial novel. "The Beacon Press Upset" formed a chapter in *Cocktail Party for the Author*. When the book was ready, the publishers, Challenge Press of Boston, wanted some quotes. Tom replied:

> Not many authors have the good luck to choose their agents as the result of dealing with them at the other end of the transmission line, as editors and buyers. When I was Director of Beacon Press, the agent who impressed me the most was Alex Jackinson. I like his honesty, his industry, his obvious concern for his clients, and his willingness to

meet a publisher more than half way. What really sold me, however, was one incident. After I had bought a good, controversial, hard-to-sell first novel—he specializes in these, thank God—BLACK AS NIGHT, by Dan Nern, I discovered that I had taken it on its thirty-first submission. Thirty previous submissions! The average agent would consider six submissions of an unpublished author a performance well above and beyond the call of duty, and the book would be on its way back to the author with a note of polite regret. Alex hung on—as few other agents would—and the book was published. When I became an author myself, there was no doubt as to the agent I wanted to represent me. I've never regretted it, and, to his credit, he doesn't seem to have either. A man, like I said, of uncompromising fortitude and impeccable taste.

Tom liked to recommend writers, one of whom was Abbott Reeves. Reeves submitted a novel, *Curiosity Rock,* which I rather liked. I couldn't place it with a hardcover house, but Gil Orlovitz, then an editor at Universal Books, accepted the novel as a paperback. My initial contact with Gil predated my becoming an agent; we appeared in the same poetry magazines. Aside from editing "sexy novels" at Universal, Gil was also an editor at *Trace,* an influential Little Magazine about Little Magazines. I appeared there, and when I turned agent, I submitted to Gil at Universal.

In that period Tom was between jobs, and there was no income at all from his writing. He paid me a call and said, "Universal has an opening for an editor. Ask Gil to recommend me."

"Would you want to edit sexy novels?"

"Sure. Why not? It won't tax me as much as serious editing."

I brought Tom to meet Gil, and they hit it off beautifully. Two iconoclasts. Kindred spirits. Two star Shakespearian actors finding themselves playing burlesque. Gil had hated it at Universal, more than once calling it a "whorehouse." But he found the work itself easy, and there was the exigency of needing to make a living. Gil's recommendation to management was warm, and Tom was considered. But the job finally went to an editor who had had experience in that special line.

As a free-lance writer, Tom starved. He wrote voluminously, but *his* way. He was a rebel who had to function within the system—or perish. He was ready to bend, compromise as an editor, but not as a writer. Each rejection left scars. And there were many. He couldn't stay on a job long. He wrote five novels, two of which were published by Swallow Press. Tom and Alan were old personal friends. The income from both novels never exceeded the token advance—one hundred dollars for *Dear Uncle Bramwell,* one hundred and fifty for *Meanwhile Back At The Henhouse.*

The lack of acceptance as a writer hurt Tom much more than his failure as a publisher. Betty, Tom's wife, would say that Tom also failed as a husband and a father. They eventually separated.

Tom felt happiest at Beacon. His plans were grandiose, but it doesn't take much time to run through a lot of money when you publish some twenty trade books, none of which did even moderately well.

At that time Tom wrote to me about Anderson's *Seven Hundred Wives:*

> I would like to do the Anderson, but there are problems. I still remember Bowie in *Thieves Like Us.* That book moved me! This new book moves me in a totally different way. I endorse what Anderson says about organized religion, especially the Catholic hierarchy, but I can't accept his implied praise of Jehovah's Witnesses. Like the Catholics, J. W.'s also spread the shit that they alone interpret "God's word" correctly. Anderson has a god-awful title, and a lot of the characters are on the fuzzy side. Yet the book has a dull brilliance, if that makes sense. If Ed will sit for some absolutely needed recasting, it could be another contract for you.

The letter went off to Anderson. There was an immediate reply. "No problems on revisions. I've done some reassessing. Tell your friend I'll go along on the changes." Less than a week later I again wrote Anderson, giving him a rundown on what had so unexpectedly happened. He replied: "The most accursed *business* in the world is the Vatican, with Medicine running a close second. But I'll be damned if Publishing isn't a close runnerup."

Tom collapsed in Los Angeles some ten years after the Beacon Press upset. Officially, the death was called "respiratory failure." Actually, he died of a liver ailment brought about by excessive drinking.

A stranger had walked into my office. He was holding a copy of an ad I had run in the *New York Times* for my book.

"Can I buy this book?" he asked.

He paid for a copy of *Barnum-Cinderella.* As he was leaving, I said, "I keep a record of local sales. May I have your name?"

He gave me his name, which I'll change to John Rayson. He added, "I'm a producer. Or I would be, if I had the right play to produce."

I reached for a copy of Ken Edgar's novel, *End and Beginning.* "Are you familiar with this book?"

"No, I'm not."

"It first came to me as a play. Would you like to see a copy?"

"Yes, very much so."

He walked off with both the play and the book. Nothing came of it, but the would-be producer and I remained on friendly terms. He'd stop by the office quite often. One day he said, "You wrote of Gil Orlovitz. I once read his play, *Stevie Guy,* and I liked it very much. I'd like to get a copy to read again."

I replied, "I've been out of touch with Gil for some years, but I could easily trace him, either through Universal or one of the poetry magazines."

And I did track him down. Gil was then living in a fleabag hotel in Harlem. I called, and left a message. Gil called me right back. After the amenities, I explained why I needed a copy of *Stevie Guy.*

"I have no copy here, and my wife won't let me into the house. But it appeared in a literary magazine, and there should be a copy at the library."

"Swell," I said. "You could make a Xerox copy right there."

"I can't," Gil returned. "I'm broke."

"I'll put a check in the mail immediately," I told him. "You should have it in the morning. And since you're broke, something will have to be done about it." That "something" I mailed him called for a bit of writing-editing. It would have meant quick income. He received it the next day and promptly brought it back.

At first glance it seemed that I was facing the old Gil, a big, handsome man. Craggy face, topped by a head of hair which remained full and black. But I quickly realized that I was looking at a shell. There was alcohol on his breath.

"Thanks for trying," he apologized. "At one time it would have been a cinch, but I'm washed up as a writer. All I can manage is a poem once in a while."

"How about editing? I could get you free-lance editing assignments."

"I can still edit."

"Let's see what you can do with an Edward Anderson novel which needs some skilled touching up." I explained about the author.

Gil held the manuscript a number of weeks and ultimately returned it. It was virtually untouched. All he did was write "Style" on each chapter head, and change a bit of grammar. I wondered how there could be such a total eclipse of a once vivid talent.

I made many copies of *Stevie Guy* and arranged a meeting between the author and the possible producer. Later John Rayson said, "Orlovitz has a drug problem; you can see it quite clearly in his eyes."

"I thought it was drink," I said. "Now it's probably both."

I attended memorial services for Gil Orlovitz, which were held at St. Clement's Episcopal Church many weeks after his death. The *Times* obituary page (8 September 1973) gave him a belated but impressive farewell:

GIL ORLOVITZ, POET, DIED IN JULY
TRACED TO CITY PAUPER'S GRAVE

Gil Orlovitz, prolific writer of avant-garde poetry, plays and novels, died July 10 at Knickerbocker Hospital. He was 55 years old and had lived alone in a single room at 235 West 107th Street.

Mr. Orlovitz apparently collapsed July 9 in front of 246 West 110

Street. He was in a coma with a 108-degree temperature and died the next day without regaining consciousness.

Mr. Orlovitz was buried at public expense on July 19 at the city cemetery on Hart Island, in a grave for paupers without family, though he had collapsed only a few blocks from the home of his wife and two young sons. Hospital and police officials had been at first unable to locate any relatives.

Mr. Orlovitz's wife, Maralyn, who was separated from her husband, said she first learned of the death on July 21, when she called the police Bureau of Missing Persons to report his apparent disappearance. Mrs. Orlovitz said that her husband had been in weekly contact with his family . . ."

After I saw the *Times* obituary, I wrote to Maralyn, the estranged wife: "What a tragic waste! But I was aware that Gil was broke and broken when we reestablished contact a few months ago. When Gil said, 'I have a copy at home, but my wife won't let me into the house,' I knew what lay behind that—the broken promises, the abuse, the neglect, the nonsupport. My sympathies were with *you*. . . ."

The *Times* story went on to report:

Mr. Orlovitz, who was born in Philadelphia, attended Temple University and Columbia University, and served in the Army Air Force from 1941 to 1945.

Nine volumes of his poetry have been published, and his poems have been printed in a variety of magazines, including the Quarterly Review of Literature, the Literary Review, Poetry, and the New Republic.

Three of Mr. Orlovitz's plays were produced Off-Broadway—*Case of a Neglected Calling Card,* in 1952, *Noone,* in 1953 and *Stefanie* in 1954.

In his later years he turned to writing novels. *Milkbottle H* was published by Delacorte in 1968 and *Ice Never F* was published in Britain by Calder & Boyers in 1970.

Mr. Orlovitz also worked as a screen writer for Columbia Pictures, as a television script writer in the nineteen-fifties and as an editor for several publishers in the nineteen-sixties. . . .

Gil knew the commercial mold, and he had a good deal of grudging respect for the income-successful writer. He wanted to turn out a popular success, but when it came right down to it, too many disaster wires crossed in the dark regions of his psyche.

Unlike Tom and Gil, Edward Anderson I never met. But he had been with me many years, and I had gotten to know him quite well. This is from the Sunday *Times* Book Ends section (March 1974).

Found. Whatever became of Edward Anderson? That question was raised recently in a favorable review by Pauline Kael of Robert Alt-

man's movie "Thieves Like Us," based on a novel called "Thieves Like
Us" by Edward Anderson. The novel (reviewed here Feb. 10) is a small
classic of the thirties, about little people's dreams and how they chase
them and inevitably fail. Avon brought out a paperback edition without copyright because the copyright had not been renewed and further Edward Anderson had disappeared from sight. After the Kael
review, however, he turned up—or rather his son Rader Anderson
did. Edward Anderson died in September, 1969, at the age of 63. The
bare facts of his life provided by Rader Anderson, an opera singer,
sketch out something of a prototypical thirties writer. There were the
newspaper jobs—10 cities in Texas, Arkansas and Oklahoma—then a
stint as a deckhand, then writing crime and prizefight stories for the
pulps. (He had been a professional fighter briefly.) His first novel,
"Hungry Men," about men on the bum, was published in 1935. This
was followed in 1937 by "Thieves Like Us," which was the co-winner of
the Doubleday-Doran Story Magazine award as the best novel of the
year. The reviews were laudatory, and one reviewer compared Anderson to Faulkner and Hemingway. The remainder of his life Anderson
bounced around from one newspaper to another and worked as a
scriptwriter for M-G-M in 1941. The family wandered a good deal but
often returned to Weatherford, Tex., where Anderson was born. His
last newspaper job was in Quero, Tex. He never published another
book after "Thieves Like Us." Those, as we said, are the bare facts. . . .

I wrote to the *Times:*

   I can fill in some missing links.
   Anderson became a client around the mid-fifties. He had lived then
in Laredo, Texas, and moved very often to other border towns,
Harlingen, El Paso, Brownsville, to recall three. His first submission to
me was a befuddled sort of "Biblical" novel he called SEVEN HUN-
DRED WIVES. It was not a good work, full of confused religious
overtones. The allusion was to the reputed 700 wives of Solomon, but
Anderson ran all over both heaven and hell. He wrote in a letter:

> Certainly WIVES is designed to be sensational. And I think the con-
> cluding chapters which I hope to have with you in another ten days, will
> show that the clergy of today, the "whore of Rome," the Catholics and her
> illegitimate offspring, the Protestants, are the Public Enemies #1. The
> whores and the politicians (publicans) have a better chance for the Kingdom
> of God. . . ? I am serious: Revelations (the Apocalypse) makes it clear that
> "The Beast" will triumph over Babylonia (the churches) and is it not hap-
> pening right before our eyes in Europe? There is no question in my mind
> but that the Force right now known as Communism will triumph the world
> over. . . .

   And who else can do a better job of describing the *state of religion* in this
country today than *Jehovah's Witnesses?* And you must give them credit,
the devil's due, you know. They are not offering you *tea,* but *strong
meat! They are telling more truths today than any other given, or cowering*

religion. They are persuading people no end because it can be very effective—
truths mingled with lies.

Along with the concluding chapters, Anderson wrote: "Perhaps once
more I am self-deceived, but if WIVES is not a saleable work, then I am
at an utter loss. For never did I write even a newspaper story with so
much confidence."

Despite my disagreements on the muddled religious references, as a
courtesy to a deserving author, and because Anderson was in desperate
need, I tried any number of publishers. I kept the book circulating many
years. My hope was to strike initial interest, with needed revisions to
come. Twice I was close to success; the second time it was an "almost"
with Arthur Fields, then of Crown.

Anderson subsequently sent in another novel, *Hell Has Its Own Stars.* It
dealt with some raffish American expatriates in Mexico. The time, 1916.
Villa and the Mormons figured prominently in the story. This was
superior to *Wives*, but it didn't measure up to Anderson's earlier works.
He wrote at the time:

> Alex, I am so out of step that I have been reduced to the welfare
> role.
> In the summer of 1964 I hotel-clerked in Dallas, nights, and spur-
> red by a rich surgeon's suggestion that I ghost a book for him, I
> researched industriously. But, alas, I found myself going just opposite
> from what the doctor wanted. It became overwhelmingly my con-
> clusion that, next to our cur-rianity (Christianity), medicine is the
> nation's top racket. . . .
> It explains why every generation of medical men claim superiority
> over the preceding one, and why it could be said today as it was in his
> time by Dr. Oliver Wendell Holmes, that if all the medicines were
> thrown into the sea, it would be better for mankind although worse
> for the fish.

Hell also came close a few times. Generally, since some convenient
excuse is always needed, a handy rejection tag was the assumption that
Mexico-background novels did not sell. Because of Anderson's pro-
longed economic plight, I sent him $500. In exchange, as it were, he gave
me the power-of-attorney on the book.

The late Sam Roth—an offbeat publisher who ran afoul of the law and
censors—took a strong liking to *Hell.* He was going to publish it under
his then-quiescent Seven Sirens Press. Roth wasn't sure when, and I did
not want to press him. His interest was too genuine. Publishing is a
mercurial fish. Shortly before his death, Roth returned the submission.
He was ill, and hadn't the strength to revive his ebbing interest in baiting

self-declared morals-watchers. I was in sporadic correspondence with Anderson, but in 1969 a letter came back. Deceased.

In letter after letter, Anderson stressed that it was his brief Hollywood period that seeded his later collapse. Success meant a swirl of parties. He started to drink excessively. Marital trouble developed. He turned into an alcoholic and tried AA, with spotty results. In a person's collapse, the roots invariably go deep; I can rake over the topsoil only.

20
Steps beyond the Initial Steps

Clark Howard's breakthrough was with *The Arm*. After that two other hardcover books followed, *A Movement Toward Eden* (Moore Publishing Co., 1968) and *The Doomsday Squad* (Weybright & Talley, 1970). Neither publisher made a go of it. Clark needed something *big*. I probed around.

The Dial Press was a firm I had long respected. They experienced difficulty in selling the "literary" novel, even the *fine* literary novel done by established writers. These were novels that had delighted critics but failed to haul in revenue. So they became more receptive to the "promotable" novel. It was less "surrender" and more an accommodation to *need*. I saw an opening for Clark.

Dial did not have a separate crime-mystery book department, but they have long published the better suspense-action story, in which Clark specialized. Dial did several of the popular *Shaft* books. I hoped to interest Joyce Engelson, herself a writer before she turned editor, in Clark *the author*. And it so worked out.

As a trial run, I felt safe in showing her two action novels, *Last Contract* and *Siberia Ten*. Both were rejected, but my prime objective was achieved. Joyce wrote: "We like the way Clark Howard writes, and the way he tells a story. If his next book outline will appeal to us, it will be a contract." Clark had then in work *The Killings* (1973). I showed Joyce the synopsis. It appealed. Dial Press saw no writing at all until I delivered the completed novel. Easy? So it would seem, but the author *earned* the right to command attention.

Siberia Ten and *Last Contract* next went to Pinnacle Books. I was impressed by the know-how of this new and growing paperback house. Although I'm a strong partisan of prior hardcover publication, much depends on what, when, and for whom. Clark already had three hardcover book credits. There would be *The Killings*, and no doubt books to follow, novels which would fall into the "impressive" category. So I was more receptive to Pinnacle's offer. Both novels were contracted for and quickly scheduled for publication. This should be of interest to the unpublished writer: Clark's very first submission was a suspense story that did *not* go out. I suggested that he *prove* himself by starting that vital second novel, inasmuch as he was entering a bitterly competitive field. He *did* win his chevrons.

This is from the Dial, Fall, 1973, catalog:

A major crime novel, THE KILLINGS is to modern police procedures what *The Detective* was to private investigation, *The Godfather* to contemporary lawlessness. Bold, even brutal, it spares no frankness as it explicitly details the efforts of two Los Angeles policemen charged with finding a mystery killer who has hideously slaughtered, and possibly raped, two young women.

Detectives Fenner and Cascade, long-time partners, handle a call from a nurse too terrified to enter her burglarized apartment. Investigating, the officers discover her roommates; twin sisters, throats cut, nude bodies tied together in a suggestively homosexual posture. The nightmare of hectic specialized emergency procedure begins; and for the detectives, the examination of a dozen plausible suspects, not excluding the nurse herself whose ambiguous sexuality proves irresistible to unhappily married Fenner.

The violent crime, surrounded by an ambience of depravity, and involving girls of an important family, becomes a city-wide scandal as it remains frighteningly unsolved. Hard clues dissolve, the slush work begins: down into the underbelly world of a big city: lesbian parlors, known "switch-bladers," an uneasy Chicano population. Clearing the innocent to find the guilty supplies a tightly plotted surprise climax to this novel which neither moralizes nor sentimentalizes about crime, cops and the law, but strictly fills out an absolute reality in the mosaic of a baffling crime."

The Killings had a relatively easy trip from publication to movie option.

On Thursday, 16 August 1973, two days before I was to leave on my annual busman's holiday, that is, lecturing at a writer's seminar in Vermont, there was a call from Hollywood. It was producer Herb Jaffe, once a front-rank literary agent.

"How much do you want for *The Killings*?" the producer asked.

"One hundred thousand," I said. "And 5 percent of the gross."

"The *gross*?"

"Yes, the gross," I emphasized. Generally this extra dividend is based on a film's *profits,* which isn't nearly as good. Costs can be so manipulated that no profit will show. But gross is fixed, and thus holds much greater value.

"I don't think I can get you that much," Herb Jaffee said. "Let me talk it over with my associates and I'll call you back. Tomorrow or Monday."

"Monday I will be in Vermont. Each August I lecture on marketing at a writer's seminar."

"Can you give me your Vermont number?"

"Yes, I have it." I read off some digits from a brochure on my desk. But the call came the next day. I scaled down the 5 percent to 2 percent, but it remained a very good deal. I called the author in Las Vegas and Clark was pleased. I called Dial Press and they were pleased. I spoke of the sale to the conferees, and they were pleased. This, like the book placement, came off easily, but a lot of rough terrain first had to be smoothed out.

In December 1972, Herb Jaffee had written to me:

Dear Alex:

Just a note to tell you that after eight years as an executive of United Artists I am going to produce films for this company under an exclusive arrangement. Needless to say, I'm going to need material and would greatly appreciate your thinking of me with regard to anything your office handles that you feel has motion picture potential. . . .

I offered many books, not only to Jaffe; I was actively submitting to the major studios, and to established independent producers.

At the drop of the smallest sale, authors tend to give way to some wishful thinking: *Now I'll quit my job!* They shouldn't. Not until they are in more solidly. Clark became a full-time pro, but then he held on to his job as P.R. man for a Las Vegas utility company.

As I pointed out, there is always a wide gap between an option and actual production. Once it comes down to basics, some hard decisions must be reached. Is that star available? That director? Financing comes in. What seemed great to a producer might hold no appeal to a prospective backer, a star or a director. More questions need to be resolved. Did social conditions change? Will audiences be apt to respond? Would it be better to do Story X? So the initial advance is in most cases lost. But where a producer invests ten thousand in a first option, it generally tends to indicate a production. A crack scenarist, Barry Beckerman, had been assigned, and *Variety* reported that "Jaffe will begin shooting *The Killings* for United Artists after he completes *The Wind and the Lion* for same distrib."

When the time came, Herb Jaffe did not renew. He said that he still liked *The Killings,* but, in just that period, "too many cop pictures appeared." His POV—point of view—could be defended.

Many writers wonder: will I learn anything of value at a Writer's Conference?

The seminars of which I was a part for some ten years began on the campus of Franklin Pierce College in New Hampshire. The year, 1965. They were started by George Abbe and Ray Swain, a poet-writer. The cast was all-star: I quote from the brochure.

JUVENILES: Phyllis A. Whitney—Instructor of Juvenile writing at New York University, and many other conferences. She won the Reynal-Hitchcock Award, among many other awards. Her 38 Juvenile novels are such best-sellers as PLACE FOR ANN, WILLOW HILL, STAR FOR GINNY, as well as two text books on juvenile writing. Just out is her novel, SEA JADE.

POETRY: George Abbe—Poet-in-Residence, Russell Sage College, Troy, New York. Teacher and writer. Published work in *Atlantic, Saturday Review, Yale Review;* two poems in Bantam anthology, THE WORLD'S LOVE POETRY; a novella, ONE MORE PURITAN. COLLECTED POEMS, 1932–1961. Winner of the Shelley Memorial Award.

BIOGRAPHY. Margaret L. Coit—Associate Professor of English and Social Science at Fairleigh Dickinson University; Pulitzer Prize for first book, JOHN C. CALHOUN. Frequent contributor to *Look, The Saturday Review* and *Book Week.*

THE NOVEL. Shirley Barker—Novelist and poet. Among her published books: THE DARK HILLS UNDER, TOMORROW THE NEW MOON, LIZA, SWEAR BY APOLLO, STRANGE WIVES and a Literary Guild Selection, THE TROJAN HORSE.

SHORT STORIES. Charles Angoff. Professor of English, writer, editor, is the author of MENCKEN: A PORTRAIT FROM MEMORY, THE WORLD OF GEORGE JEAN NATHAN, and SUMMER STORM, published in December, 1963.

Others on the faculty were Frangcon L. Jones, Loring Williams, F. Alexander Magoun. The seminar was a rousing success, but a policy rift developed between the co-sponsors and the school administrators. The next year we were welcomed by a posh hotel at Rye Beach, New Hampshire. Management thought that "a touch of culture" would be a welcome attraction. It no doubt was; we were called back for a second time. Then there was another move, this time to East Dover, Vermont. There we settled down for a seven-year stay.

An old barn had given way to a new, modern structure, surrounded on all sides by gardens. It stood on the grounds of Miriam and John Williams Andrews's home. Husband and wife published *Poet Lore.* The event became known as the Cooper Hill Writers Conference, also called The Barn.

Over the years, conferees and faculty changed, but not the underlying purpose, which was to give writers an opportunity to learn. The faculty always was picked with care—leading writer-teachers were on hand to instruct on every possible phase of writing. My slot always remained marketing, marketing every conceivable type of writing.

Phyllis Whitney turned her full attention to the best-sellers she continued to turn out, so she did not again join us. But, because children's books are such an important branch of publishing, she recommended an excellent replacement, both for the seminar and her class at N.Y.U. This was her friend Lee Wyndham, who also had excellent credentials. This author of some forty books brought not only great expertise to her classes; she also exuded a great love for what she was doing. Anyone interested in writing for children should get her book *Writing For Children And Teen-Agers,* or the Whitney books.

Who attends these summer conferences?

There are pseudo-authors who *play* at being authors. They had at one time written a novel, or a part of a novel, and while they had long ago given up any hope of advancing, they tote the dog-eared manuscript from one summer conference to another. It keeps the old dream simmering. They mix with other writers, consult with the instructors. If nothing else, they enjoy a gratifying vacation. Serious writers also attend, hoping to pick up some valuable tips on writing and marketing.

Ardath Wise nursed a leaning toward the mystery. She learned. She became a client. Four of her gothics were published in hardcover by Crown/Lenox Hill Press.

Dr. Naomi Faust (Ph.D.) learned. She teaches teachers-to-be at Queens College. I placed an important book of hers on education, *The Bridge: Between the Privileged White Child and the Underprivileged Black Child.* As a black writer, Dr. Faust brings some real insights into the problem. Views inevitably differ on how a livable balance can be struck between the races; strife creates issues and issues inspire books.

I considered the subject so worthy of a hearing, I promised Dr. Faust that I would publish her book under Impact Press, if I could not find a better publisher—better in terms of that special project. It isn't always a matter of *size.* Or resources. If a title could get lost on a big list, but is important to a small publisher, that small publisher becomes better. Ultimately The Dunellen Co., publishers of the University Press of Cambridge Series, became interested. Dr. Faust was eminently pleased.

When the book was accepted, there was a call from Judith Govak. She said, "Mr. Jackinson, we want to contract for Dr. Faust's book, which you submitted, but would you mind if we wrote directly to Dr. Faust? We've never dealt with an agent before."

"No, I don't mind," I said, and smiled. Some publishers of the scholarly book take undue advantage of the Ph.D. author. Textbook publishers send travelers to the campuses to recruit professors who specialize in specific topics. Professors rarely use an agent, and many publishers are not reluctant to take advantage. These scholars do not depend on book income for a livelihood. Some are so anxious for professional reasons to see a book in print, they even subsidize the publication.

The Dunellen contract called for royalties to start at 7½ percent rather than the usual 10 percent. I found this part objectionable, but not *too much* so. This needs some explaining.

When Nash Publishing of Los Angeles first came upon the scene, I submitted to them a book by Stanton A. Coblentz. Edward Nash wrote that he was very much interested. Royalties at Nash, he explained, start at 8 percent, at least for non-name authors. He stressed that the subtracted 2 percent went into advertising-promotion, so that, in the end, the author profited. I had to reject this reasoning on a matter of principle. Nash was a *commercial* house, and I did not want to add to what was a bad precedent. For the Dunellen type book a concession seemed more justified.

"Front Matter"

Bob Wyndham, Lee's husband, was also a writer. One of his books was called *Enjoying Gems: The Lure and Lore of Jewel Stones.* The small book was published by Stephen Greene Press.

Stephen Greene had been invited to speak at one of our seminars. We met, and he also met the Wyndhams. We three were invited to Brattleboro to discuss book possibilities. Bob offered the gems idea; the publisher accepted. The book carries an interesting dedication:

> An ancient legend tells that the Devil prized his wife above all his worldly possessions, and kept her locked up in a magnificent palace he designed like a great jewel box constructed of every beautiful gem stone on earth.
>
> Now, I prize my wife in the same way, but never possessed the power to fashion so grand a castle or even keep her locked up. So, I built this book with words about joyful gems and dedicate it to my Genia.

A dedication page is understandably important to an author, and to the person, or persons, receiving the accolade. Show me the person who does not relish some form of praise, recognition, and I will point to the twin of some colorless dullard. But there is a right and a wrong way to go about it.

Not until I opened a copy of Clark Howard's *The Killings,* did I see this touching tribute: "To Alex Jackinson—agent—adviser—friend—with gratitude." I did not know that this would be in the book. It was a surprise Clark had arranged with Joyce Engelson, his editor at Dial. Many years later, when I opened a copy of *Brothers In Blood,* I was in for another surprise: "Once again to Alex Jackinson, my friend first, and then my agent." And that is the proper way to go about it—wait until a book is accepted before inserting a dedication.

Many writers conceive a dedication page before a book is written. It may serve as a spur, since the person to be honored is close to the author.

But it becomes a meaningless ego-sop unless held in check until the cake is ready to be pulled from the oven.

Dedications, acknowledgements elaborate or simple, quotes—all that belongs to what is called "front matter." It means utterly nothing to an editor at the submission stage. Editors want to get at the core of a narrative as quickly as possible, and they look with disfavor at distraction. But once the desired result begins to happen, the climate shifts from cool to warm. Relationships change between author and agent; more important, between author and editor.

I am aware how easy it is to say "wait," and how difficult it is for most authors to cultivate patience. Manuscripts are shipped off much too hastily. When they return, there is keen lament. *Why didn't I wait a bit? I see so many errors I overlooked.*

When I offer a manuscript to editors, I hold back the pages, at times many pages, that have no immediate relevance. A road needs to be paved before it becomes safe to drive over.

21
Back to Angry Writers

The Pushcart Press Rescue Operation

An agent can easily become cynical, but I remain a roadside believer in that old Chinese homily that it is better to light one tiny candle than to curse the darkness. That would apply very much to the annual Pushcart Press rescue operation. Bill Henderson calls it the Editors' Book Award. William Kennedy says, "The Editors' Book Award is an extremely valuable idea."

Kennedy's "Cinderella story" received very wide coverage. *Ironweed* had scored thirteen rejections before Corlies Smith, then with Viking, became the sponsoring editor. A boost from Saul Bellow helped. The novel copped the National Book Critics Award, and then the Pulitzer Prize. This meant national exposure in ways that transcend mere book news. Reporters featured the thirteen rejections. Major talk shows invited Kennedy. To the uninitiated this was *news*. How could it possibly have happened? It could happen simply because too few book buyers respond to the worthwhile novel until that neglected stepchild somehow begins to crawl into the glare of publicity.

Pushcart Press did not publish *Ironweed*, but they pull from anonymity a handful of tiny candles. This is done because every year, between 15 May and 15 August, "Pushcart Press celebrates an important and unusual book manuscript that has been overlooked by commercial publishers. Pushcart Press publishes that manuscript with national advertising and promotion, plus a cash award to the author." (For details about the Editors' Press Award, write to Pushcart Press.)

Ironweed has many counterparts. *Many?* That depends on what calculator is used. Measured against the forty thousand or so books published annually, the percentage of rescued books is very small, but more is involved than just numbers. The possibility gives countless authors a chance to *hope,* and that is very important. The publicity "made" Kennedy. His previously neglected books were republished. He is now a NAME, but the success of *Ironweed* is not going to change the way books are picked.

"It Falls between the Cracks"

Patrick O'Connor, senior editor at Warner Books, wrote me: "First, thanks for sending on the two Raboo Rodgers novels. He is, as you say, quite a good writer, and he tells his story well. The trouble is that books such as his are difficult to package. They fall between the cracks. They're not romance as one ordinarily thinks of romance, and they're not adventure."

Peter Guzzardi of Bantam wrote: "Thank you for sending me GOD'S LAST WEEKEND by David Comfort. As you may know, Bantam's need with regard to original fiction is very specific these days. The hardcover list is oriented toward bestsellers, and the paperback originals we publish tend to align with staple categories: romances, thrillers, westerns, mysteries, etc."

Another letter from a Warner editor: "I am returning A CARNIVAL OF TERROR by Donald Jordan reluctantly. This is a very suspenseful story and I enjoyed reading it tremendously. Unfortunately Warner has no place for it as it does not easily fit into any category for marketing purposes."

Rosalind Magzis, of one of the leading mass-circulation women's magazines, wrote: "As we say in the trade, Marianne Landon's story falls between the cracks. It is not for *Redbook,* and it would not qualify as a 'quality story.' "

From Linda Grey, Bantam's editorial director: "With regret, I will not be making an offer on THE HAND HAS MANY FINGERS by Donald Platt. It doesn't seem right for us. I'm afraid that I felt that the book uncomfortably straddles a number of genres, making it difficult for us to position it successfully on our list."

"Category" was a familiar term to me when I had been free-lancing, but never in my long experience have writers been subjected to such rigid barriers or such straightjacketing.

If called as an expert witness, I would testify in a court of law that a score of writers like Jordan-Comfort-Rodgers, are *better* writers than those who turn out the blockbusters, but that would mean less than nothing. Good writing is only a component piece of the puzzle unless one is aiming at the literary publications.

George Abbe is a classic example of the *fine* writer who is caught between hell and a hard rock. The answer would seem to be, "go the other route," which means go to the small presses, but this sounds better than it actually is. Out of about fifty books published by these "God's frail children," at least forty-five will be nonfiction.

Authors and certainly the Writers Union tend to regard publishers as *adversaries*. This is totally erroneous and damaging to writers.

An excellent small publisher would be *The Smith*. Harry Smith is cast in the mold of Alan Swallow-Tom Bledsoe, Don Quixotes whose hearts are with the maverick author. In 1967 *The Smith* published Abbe's *The Funeral*, previously rejected by eighteen mainstream houses. I turn to the publisher's own comments:

> George Abbe's fifth novel might be advertised as SEX AND VIO-LENCE AT A FUNERAL. But we won't advertise it as such.
> We will tell you that the occasion is a family reunion at a funeral. That, gathered together in decaying Poughkeepsie mansion of the deceased, family lusts and animosities flare anew. And that passionate hate and search for God transpire in the shadow of the coffin.
> We will tell you that *The Funeral* is a novel of falling and finding. Of fornication and fortitude. Of pity and pride. Of love and death.
> We will tell you that George Abbe has won impressive acclaim both as a novelist and a poet. A protege of Stephen Vincent Benet, Abbe's picture was on the cover of SATURDAY REVIEW as a result of the praise accorded his first novel, *Voices In The Square*. He is also a winner of the coveted Shelley Memorial Award.

Voices found a sympathetic publisher in Coward-McCann. Today the imprint is in the same dark zone sheltering the many publishers I had named. The past ten years or so saw the eclipse of many houses that might have published an *Ironweed*-type novel: Gambit, Corwin Books, Wyden Books, Liveright, Vineyard Books. The list could be extended over many pages. *The Smith* and other small publishers are also in the shadows. Not because Harry Smith *wants* it so, but because there remains the problem of staying above water. The question remains: adversaries or victims? Where lies the basic blame?

Granted, "intelligentsia" topics do not rate high scores, but more should be done than is being done to stimulate the sale of poetry and the unknown but *good* novel. Could a union reeducate readers? That is where reform is badly needed, an uplifting of taste and book-buying habits.

The Books I Am Most and Least Proud to Have Agented

This sequence is not about sin and tell, but the confession story was the link, the joining glue, which welded into a rather special topic—the books I was most and least proud to have agented. A book can assume special importance for many reasons.

When I received Judge Tom R. Blaine's manuscript, *Goodbye Allergies*, I was impressed. I have never suffered from allergies, but people close to me have, and I thought that Judge Blaine made a sound argument. He presented what had gotten to be known as the "hypoglycemia viewpoint." I sent the manuscript to Herb Michaelman of Crown. He called me and said, "Thanks for sending over *Goodbye Allergies*. Books on allergies sell. But Judge Blaine is not a doctor; would you mind if we gave the book for evaluation to two allergy specialists?"

"I'd be delighted," I said.

Two weeks later Mr. Michaelman called again. "We could not publish this book. Our specialists say readers could be hurt by it."

The one thing I could never be a party to was a book that might *hurt* readers. I was puzzled. I would have returned the submission save that, just then, the Hypoglycemia Foundation was holding a dinner at the Overseas Press Club. Matilda and I attended, and we encountered what we knew existed: sharply divided medical opinions. Qualified experts highly praised the viewpoints expounded by Judge Blaine. I knew I'd resume seeking a publisher.

The next submission was to Citadel Press. They wanted endorsements from qualified doctors, and they got more than they could use. Sam E. Roberts, M.D., Professor Emeritus of Otolaryngology, University of Kansas Medical School, said, "Every person who has any type of allergy—mild or debilitating—should read this book. Every practicing physician should have this book in his private library."

A year after publication Citadel Press sent me copies of very grateful letters Judge Blaine received from former allergy sufferers. This successful first book paved the way for publication of four other medical-type books by Judge Blaine. All the books became important to me.

The Discovery of Love by Malden Grange Bishop assumed importance for a totally different reason. This book was one of the first published about LSD. For the author, taking LSD was an intense religious experience, a discovery of God, or love. The experiment was conducted under strict medical supervision, and Malden was not to repeat the experiment for at least six months. The book clearly left readers wondering about this new drug. Shortly after the book's publication, LSD was picked up by the Beats. Then I was sorry I had had a hand in what seemed to be a new plague sweeping the country.

The Dutch-born Joost A. M. Meerloo, M.D., was given a booklet of my poems, *The Claws of the Butterfly—The Song of the Viper*. His colleague, Dr.

Alfred Dorn, was the donor. Dr. Meerloo thought it a bit odd for an agent to write poetry, but he was used to encountering strange turns. "When can we meet?" he asked the first time he phoned. "I'd like to discuss my new book. Two books, in fact."

"Dr. Dorn said you live at 300 Central Park West. I take the "D" home. There's a station right there. I could stop off any day around five."

"That would be wonderful. Today, perhaps?"

"Today would be fine."

Many of my clients also become friends, even though they do not live in New York. Most do not. Dr. Meerloo I met many times. He was a warm, compassionate man, and he remained warm and compassionate despite having seen the very worst of human degradation. A good part of his family had been wiped out by the Nazis.

Born in 1903 in The Hague, Dr. Merloo earned his professional degrees at Leyden University and the University of Utrecht. Following the Nazi occupation, he escaped to England in 1942. He served as chief of the Psychological Warfare Department of the Netherlands. Arriving in the United States in 1946, he became a diplomate of the American Board of Psychiatry and Neurology. Despite all that he had lived through, Dr. Meerloo was able to maintain a sense of optimism.

When he became a client, Dr. Meerloo had had two books published by Grune & Stratton, *Suicide and Mass Suicide* and *Justice and Injustice*. I placed his *Mental First Aid* (Hawthorn Books) and *Illness and Cure* (Grune & Stratton).

I mentioned that there had once been an active crime magazine, *Manhunt*. I sold to them. When the magazine folded, one of the editors, Walter R. Schmidt, resettled in Los Angeles. Many years later he turned author and undertook to do a fact-fiction book based on the life of Johns Hopkins.

Johns Hopkins is a household name, but almost no one knows anything about the man himself. The material I received from Mr. Schmidt was interesting in terms of content, but it was not handled effectively. Walter himself suggested a collaborator. I at once thought of Lucy Freeman, with whom I had remained in touch through the years. Lucy liked the basic material very much, and agreed to come in as a co-author. I now have *The Story of Johns Hopkins* very actively on the market.

Asked which book I am most proud to have agented, I would find it very difficult to reply. There were many. My home library contains shelves of books which gave me great satisfaction to have piloted to publication. Each placement represents a campaign if not a protracted struggle. There are books from Alfred Dorn and his co-author, Alfred E. Eyres; Cy Rice, Clark Howard, George Abbe, Stanton A. Coblentz,

Ken Edgar, Dr. Twerski, Dr. Meerloo, Judge Blaine. Then there are many single titles: *The Joy of Dieting* by Albert B. Gerber; *The Battered Parent:* James O. Palmer; *The Postage Stamp Garden Book, Jadoo, Defender of the Damned*, the biography of the famous Gladys Towles Root; *Every Diamond Doesn't Sparkle*, a baseball book about the Dodgers. Stacks more. *Magnum Fault*, the juvenile book by Raboo Rodgers.

In 1973 The Poetry Society of America had asked me to be one of three judges in selecting the best book of poetry published that year. From the hundred-odd books I received, I picked ten choice selections. There was no *one* best. Still, the rules were set and I had to settle on a single title. This time if I had to pick *one* book of poetry or prose, it would be Dr. Meerloo's *Illness and Cure*. What hits home more than the very basics of living—illness and cure?

I mentioned in the Foreword "splendid human beings who restore the heart." That would cover many of my clients and nonclients whom I encountered in my work. It would certainly include Dr. Meerloo. Despite having authored many books, all dealing with basic humanism, he never became as well known as he should have been, for this great humanitarian had some important contributions to make.

In reviewing *Suicide and Mass Suicide*, the *New York Times* reported: "Dr. Meerloo, a practicing psychiatrist, is a wise man. His book is fascinating, with its deep insights of hidden destructive urges; of relationships which lead to tragedy; and of 'welfare suicides' in states which care for all of one's needs."

Let's turn to the other side of the coin. With the question reversed, which book am I *least* proud to have agented, I would have a very quick answer. It would not be *merchandise* like *The Astrological Guide to Sex*, which I had considered pure bunk-junk, but which Popular Library had welcomed; nor would it be any of the sexy novels. It would, oddly enough, be a serious work—Dr. Edward R. Pinckney's *The Fallacy of Freud and Psychoanalysis*.

Because I had sold many stories to the Macfadden books, I got the tip that *True Story* was considering a new monthly feature, a medical column, and could I recommend an M.D. who wrote? Almost from the start I represented many M.D.'s who also had writing ambitions. No one in my orbit seemed right for a monthly column, so I wrote to the editor of *Today's Health*. In turn I was directed to Edward R. Pinckney, M.D., then an assistant editor of an AMA Journal. The column idea was subsequently dropped, but my association with Dr. Pinckney flourished. I placed his *Making the Most of Your Doctor and Medicine* (Follett Publishing Co.), and *The Fallacy of Freud and Psychoanalysis* (Prentice-Hall).

The second book grew out of an assignment. Gladys J. Carr, one of the most astute editors around, was then on a high rung at Prentice-Hall. She had signed Dr. Hyman Spotnitz to do a pro-Freudian book, to be written with Lucy Freeman. As if to balance the scales, Ms. Carr thought that it would be sound publishing to do an *anti* book as well. I had submitted to her a Pinckney proposal on child care. She did not welcome the topic, but she liked the sprightly way Dr. Pinckney handled his material. And she was impressed with his track record. She invited me to lunch and posed a question: would my client like to confute Freudian theories? Dr. Pinckney responded with alacrity: he certainly would!

Once the book was in galley, it set off a mild war within the Prentice-Hall atheneum. The textbook people considered the work so unscientific that they were sure the medical fraternity would pounce on it vehemently, which might hurt textbook sales. Dr. Pinckney proclaimed, "Psychoanalysis is the biggest hoax ever perpetrated on the American public." Since textbooks are always a publisher's staple, trade books might have been forced to scrap the book or turn it over to some other publisher, save for one factor—Dr. Pinckney threatened to sue. And he certainly would have.

Like most people, Dr. Pinckney could be extremely generous, gracious—and very hard, unyielding. He was also a lawyer. Prentice-Hall, he insisted, had to honor the contract. They did. The book drew a bad press. In retrospect, I believe that Dr. Freud had been very badly served.

22
Some Good Stories

Clients I Hated to Lose

Novelist Ron Kurz had once written:

Dear Alex,
    I had this all prepared for mailing when your letter arrived. So I'll let it stand. Reading your letter only reenforces my hope of having you represent me.
                                    Best,
                                    Ron

Just then Bud Yorkin wanted to option a previously published Ron Kurz novel which had long interested him. Ron stressed that he wanted the agreement to go through me. I accepted the generosity, hoping, of course, to make up for it in what I thought would be a long association. I regretted that it was a short partnership. Any special reason? There often is no *reason*—not anything that could be specifically pinpointed, like holding a check too long, which some agents do, or like sending out a manuscript after reading only a few pages. This is also something some agents do.

Ever since I had encountered *The Bashful Billionaire,* I had wanted to write to the author, Albert B. Gerber. For *Barnum-Cinderella* I did not need "inner facts" on how the Hughes biography originated, but I did want to ask a few questions for *this book.* So a letter went off. On its receipt, Al Gerber phoned me, and then wrote:

Dear Alex;
    Thanks for sending me your book, your collection of poems and other materials. As I told you, I am looking for a new agent. I have talked to Lyle Stuart, and he says you are one of the "good agents" of the world. In fact, I believe he says that you are the only good agent. I

have several books in the works, and some of them actually completed. I would like to set up a fairly lengthy appointment to discuss these projects. . . .

("The only good agent" is, obviously, from the humor department, but flattering, and so I did not delete the passage.) *The Bashful Billionaire*, I learned, had been commissioned. Al Gerber had completed *Sex, Pornography & Justice* for Lyle Stuart. One night when they and their wives were having dinner at the Algonquin, they reached a decision: the publisher decided that Al Gerber's next chore would be to take over on the Hughes mess. Gerber, a first amendment lawyer, retired to devote full time to writing.

A book I especially enjoyed placing was Gerber's *The Joy of Dieting*. The publisher (Dodd, Mead) proclaimed on the jacket: "At long last, the technological diet. Here's a foolproof diet that lets you take advantage of modern nutrition's latest technology—savory foods that are sweet without sugar, salty without sodium, bulky without calories. *The Joy of Dieting* presents the best in low-calorie foods, some common and others rare, and shows you how you can take off weight while enjoying a complete and balanced diet. Introduction by Paul Gerber, M.D."

The original title was *The Technological Diet*, which I liked. It was at the publishing end that it was deemed wise to cash in on the "Joy" bandwagon, and they appended a title I did not like. For most people who are overweight, there is no *joy* to dieting. Dieting is essentially a painful process of denial that has to be maintained through a lifetime to be effective.

We live in a chemically orchestrated society, and little can be done to reverse the tide. What we eat is a product of our time. In that sense this is a good book on an over-exploited subject. It tells the homemaker which adulterated foods are safer than others, and which chemicals will do the least harm. The author would not be a party to a false-claims book. Nor his M.D. brother, Paul.

Al Gerber had formerly been represented by Scott Meredith, and before that, by Paul Reynolds. Each is a leader in the field. Each is an agency I would love to have if I were an active free-lancer. Why, then, was Mr. Gerber dissatisfied? Why did he become disillusioned with me? A broad answer is that chasing after contracts is leaping over obstacle courses rather than a straight run.

I had also lost John A. Keel. Keel spoke for others as well as himself:

Most people who bleed all over pieces of paper have an incredibly inflated opinion of their own worth and when an agent fails to verify that opinion through fantastic deals they move on to someone else. Despite my innate modesty I concede that I have never been able to find an agent who could match my staggering genius. . . . From conversations with other writers it seems that most are searching for some kind of miracle man who can whip million dollar deals out of thin air. I was never that naive. Writers go from agent to agent just as hypochondriacs go from doctor to doctor. . . .

When I had to turn from books to television it was necessary for me to acquire agents in that field. I was with Ashley-Famous for a time, and then with other equally big (e.g. MCA) agencies. I found, to my chagrin, that the big agencies were primarily concerned with package deals. They sold performers, directors, writers, etc., all in one package. It was a lousy system, particularly for a hyper-creative super-independent type such as myself. Perhaps I unfairly blamed you for some of my problems.

Why So Many Clients Agent-Hop

Hypochondria, poverty, and most of what Keel wrote would not apply to Al Gerber, but some of my own experiences might.

Two years before I became an agent I decided to permanently end being a furrier. Could I make a living from writing? I tried. I wrote a novel. A few new short stories. I had no valid reason for seeking a new agent, but there had been a period of silence. No sales. I wanted to move from the pulps to the slicks. I decided that a new agent might offer some new insights. And he or she might have better contacts. In three years I went to four different agents, all of top caliber. I now realize that my groping for the lucky strike was unwarranted agent-hopping.

I constantly wondered: if an agent liked my work, why not an editor? There were complexities involved to which I did not have the answers, though I thought that I had. I kept writing. Another novel, more short stories. There were sales, but not any that really satisfied me. Nor, for that matter, the agent. I kept searching for new portals.

Writing is full of mystic "What-ifs." What if Lynne Lumsden had not gone to Growth Associates? What if Mike Dewell had not reminded himself of Paul's submission? What if Joyce Engelson had not risked an advance on *The Killings* outline? What if Farr had not contacted me? What if I had placed Al Gerber's novel, which I had failed to do and it clearly displeased him? The speculation is endless.

My last contact with an agency was in 1951, with the large Scott Meredith office. I quote two short notes, both signed by the boss himself.

Dear Alex Jackinson:
Here's your check for TAILORED FOR A SHROUD which Trojan has taken.
Keep them coming.

Dear Alex Jackinson:
  Thanks for sending along MOURNING BEFORE DAWN, which is
a very nice job indeed.
  I wish you'd continue to send your published poems along to me
from time to time. I may not handle serious poetry as an agent, but I
still enjoy reading it.

All good wishes,

Had I continued as a writer, I would in all likelihood have stayed with
the agency, an agency that had always puzzled me. They represented
some our most famous authors and worked out deals writers fantasize
about. They also advertised extensively at that time and employed a staff
of editors busily working on the heavy influx of submissions. I know *why*
this was done—the income from fees was considerable. But wasn't there
a risk that the prominent writers wanted to be associated only with other
NAME writers?

  I had paid this agency a fee, the first time ever. This pours over into a
grossly misunderstood aspect. It is erroneously assumed that "good"
agents do not charge a fee. I had reported in my previous books how
Eric S. Pinker, a penthouse-swimming pool agent, had been indicted for
stealing clients' money, most of it from P. G. Wodehouse. Pinker was too
refined to charge a fee. Mr. Wodehouse then turned to Scott Meredith,
and I learned a valuable lesson.

  Agents who charge no fees work only with established authors. They
do not turn out *reports.* I had learned from that Scott Meredith report,
and that's the key to it, what one learns from an agent.

  When I felt a need to advertise, I charged a nominal fee. Not for
reading a manuscript, but for the guidance I offered. When I had my
"family of clients," I stopped advertising and dropped the fees. I also
stopped sending out lengthy, time-consuming reports.

Books I Would Not Handle

  My friend-client, Frederic Young, told me about a manuscript that he
thought would be offensive to Jews because it was supposed to have been
a satire on the Holocaust. I declined to read it because the extermination
of six million people did not seem to be a proper theme for satire. Young
asked me to reconsider, and I did read the novel. I refused to handle it
for other reasons than that it would be offensive to Jews; I simply found
it to be a badly handled work.

  Some ten years ago I almost became the agent for Bob DePugh.
DePugh hasn't been in the news lately, but a decade ago newspapers
throughout the country proclaimed:DE PUGH, MINUTEMAN'S FOUNDER,

GRANTED PAROLE AFTER 6 YEARS. From the *New York Times:* "Robert Bolivar DePugh, founder of the Minutemen, a right-wing paramilitary organization, was granted a parole today after serving a little more than half of an 11-year prison sentence for the illegal possession of firearms."

There was understandably a lot of anti-Semitism in that militant right-wing organization, but that would not have deterred me. One can't have an open policy on one issue and not on another. It all started with a letter from W. David Arnold, chairman of the Department of Speech and Threatre Arts at Baker University. He wrote: "If I may suggest a possible idea for you, I write to Robert DePugh who is the former head of the Minutemen. He is currently serving time in the Federal Prison at Atlanta, Georgia. Bob is a very good writer and he has a book ready for publication. Although I don't agree with him or his political philosophy, I believe he would have some valid comments to make on this subject."

De Pugh and I had a lengthy correspondence. In one letter I wrote: "I once thought that all the world's ills would alter if you just change the system. I've seen systems change at the Left, and at the Right, and each left me delighted that we have America, with all its middle-ground imperfections."

De Pugh once wrote: "My unexpected parole caught me with eleven different oil paintings in progress, some nearly finished, others just started—so I'm busy trying to finish them before going out. . . . What do you think of the Watergate affair? A real circus, I'd say. Keep in touch."

I never got to see DePugh's book. Finally he decided to publish it himself through his organization's publication arm. Politics aside, I got to like the fellow. It may be that he was an artist. The point is, I would have handled his book.

When Arthur Bremer gunned down George Wallace, he was reported to have exclaimed: "Now I will become known! How much do you think I'm going to get for my autobiography?" And becoming known was certainly going to help him get published. Indeed, the prestigious Harper's Magazine Press published *An Assassin's Diary.* I never had an opportunity to represent this twisted fellow, but Bremer was one "author" I wanted to have no contact with whatsover. I loathe the thought of representing a writer who needed a blazing gun to focus attention on himself. I did have a fringe opportunity to be involved with the Son Of Sam.

Good Housekeeping had paid $8,000 to run an article called "The Startling Story of 'Son of Sam's' Real Mother." The display copy read: "David Berkowitz Murdered Six People And Maimed Seven. Not Until He Was Caught Did Betty Falco Learn He Was The Son She'd Given Up 24 Years Earlier. By Susan Wishengrad."

The material had come to me some months before. I reported to the author:

June 20, 1978.

Dear Susan Wishengrad:

I made it my business to read the manuscript quickly and I'm sorry to say that I will decline to serve as the agent.

David Berkowitz has become a fixture in crime annals. His own story will command great attention. A book written by one of the involved psychiatrists would interest editors. His mother and sister cannot tell the "real" story because they had no idea how Richie lived his double-identity life. Still, a story under their byline would interest one of the mass-circulation women's magazines. . . . DAVID BERKOWITZ WAS MY SON . . . MY BROTHER. What would give the story poignancy is how their lives were changed since the headlines broke. Your best bet might be to go to McCall's or Ladies Home Journal directly. One of their editors would be assigned to do the needed pruning.

Best wishes,

As an agent, I function as the conduit between author and editor. I often bring to editors books that I personally disliked, but for which I thought that there was a market. (*The Foundation Book of Astrology* was one of many examples.) It is not my business to draw moral-ethical judgments, but with David Berkowitz I reacted in a strongly personal manner.

I can safely call myself a compassionate man. I can express sympathy for almost any person accused of murder. But in the Berkowitz case all my sympathies went to the victims, especially the young men and women who were left crippled.

Berkowitz offers a great study in schizophrenia, but, as commonly understood, he was certainly *legally* sane. Great skill and cunning went into the plotting and execution of the many assaults, and then the return to being the "nice," even-tempered Richie the postal worker. He was preparing for another rampage when the police cornered him.

Such intense public interest was generated by the slayings, it was inevitable that media would make a carnival of it. When the submission came to me, the tempest had somewhat subsided, but I still regarded Berkowitz as one of the most loathesome human beings I had yet read about, in fiction or in fact.

Among his victims I would certainly include the "real" mother and the "real" sister, but theirs is a story apart. I would not have advised Susan Wishengrad to approach the women's magazines unless there was a fair chance of a magazine showing interest, but even if a crystal ball had predicted a large commission, I still would have shunned even a peripheral involvement.

1984 update.

Ninety thousand dollars in royalties for Berkowitz's book is being held in escrow pending some court decisions. The state of New York had passed a bill prohibiting convicted killers from profiting on books based on crimes they had committed. The income, it is argued, should go to the victims or their beneficiaries. "Justice."

Susan Wishengrad had come to me on an esteemed recommendation; fortunately, she was not a client to whom I owed any special consideration. Had she been, I would have overcome my reluctance. But for other aspiring writers there is a clear lesson—to keep plugging, especially in the face of a rejection by an agent.

Addendum.

As I had surmised, a psychiatrist, David Abrahamsen, did write a book about Berkowitz *(Confessions of Son of Sam).* The review is from *Publishers Weekly* (1985).

In August of 1977, Abrahamsen, forensic psychiatrist, criminal pathologist and author of 13 books including *Crime and the Human Mind,* was engaged by the Brooklyn D. A.'s office to examine mass murderer David Berkowitz and determine whether he was sane and able to stand trial. Three psychiatrists had previously declared Berkowitz insane; Abrahamsen disagreed, believing the accused man's story of having been ordered to kill by "demons" to be a fabrication. Berkowitz was subsequently tried, convicted and sentenced to several hundred years in prison. In 1979 he admitted that he had lied about the demons, and invited Abrahamsen to study him and write his biography. The result, based on extensive interviews and correspondence as well as a thorough investigation of Berkowitz's past, is a psychiatric study of the killer's progress from an angry and ambivalent adopted child unable to deal with his feelings of rejection, to a psychopath who hid behind a passive facade by day and sought the ultimate revenge against women by night. Oddly enough, one comes away with very little sense of Berkowitz's personality, even from excerpts of his letters, which reveal little other than his enormous self-interest.

I had called agenting a "link" business, which it indeed is. A very unusual link will unravel.

At one of the seminars I was surprised to see three Catholic Sisters in my class. Each was a poet. We became close friends, and when I returned to New York, I undertook to market *The Nun's Book of Poetry,* a collection devoted exclusively to the work of nuns. Many were very fine poets.

When *Congress Weekly* had accepted my article, "e. e. cummings and Anti-Semitism," the editor, Harold U. Ribalow, saw an opportunity to make something of it. He invited some prominent writer-critics to participate in a symposium on the subject. Ludwig Lewisohn, whom I had greatly admired since reading *The Island Within,* responded:

For a good many years now I have relished the subtle and sometimes brilliant poetic antics of E. E. Cummings. But I think it is absurd to take him so seriously. He who is indiscriminately bitter about everything evidently has no balanced judgment or assured sense of values. He can in his amused and amusing universal disgruntlement be made out anything—fascist, anti-Semite, what you will.

The charm of his work is in the sprightly dexterities of his use of language. As to the whole question: Often I assign readings to my students who come back aggrieved: "But Gibbon (or X or Y) is an anti-Semite." Answer: "Who is not—from Horace and Juvenal to Aldous Huxley, Scott Fitzgerald, Thomas Wolfe? And would you stop reading on that account?" "What must one do?" they ask. "One must understand the legendary and mythical character of literary anti-Semitism from a creative and self-affirmative Jewish point of view and—call it a day."

A book I am totally dedicated to placing is the autobiography of Ludwig Lewisohn's son, James E. Lewisohn. James, paroled in January 1985, spent ten years of a life sentence in a Maine prison. He was convicted for killing his wife, Roslyn, whom he had deeply loved, and for whom he had written some exquisitely moving poems. James received a thoroughly Jewish upbringing and later converted to Catholicism. It was that Catholic link which had brought him into contact with Sister Mary Venard, one of the three nuns. Sister Mary Venard suggested that this tormented man contact me.

23
Merchandising Poetry

From *Publishers Weekly:*

Unlike last week's rumors, it can be officially stated that Harper & Row is very pleased at the way the latest Rod McKuen is selling (he used to be with Random House, remember?). *Sound of Solitude* is up to 30,000 copies just after publication; one in the eye to those who thought McKuen went out with flower power and body paint. McKuen is a man who knows how to merchandise his work. He's even sold it mail order. These days, his own music is piped in at his autographing parties, so you can listen to the warm while you're in line clutching a book. And Rod has gifted all the Harper sales reps with luggage stamped "Rod McKuen," lest they forget. We were once a fly on the wall at a dinner party where Rod and John Ashbery were talking about poetry, unbelievable as it sounds. There they were, one each of the world's most and least accessible poets, and Rod was giving John tips on how to get people to turn out strong for his poetry. In short, merchandising. "You're talking to the wrong poet," said Ashbery wistfully. Period.

For one who has been involved with poetry as long as I, the above quote is specious. In America poetry cannot be merchandised—only names can be. Rod McKuen and Bob Dylan had achieved reputations as actors, troubadors, folk singers, composers. They wrote poetry. Their poetry was accepted because they were NAMES. And because they were NAMES, publicity followed them. In no sense did their poetry come first.

James Dickey and Erica Jong were poets before they turned out best-selling novels, but it was only *after* that their fees and turnouts upped considerably at poetry readings. Allen Ginsberg became a NAME as an advocate of the free use of drugs and as a guru in the Beat Movement. He now rates attention with brand-name publishers.

Poetry in America is supposed to be booming; in many ways a supporting case could be made. Poetry readings are honored on TV, and not only on Channel 13. There *is* interest in poetry; but to what extent the candle burns, or flickers, is not a matter of conjecture—it is more a cause for national lament.

The most lacerating disappointment an agent can endure is to try to place even an excellent collection of poems with a mainline publisher. Dan Wickenden, for many years a top editor at Harcourt Brace Jovanovich, once wrote to me:

> Dear Alex,
> Any veteran agent who consents to take on a poetry manuscript deserves a medal of, at the very least, bronze. But at the moment we're out of putty medals, even, so I can't bestow one on you. A contract, of course, would be even more gratifying than a medal of the purest gold, but I'm afraid I can't offer you one of these, either. You sent over a thoroughly enjoyable collection, but except for present commitments, some of them of long standing, we are having to be strongly resistant to poetry these days.

From Doubleday, the same collection;

> I'm sorry, but we cannot make a contract offer at this time. The poetry situation here, and in general, is bleak. We have been forced to cut our poetry list by half and are committed through the next year. Under the circumstances, we tend to publish only authors with a well established audience.

Harper & Row, Viking, W. W. Norton, and others of that level phrased it differently, but each editor I approached said essentially the identical thing—that poetry was difficult to sell, so they were confining to poets who already had established some sort of a name.

Rejected at the top, where does the *good* poet go? There are the university presses. There are the cottage publishers where poetry is welcome. I'd guess that 90 percent pay to see their work between covers.

I take a dismal view of the *size* of the American poetry audience; conversely, if one looks into the published books of new poets, one will find much excellence. It is like fearing to fall into some verbal fumarole, and encountering persimmon and orange groves instead of volcanic ash. The ash is there, and it is bitter on the tongue when one measures the number of rock records sold in contrast to books of poetry, poetry even by poets libraries must have.

A high percentage of the known poets teach poetry, or are in some way connected with English departments of colleges and universities. Their pupils appreciate poetry, at least while classes are in session. Some will write poetry. In or out of academia, poets build reputations step by step by appearing in poetry magazines. Many are subsidized by the National Endowment for the Arts. But most college graduates, even from the Ivy League group, do not support poetry once textbooks are put away.

One reason for the disinterest is that poetry is taught very unimaginatively in most of our public schools, where the elementary training should properly start. It is not surprising that so many adults will say, "Poetry leaves me cold." I can recall an interesting anecdote. A ten-year-old girl, very bright, read a poem aloud to her mother and me. She read it in such a colorless, sing-song tone, I groaned inwardly. I asked why she did not read the poem *naturally.* Her mother replied defensively, "I know, but that's the way she's taught in school and I don't want to go contrary to her teacher."

There used to be a semi-official trade estimate that only 2 percent of the American population bought books. No doubt the percentage rose to 2½ or even 3 percent, shamefully low in comparison to other countries. But the percentage of poetry book-buyers is even lower.

A vast number of people *write* poetry. Good, bad, atrocious, poetry pours into poetry magazines and other publications. Utter novices send me collections. I try to explain as best I can why I must decline. I try to point to the *preparation* they will have to go through. Unhappily, this vast potential audience does not *buy* books of poetry. As I said to Lillian, "Publishers would be happy to publish poetry providing the books could be sold." And why can't they be?

Ted Hughes is the new poet laureate, and libraries must have his book. So publishers will not *lose* on him, but even he can't be "merchandised" unless the publicity people will want to exploit his marriage to Sylvia Plath. Let's veer into a fantasy.

Words are the stock-in-trade of Brooke Shields and Michael Jackson. Song lyrics are webbed into their lives. It may well be that they also read poetry. And *like* poetry, which is quite likely. They might even *write* poetry. Imagine the scramble among publishers if either one offered a collection????

I laud the many fine poets who are not phased by the muted rewards, for a Rod McKuen stands out as a rarity, a phenomenon. Before Simon & Schuster took him on (prior to Random House) McKuen served a fifteen-year *growing* period. Consider this letter, dated 13 May 1970.

Dear Mr. Jackinson:
Thank you for your letter concerning Rod McKuen and Cheval Books.
Cheval-Stanyan Books, at the present time, has over 50 authors on its list and will be publishing between 20 and 50 books a year. However, Rod McKuen is the only poet that we have on our list and our arrangement with him is such that we cannot publish any other poets. At this point our roster of authors and books to be published is

complete through the end of 1972. Cheval-Stanyon Books are distributed through Random House, Grosset & Dunlap, and World Publishing.

If there is any further information that we can give you, we would be happy to do so.

Cordially,
Wade Alexander

I did not write to Cheval-Stanyan again. I did not see it as an open market for my poetry writing friends.

Before I offer two of my poems, I want to extend kudos to the select groups around the country which *do* support poetry.

Split Infinitive
In Memoriam, Matilda (1910–1972)

You gently stepped to touch the robin's wing—
and cobra sounds were your reward:
You offered maypole bells so set to ring—
and vultures opened up their devil's hoard.
You spoke of art to which you were so prone—
and bats poured forth from darkened eaves;
In sheer despair you hurled an angry stone—
and roses sprouted from dry, withered leaves.

Past and Present

To predict the future we must understand the past.

In moons to come, love
could wear a madman's cloak; birds
might hobble on winged crutches,
and grass would grow on fields of skulls.
Hangman scenes the prophet paints
will surely be, if atom-dogs,
now on leash, are allowed to break restraints.

The future is yet to unveil, but the lizard ooze,
Man's early efforts to survive can easily be traced.
Go to your museums. They have the Magi touch
of rolling back the years. On walls, display cases,
one sees replicas of dwellers of the cave.
Step from room to room, age to age;
note the pristine wireless, the frantic
efforts to communicate. Also to enslave.

Read the ancient books. Marvel at the *savage*
eager to cope, learn, advance.

Watch the steady growth of wisdom—and, parallel
the rapid strides in weaponry. Once it was the lance,
then the gun, the tank, the jet. Each tool,
so often used, was fiercer than the one before,
tested in the flaming carnivals of war.
    A new eruption boils. How far? How near?
    Level is the hill where stood the seer.

24
Summing Up

Unless there is something stop-press involved, a publisher needs some six months in which to "turn around," since a lot of preliminary steps need to be taken. Copy-editing. Preparing jacket text and a mailing piece. Insertion in the next catalog. Designing a jacket. My original cut-off date for this book was 15 February 1985. That month I received from Dr. Twerski a highly inspirational book, *Wisdom in Rabbinical Tales.*

In this new work, Dr. Twerski called upon his vast knowledge of rabbinical lore. They are survival stories handed down from generation to generation. What stands out is sheer *survival,* and that crosses ethnic-ethical lines. In terms of theme, Prentice-Hall was automatically eliminated, due to their change of policy. My initial submission was to Ted Solotaroff, a Senior Editor at Harper & Row. He replied: "I am returning Abraham Twerski's manuscript. I'm afraid I don't see enough of a market for it, though you might want to try our religious division in San Francisco." I did, aware that Harper & Row had shifted their religious books department to the west coast. Two letters followed: each expressed interest, and also fear that the book was too restricted to a Yiddish readership. The revisions they wanted would have made it a different book.

I went to other publishers. The results were identical, too limited an appeal for a general trade book. I felt that the book's message could appeal to Gentiles as well, just as *Fiddler on the Roof* generated a universal acceptance. The ending was again a happy one for the author. He wrote that a cousin had bought a Jewish-interest publishing house, and offered him a contract. Dr. Twerski was glad to accept.

When my first book went to the typesetters, I had so many properties in transit, I began to plan my second book. The same applies to this third reminiscence. A fourth will be needed if I am to catch up.

February 1985 has been a very active and a hopeful month. I have a

Paul Fitzsimmons story at the *Ladies' Home Journal*. Books are out from all my active clients. A letter from Joni Evans prompts me to quote:

> *The Man Who Was Johns Hopkins* may be a wonderful subject for a book. For some reason this outline does not convince me one way or the other. If Lucy Freeman and Walter Schmidt do a sample chapter or two, I would be happy to take another look. I just don't feel there's enough here to know for sure.

A SOMEWHAT ROSY VIEW OF AN UNHEALTHY INDUSTRY was the heading of a review of *Barnum-Cinderella* by Robert Evett, a staff writer for the Sunday *Star,* Washington, D.C. (2 January 1972). I quote the last two paragraphs:

> In short, it is a book for Pied Pipers and fools, and unfortunately, neither category is in short supply. So far as imaginative literature is concerned, the publishing industry is at the point of blowing itself up. If it finally succeeds, authors, agents, publishers, students and teachers of "Creative Writing" will have to find some other way to occupy themselves.
>
> Failing that drastic and dreadful conclusion, there will continue to be fraudulent correspondence courses in writing, and books such as this, all designed to gull people into thinking that they can make it in this highly competitive field. I submit that all methods used to encourage people to enter this hazardous profession are equally immoral, regardless of their claims to respectability.

This review drew this letter:

February 2, 1972

Dear Mr. Robert Evett,

I am one of those "Pied Pipers" who was strongly encouraged by Alex Jackinson to fight my way through to publication. This was in 1964, when his first book, COCKTAIL PARTY FOR THE AUTHOR, also offered "a somewhat rosy view of an unhealthy industry." Eight years ago, as today, Publishing had its hangups and dislocations. The American Theatre (and Hollywood) have long been in the Recovery Room. My Medical realm is another "hazardous profession," I can attest. Should anyone be discouraged from daring to break through in these ailing professions? It is to Jackinson's everlasting credit that he passionately discourages writers from becoming discouraged.

A case in point would be Dr. Ken Edgar, whose first novel will be published this fall by Prentice-Hall. I had seen a letter from him to Jackinson, lauding our agent for persistent support, such as I received. Ego is unseen, hidden, but what weight can measure its centrifugal force as it pertains to the individual? I wanted very much to be published, and I was—after Jackinson pointed out what I was doing wrong.

The last paragraph of your review, and especially the last sentence, is incredibly defeatist. You wrote: "I submit that all methods used to encourage people to enter this hazardous profession are equally immoral, regardless of their claims to respectability." Immoral? If your review could be seen by all those who had been in contact with Jackinson in the eighteen years that he has been an agent, I think that almost all would laud him for his unfailing and unflailing *encouragement*.

> Respectfully,
> Max Goodhart, M.D. [who writes
> as Alfred Dorn, M.D.]

Let me again stress the sheer importance of *patience*.

My first book featured two significant cocktail parties. One was held at the Metropolitan Club in Washington, D.C. The host was the Chilton Co., publishers of Admiral Arleigh Burke's DESRON 23—*Destroyer Squadron*. The "With" author was Ken Jones. I journeyed out to "meet the admirals," as I had then put it. I especially hoped that Admiral Rickover would attend. He didn't, but many admirals did turn out to toast their triumphant fellow-officer.

The other celebration was held at Central Park's famous Tavern-on-the-Green. The sponsor was Abelhard-Schuman, which had published Charles Pearson's *The Indomitable Tin Goose: The True Story of Preston Tucker and His Car*.

That (then) revolutionary automobile was introduced in 1948. The motor was in the rear, at that time a sharp departure from the mass Detroit output, and the car aroused controversy. The car was driven to Central Park from Florida by a Tucker enthusiast. The author, Charles Pearson, assured me that based on his extensive research, the Tucker was a *good* car, and should have succeeded. I rode in a Tucker, and felt that it *was* a very fine car.

A third party should have been held. For Cy Rice's *Nick The Greek* (Funk & Wagnalls, 1960), the biography of the original and *only* Nick The Greek. That was Nicholas Andrea Dandolas, who had died broke and unattended in a Los Angeles hotel room.

Nick The Greek had been under option before, but a new option came through in 1984. The year also brought an option offer on *The Preston Tucker Story* by Arleigh Burke. The book intrigued a Canadian producer, and negotiations began. The story was bought for reprint by Bantam Books. Conditions had changed in the past twenty years. There evolved a new and spreading interest in naval and military affairs, and people associated with those events.

The unhappy part is that death claimed all three authors and the subjects they wrote about. Ken Jones had died of cancer, Charles Pearson of a number of ailments. Cy Rose, an athletic sort, was jogging on a beach close to his native Los Angeles when he felt a sharp, unexpected pain in his left leg. He was rushed to a hospital. The phlebitis could not be checked before it spread to his heart.

Death has been extremely unkind to my "family of clients," and to my immediate family. Matilda, my wife of forty years, succumbed to oral cancer in 1972. Stanton A. Coblentz passed from the scene, as did John Williams Andrews. Others. For some their work will be remembered.

While *Zebra* was in the process of being promoted in 1982, Clark Howard turned in his next book proposal, *American Saturday*. Nominally, this was a book about George Jackson, but the story had a much broader social base.

Jackson was the author of *Soledad Brother*, a book that had drawn the praise of Left-oriented intellectuals, mostly white, who had helped him with his book. Jackson, a Black Panther field marshal, was originally jailed for a minor robbery. He would have been released after a short stay, save that, in prison, he broke rule after rule. The infractions included the brutal murder of a guard. That made him a lifer.

A gun was smuggled to Jackson. A violent shootout followed, and he was killed trying to escape. Also dead were three guards. Involved with Jackson and the Black Panthers were Angela Davis and many sympathetic white lawyers. One was Stephen Bingham. Did he smuggle in the gun? Bingham disappeared, and did not surface for 13 years. He has yet to face a jury.

When Joyce Engelson read the *American Saturday* book outline, she phoned me and said, "This time you get the twenty-five thousand."

The book proved to be a total flop, for several reasons. In part it was because many book buyers no longer felt the same sympathy toward black revolutionaries that they had displayed in the sixties and seventies. The Panther party disintegrated, the former leaders going many separate ways.

Another sort of "disintegration" occurred within Marek/Putnam. Marek lost Robert Ludlum. The MCA overseers, who made the final decisions, were unhappy about it. When the time came to publish *American Saturday*, Joyce and Dick were no longer around as the friendly guiding lights. So there was no advertising. The Putnam executives could not achieve a paperback sale, on which they had banked. For the publishers, the entire advance was lost.

Marek and Engelson next linked with St. Martin's Press. Clark's first book for them under the new imprint was *Brothers In Blood* (1983). Blood is symbolic. The accounting here was also in red. No reprint sale. No movie interest, though the hope flag remains out.

After two years there was another shift. I first saw the announcement in the *New York Times*. Richard Marek named publisher of E. P. Dutton.

Joyce Engelson, editor-in-chief. This venerable old house had previously been acquired by New American Library, which had wanted a tie-in with a hardcover publisher.

Publishing is beset with tombstones, tombstones placed over books that should not have died prematurely. This also applies to publishers. For me, a particularly painful amputation was Pinnacle Books. This particular eclipse means nothing to the James Clavell income author, but it is a serious blow to the huge segment of writers who have to grub for contracts in the mid-road byways.

This firm was founded by David Zentner, publisher of *Escapade* and other girlie magazines. From this low estate he branched out into decorating newsstands with glaringly sexy paperbacks. Sex sells, on as many levels as one can imagine. Success begets growth and expansion seeded Pinnacle's birth.

Their first Manhattan domicile was in an old factory loft building on East 26th Street, off Madison Avenue, an area to which numerous Uptown publishers have long started to return. A more managable overhead. Zentner had occupied an entire floor. To the right was Pinnacle, supervised by Andrew Ettinger. The left pointed to Bee-Line Publications, of which Mr. Zentner remained the active head. Their specialty continued to center around the mutilated virgin. Pinnacle's output was closer to the sort of books published by Gold Medal, with a heavy emphasis on AA–Action/Adventure. That is why they welcomed Clark Howard. Also Joe Buffer. Each rose to a higher level. Clark with books, Buffer through screenplays. It was a delight to work with Andy. It was also easy to trade with Mr. Zentner. Pay was prompt and advances were on a par with other comparative houses.

The firm's first of several transmutations was to be absorbed by Michigan General, a nonpublishing conglomorate seeking to expand profits. The Pinnacle operation, divorced from Bee-Line, moved to Los Angeles. This was to be closer to the edge of Hollywood. The book-movie tie-in was then very much in vogue. It didn't work out. Despite many staff and managerial changes, that illusive flower, profits, failed to blossom. Pinnacle once again changed coasts, this time settling at 1430 Broadway, a few steps from Times Square.

Patrick O'Connor came in at the editorial end. He brought with him vast paperback experience, having occupied high slots at NAL and Popular Library. But Pinnacle was in no position to bid for the big properties or entice high-income authors. Room at the mid-level was restricted. Results modest, Management sought a new team. Sondra T. Ordover came in as Publisher. Her editorial baptism had been at Fawcett-Gold Medal, a superb training ground. She assembled a staff of top professionals. Results were good; the firm was being turned from red to black. But there were corporate heads to please, supervisors who had only a bottom-line interest in publishing. Funds were withheld, with the result that some Pinnacle checks bounced.

As with Playboy Press, Lancer Books, and other natural and unnatural editorial disasters, my clients and I escaped lucky, in that there had previously been a reversal of rights. It is generally assumed that once a publisher fails, rights automatically revert to the author, but this is not always so. A look at the fine print becomes important.

Pinnacle assets and backlist will be picked up by some other house, perhaps Zebra Books, but as an independent mid-lane publisher, kaddish could properly be said.

25
Trade Notes

I will once again have to bring in Beverly Jane Loo. Leaving McGraw-Hill, she formed her own firm, Beverly Jane Loo Associates. "I am more of a 'packager,'" she had written. "I co-publish." I submitted to her. She replied:

Dear Alex:

I've given quite a bit of consideration to REACHING OUT by Ken Edgar. It's an interesting novel, but it just misses being 'sufficiently commercial, and I can't find a way to fix that. Certainly it's publishable in its present form, but my kind of book packaging demands that I contract for those titles I believe I can help make a best seller. Thus I am forced to say no to a book I really like.

Editors are not the only ones who think up book ideas. Writers do it. Agents do it.

After that first New England seminar, I established a close tie with Margaret L. Coit. Dr. Coit still teaches history at Fairleigh Dickinson University. She is the author of two successful books: *John Calhoun,* which won a Pulitzer Prize, and *Mr. Baruch.*

Margaret Coit is a Houghton Mifflin author. When she has a book idea, H-M automatically gets first refusal, but the publisher allows her to do outside chores. Thus she was asked by Prentice-Hall's college department to edit a book of opinions on Calhoun. Later the University of Kansas Press invited her to do a book on Andrew Jackson. I was asked to handle both negotiations.

Life magazine once featured a score card of President Kennedy's ten favorite books. It included Ms. Coit's *John Calhoun.* So I had a client with considerable clout.

Gladys Carr enters the picture. She had shifted from Prentice-Hall to head McGraw-Hill's American Heritage Press. She would also funnel books to the regular trade books department. I was quite certain that she would be interested in Margaret Coit. And, of course, she was.

I explained why *we* had come up with a proposal. I suggested a book on Santa Anna. The McGraw-Hill editor agreed that it was a sound idea, that a new biography of the nineteenth-century Mexican dictator who had such a strong influence on American history, especially the Southwest area, would sell. And we certainly had the right author. It was Margaret Coit who killed this budding attempt at packaging. She said that it usually took her three years to do research on a book, and she had several other ideas of her own.

Publishers often need to hire writers, but the novice cannot profit from this need. Whether a novelization of a screenplay or ghosting a diet book is involved, publishers will want to know about an author's credentials. Where a promising new author lives in the Metropolitan area, I urge that they take a professional writing course at one of three schools I like to recommend: N.Y.U., Columbia, and New School for Social Research.

Postscript

Soon after my meeting with Greg Bautzer, Stephen Longstreet came in from Beverly Hills, where he still lives. We met for breakfast. I was then active on the stage adaptation of *The Pedlocks*. I asked the question which had long been on my mind, if he would like to do a book on Hughes. "I'd love to!" Longstreet replied enthusiastically. "I did some cinema work for Hughes. I know a lot about him." I wrote to Greg Batzer and he replied:

Dear Alex;
  Your suggestion regarding Longstreet is excellent. I will take it up with the man (when I can catch him) and advise you. In the meantime—
                                        Best regards,
                                        Greg

Nothing materialized. I sent a prod a year later, and there was this reply:

Dear Alex;
  Thanks for your note regarding the Hughes biography. There is nothing new on the subject, but I'm still very hopeful . . . however faint it may be.
                                        Best regards,
                                        Greg

Rosalind Magzis is a veteran magazine and book editor whom I have known since she was a kid. Roz had started as an editorial assistant at Dell, long before the Doubleday takeover. She read a typescript of this book and brought it to me at my office. She had made a sheaf of notes, and started firing away.

"At the time that you were putting together *Syndromes,* you were friendly with Dr. Pinckney and Lucy Freeman. I wondered, and readers will wonder, why they declined to be in the book?"

"They didn't decline," I said. "They declined only to write for free. Each wanted an up-front payment. I saw their side of it, but I couldn't pay them and not the others."

"Did you read that new Hughes book?"

"No, but I will. I did catch that '20/20' show. I'm surprised they picked Bob Maheu as the Hughes aide. . . . He was fired a long time ago. As I said, a look at those private papers was needed for an accurate biography—now much of what was private is in the open."

"In writing of Pushcart Press, why didn't you mention *Saul's Book?*"

"I thought it was too sordid a story—a talented writer beaten to death by his adopted son. It sickens me."

"You mentioned suicides in your family of clients. Readers have a right to know who."

"Robert Lund is one. Iris Wells another. I told both stories in my last book. Shirley Barker was not a client, but we were in close touch. She self-terminated."

"It was a very amusing bit, James Whiton and that telegram, "You are a pain in the ass." Each time I see Vincent Price on TV, I am reminded of Dr. Phibes. What happened?"

"I really don't know. I lost contact with Jim Whiton. Jerry Silva and his wife divorced. That ended Silva Productions, but the husband started a new firm, Double Helix Films. Jerry wrote me. "Jim's story is inching along to production, and one day Montgomery Clift will become a television feature.""

"I take it Sara Grimes is an actual name."

"It's a pseudonym. I once had a close relationship with the author, but I lost track of her. When a mailing piece is ready, I will make a new effort to locate a lot of people with whom I have lost contact."

"If you want a quote from me, say I think your story reads like an exciting suspense novel. You grip the reader from the very start and hold the interest throughout. It's the best of your books."

Final update, January 1986.

For several reasons, publication of this book had to be postponed to this year. And I am vastly pleased over it. What follows explains why.

A book to which I have a strong personal attachment is *Six Against the Rock*. It was published just when the 1978 ABA Convention—American Booksellers Association—was held in San Francisco. I was at that annual gathering. I attended the boat ride to Alcatraz which Dial/Dell had arranged. Everything connected with that convention forms a very warm memory.

I chose the title for this book, *The Romance of Publishing,* very carefully. Since book publishing is so precarious, so beset with tombstones, where is the *romance?* For me it lies in the unexpectedness with which events erupt . . . like a phone call from Gaylord Productions. The story explains itself in a letter that went off on 8 January 1986.

Dear Morton Smithline,
Thank you very much for sending your letter via Federal Express. It arrived less than 24 hours after we had spoken.
Let me detail why I needed a letter. Once a phone conversation is transmitted, there is always the danger of misinterpretation. But copies of this letter are going to Clark Howard and to Doubleday.
Six Against the Rock was published in 1977 by The Dial Press. As you of course know, Dial has long been a Doubleday subsidiary. The book has been optioned three times. First by Q M Productions. Merrill Karpf had then been the executive Vice President, and he knows *Rock* very well. When Quinn Martin formed *Quinn Martin Films,* he picked up the option, which had lapsed. Then he renewed. As you will see from the attached, a production *almost* resulted. It would delight all of us involved to conclude a new deal.

And a new deal was consummated. Finally it seems that a film will be made. With producers who know both the book and filmmaking. Gaylord Productions works in partnership with Schaefer-Karpf Productions. They produced "Children in The Crossfire" and "Stone Pillow," starring Lucille Ball. They are currently producing "Mrs. Delafield Wants To Marry." This will star Katharine Hepburn.

Zebra is another work that arouses strong emotions. The letter from Cynthia Totter is dated December 17, 1985.

Raboo Rodger's *It Started With Watermelons* goes back to you unread because there has been a 200% degree turn here. We will no longer be making *Movies of the Week.* Mr. Murdoch plans to consolidate Twentieth Century-Fox with Metromedia, with Channel 5 as the hub. In effect this will constitute a fourth network, the Fox Television Network. This is down the road a bit, but let me veer off into another, a somewhat unrelated and yet related tangent.
I had been in the story department of Metromedia Producers at the time that Nona Brown had optioned *Zebra.* The story had greatly fascinated me. It still does. When the dust settles here I would like to propose *Zebra* to the top brass.

What militated against production at Metromedia is still a formidable objection, namely that all the villains are black and hence it may be perceived in some quarters to be an anti-black film. Still, if I remain at Fox (heads are rolling right and left) I would like to make the pitch, if that will be alright with you.

I gave Ms. Totter the green light. I also pointed to a few sociological factors that could work in our favor.

Time and change are history's Siamese twins. The Muslim Movement itself changed, as all blood-and-thunder sects tend to splinter and diverge. The death of Elijah Muhammad ended a period. Another began under the leadership of his son Wallace, and it was (is) very different in tone and intent. The new movement welcomes the participation of whites. A rival group, the Nation of Islam, is headed by Louis Farrakhan. This faction remains as militant as it had been during the San Francisco killings. In his role as leader, Mr. Farrakhan had called Hitler "a very great man," a leader who had been good for Germany. Considering the later ruins, this becomes questionable. Farrakhan had accepted a $3 million grant from Col. Qaddafi. In a film, onus for the killings could properly be attributed to this tiny minority.

Many exciting new things happened in 1985, events which will have to wait for book four. I have yet to place the Jim Lewisohn book, or the Johns Hopkins story, or two new works from James Whiton, who actively returned to the fold. Perhaps the most interesting development was a book revolving around Steven Spielberg written by his stepmother. My letter to an E. P. Dutton editor is self-explanatory.

Dear Jeanne Martinet,
　　Thank you for sending me a copy of your letter to Fana Spielberg. Steven Spielberg is such a glittering name, I certainly hope that the manuscript will be returned to you once the revisions are done with. But let me pick up a passage out of the letter you received: "Alex Jackinson has informed that he sent you the first 110 pages of my manuscript, *The Circumcised Heart.* He was not authorized to submit the work as no contract had or has been made with him." I most assuredly had the proper sanction, but my concern stems from these words: *as no contract had or has been made with him.*
　　The one thing I never had, and never will have, is a contractual relationship with a client. Agents do at times get stung, but I would rather suffer a loss than invoke a legal stratagem. I prefer an open door, for clients to enter, and leave, where they feel the inclination.

I am friendly with an agent who regards writers as an ungrateful bunch of leeches. She will concede that four or five out of fifty are appreciative and pleasant to work with. With me it is the very opposite. I think that a small fraction casts off a stench, but overwhelmingly writers stand on a high mountain. The mountain erupts; writers falter, but they continue to hold the capsules of hope.

Hope is a light that points upward. Quote from *Authors Guild Bulletin,* Winter, 1986. "At Crown, Andrea E. Cascardi has come on board as a Children's Books editor. Formerly, she was with Scholastic and Houghton Mifflin." Houghton Mifflin had contracted for a third Teenage novel by Raboo Rodgers.